ONCE MORE
AROUND THE BLOCK

Also by Joseph Epstein

ONCE MORE
AROUND THE BLOCK

Familiar Essays by

JOSEPH EPSTEIN

W · W · NORTON & COMPANY

NEW YORK   LONDON

Copyright © 1987 by Joseph Epstein
All rights reserved.
Published simultaneously in Canada by Penguin Books Canada Ltd., 2801 John
Street, Markham, Ontario L3R 1B4.
Printed in the United States of America.

First published as a Norton paperback 1990

The essay "My Friend Martin" first appeared in *Commentary*, and is reprinted
with the kind permission of the editors.

The text of this book is composed in Janson Alternate, with display type set in
Weiss Italic.
Composition and manufacturing by The Haddon Craftsmen, Inc.

Library of Congress Catologing-in-Publication Data
Epstein, Joseph, 1937–
Once more around the block.
I. Title
AC8.E667   1987   081   86–33248

ISBN 0-393-30633-X

W. W. Norton & Company, Inc., 500 Fifth Avenue, New York, N.Y. 10010
W. W. Norton & Company Ltd., 37 Great Russell Street, London WC1B 3NU

2 3 4 5 6 7 8 9 0

For Robert Ginsburg & Norman Brodsky,
Old Friends from the Old Country

Contents

CONTENTS

A Note on the Title

F ROM THE AGE of fifteen until the age of eighteen, I,
along with the two dedicatees of this volume of
essays, spent a great deal of time sitting in a gun-metal grey
1950 Chevrolet coupé with plaid seat covers. Late into weekend
and sometimes mid-week nights we sat in this car, talking,
analyzing the world, dissecting personalities, and laughing—
above all, hooting, howling, groaning, gasping with laughter.
Life seemed so wondrous and rich and the conversation among
us so inexhaustible that we could never quite bring ourselves
to separate and call it a night. "Once more around the block,"
one or another of us would say, and the Chevy would cruise
around the block and the conversation would continue, often
ending only with the rise of the sun. Writing the essays in this
book has given me something of the same pleasure as those
conversations with those two dear friends who, thirty-five
years later and many more times around the block together,
remain dear friends.

All but one of the essays in this volume first appeared in
The American Scholar, and I wish to acknowledge the important editorial help of the editors of that magazine: Jean Stipi-
cevic, Sandra Costich, and Thomas Nieman. Through their

conscientiousness they have saved me many an embarrassment; the embarrassments that remain are exclusively the fault of the author.

JOSEPH EPSTEIN

Once More
Around the Block

Work and Its Contents

"COMES ANOTHER DEPRESSION," said my father, as he noted the patch of grass I missed in the center of our small back lawn, the weeds I forgot to pull up next to the fence, and the uneven edges I left along the pavement, "it's guys like you they fire first." I haven't yet been fired, but then neither have we had a major Depression. "If you work for a man for a dollar an hour," my father used to say, "always give that man at least a dollar and a quarter of effort." But my first job, at age thirteen, was that of a delivery and stock boy at Sanders Pharmacy and paid sixty cents an hour and was so excruciatingly boring—I mostly dusted bottles—that my problem was how to find a way to give Mr. Sanders even twenty cents an hour in honest effort.

When I was growing up my father gave me a good deal of advice about work that I could neither use nor quite shake off. But, then, what you have to know about my father is that he himself was a Herculean worker, a six-day-a-week, never-look-at-the-clock man until his retirement at seventy-five. Perhaps an anecdote will give you something of the flavor of his work habits. My father once told me, in complaint about a man who worked for him, that for fifteen years this man had come to work at 8:30 on the dot, which was the precise time his business opened. "You would think that once," my father said, "just once he would be early." "Dad," I said, "please don't tell that story to anyone else." But now I see that I have told it for him.

My father also used to say, over and over as it seemed to me then, "If you don't like your work, you're in real trouble." He began to tell me this when I was perhaps eleven or twelve, and I only came to know it was true when I was in my late twenties. Until then, work was work, a necessary evil, though not so evil as all that, something to fill the hours between sleeping and enjoying myself. "Work is the curse of the drinking classes," said Oscar Wilde, which is a remark I would once have found more amusing than I do now. Today I must own that I subscribe to the less witty, indeed not witty at all, but vaguely moralizing view of Thomas Carlyle, who in *Past and Present* wrote: "Blessed is he who has found his work; let him ask no other blessedness." If I did needlepoint, I should stitch that on my pillowcase and sleep on it, exhausted after a good day's work.

Not everyone, I realize, shares this taste for work. Far from it—so far that I sometimes think that the world is divided between those who work so they can live and those who live chiefly so they can work. I make this sound more black-and-white, either-or, one-way-or-the-other than it truly is. But the fact is, in my experience, some of the most forlorn people I know are those who haven't found their work: people of artistic temperament who have no art to practice, leaders without followers, serious men and women with nothing serious to do. On the other side, people who have found their work can seem, while at work, creatures of great dignity, even beauty. "A man blowing a trumpet successfully is a rousing spectacle," noted the Welsh writer Rhys Davies in one of his short stories. And so, too, is a man or woman working at anything he or she loves.

Contemporary novelists have tended to banish the subject

of work from their books, though work, both in its dreary and in its glorious aspects, has been of great significance in so many novels of the past. One thinks of poor David Copperfield slaving away at the blacking factory; of Clyde Griffiths, his head full of dreams, working as a bellboy in Kansas City and on the assembly line at his uncle's shirt-collar factory in Lycurgus, New York; of the figure of Levin, in *Anna Karenina*, sweating joyously as he works in the fields with his peasants, stopping from time to time under the blazing sun for a swig of kvass; of the seamen in so many tales and novels of Melville and Conrad going about doing ship's work—scrubbing down the decks, lashing up the mast—and working together to fight off typhoons and other seagoing disasters. And finally one thinks of prisoner Ivan Denisovich, of his long day's work done under the worst possible conditions of cold, hunger, and fear, from which he emerges, in Solzhenitsyn's novel, with simple but hugely impressive dignity. In the novels of Solzhenitsyn a true sense of and love for work comes through, and part of Solzhenitsyn's distaste for politics is that it is the enemy of work. As the engineer Ilya Isakovich Arkhangorodsky says in *August 1914*:

"On one side—the Black Hundreds: on the other—the Red Hundreds! And in the middle"—he formed his hands into the shape of a ship's keel—"a dozen people who want to pass through to get on with a job of work! Impossible!" He opened his hands and clapped them together. "They are crushed—flattened!"

I was put in mind of the place of work in our lives, and in the general scheme of society, by an essay in *Harper's* (December 1982) entitled "Dirty Work Should Be Shared" by Michael Walzer. The argument of Professor Walzer's essay, though its general line is conveyed by its title, is a bit blurry. Professor Walzer wishes that there weren't so much drudgery, so much

hard, unpleasant, ungratifying, ill-rewarded work in the
world. Like Oscar Wilde, from whose "The Soul of Man
Under Socialism" he quotes, he would have "all unintellectual
labor, all monotonous, dull labor, all labor that deals with
dreadful things and involves unpleasant conditions . . . be done
by machinery." Yet Professor Walzer knows this cannot be so,
and that it is not soon likely to be so. But being an equalitarian,
he yearns for a rearrangement of institutions, a readjustment
of conditions, an alteration of names and attitudes whereby the
burden of what he terms "dirty work" in society can be more
equally shared than it is now. "Hence the question," he writes,
"in a society of equals, who will do the dirty work? And the
necessary answer is that, at least in some partial and symbolic
sense, we all should do it." Exactly, or even roughly, how we
should do it he does not say. Professor Walzer does, though,
discuss such things as worker ownership of garbage collection
firms, arrangements for work sharing in Israeli kibbutzim, the
old French institution of the corvée (a form of labor for the
state). But in the end he hasn't a solution and concludes not
with a bang but with a whimper of exhortation: "Society's
worst jobs should not be the exclusive business of a pariah class,
powerless, dishonored, underpaid."

When one begins to talk about work in connection with
power, honor, and payment, one steps onto a verdant field of
quicksand. The world's work is, after all, only rarely paid for
commensurately with its worth. This is a problem compounded by the fact that commensurability between work and
wages is never an easy thing to determine, especially if one
hopes to pay for work according to what one construes to be
its social usefulness. If the job of determining such wages were
mine, I should lower the wages paid for some work and raise
those now paid for other, and some I should leave pretty much
as they are. For example, I tend to doubt that the quality of

policemen would become greatly improved if the job paid vastly more money, yet I have a hunch that the quality of doctors and lawyers might rise if they were paid less.

I used to hear the argument made fairly regularly that teachers are greatly underpaid, and at some point in this argument someone would inevitably say, "Why, even garbage collectors make more!" As someone in favor of better education —a courageous stand for me to take, don't you think?—this argument always made me a trifle edgy. I thought that garbage collectors deserved more. For one thing, teachers are usually teachers by choice, while garbage collectors collect garbage for want of anything better to do. For another, a good teacher is rather rare, but who knows a bad garbage collector? But if we are going to talk about the underpaid, what about that national treasure, that lonely yet proud figure, on whose shoulders so much of the quality of a country's culture depends—I speak of course of that splendid and stalwart chap, the essayist.

As an equalitarian, Professor Walzer, if I read him aright, would have teacher, garbage collector, and essayist earning roughly equal salaries (a true leg up, by the way, for the essayist). He would also like them, I gather, to be equally honored and equally powerful. He argues against the degradation of certain kinds of work—I am not sure anyone is arguing for it —and wants a society in which there will be "no more bowing and scraping, fawning and toadying, no more fearful trembling; no more high-and-mightiness." Somehow, I must here confess, I find myself not so much unsympathetic as uninterested in Professor Walzer's proposals. I am not sure, for example, that sycophancy is built into specific jobs. A duke can be more fawning to a powerful prince than a washroom attendant to a United States senator; some of the worst snobs I have ever seen in action have been waiters. Nor do the teacher, the garbage collector, and the essayist bow and scrape, fawn and toady before one another—or, for that matter, before anyone (unless it is in the nature of the individual to do so). I am not aware, either, that one causes fearful trembling in the others. No, it seems to me that they greet one another the way most people do who work at very different jobs—with a lively and only slightly muted incomprehension and indifference.

But, then, the difference in point of view between Professor Walzer and me is vast. As a social theorist of sorts, he likes to come at things at a fairly high level of generality, while the points he attempts to make seem to me of interest only when they are treated on a much lower level of generality. He feels he knows why certain social classes bog down in dreary work; I am more interested in how it is and what it took for so many members of these classes to have been able to climb out successfully. He is sure much modern work is degrading; I am more impressed with the competence, dignity, and ingenuity that people apply to difficult jobs. He begins his observations with a yearning for equality; I begin mine yearning to understand how even one person—I, for example—came to do what he does.

Professor Walzer feels that perhaps dirty work "should be done by society's only legitimate proletariat—the proletariat of the young." There is, if I may say so, something a touch goofy about referring to the young generally as "proletariat"— Workers of the world unite! You have nothing to lose but your sneakers!—for it gives yet another abstract twist to a word that has by now almost completely lost its relation to reality. Still, it is true that the young do get a goodly share of society's worst jobs; or at least they used to. I know I had my share of these jobs when young, and each time I would set out on another one, my father would say, "It can't hurt you. It's good experience." It took me a while to understand that the term "good experience" was my father's artful euphemism for "bad job."

Of these bad jobs, as I say, I had my share. Most of the "good experience" of my youth served to convince me of my incompetence. I found that I grew bored quickly, and could not very well sustain, on my first job, a false interest in dusting drugstore stock for the duration of my two- or three-hour shifts at Sanders Pharmacy. I tried out as a golf caddy; this was during the time before golf carts and when clubs were not yet called by number but still had such names as mashie niblick— names that seemed to me more appropriate for canned vegetables. But one had to be out of the house by five in the morning to get in two full rounds, which, at age thirteen, I found difficult to do, so I quit, thus proving to myself that I was not a person of much perseverance. ("Quitters never win," said my father.) My first year in high school I worked as a food bagger in one of the first supermarkets in our neighborhood, a place called Hillman's. Milk still came in bottles, and the reason I recall this so vividly is that milk bottles seemed to break through so many of my bags before the women carrying them were able to get up the marble stairs leading out of the store. Although for some reason I wasn't fired, it wasn't long before I was out searching for fresh "good experience."

By now I was convinced that I had a short attention span, little perseverance (or, as the moralizers put it, "stick-to-it-iveness"), and wasn't very good with my hands. Yet onward, ever onward, substituting for a month for a classmate, I next worked as a busboy in a neighborhood Chinese restaurant. The neighborhood was predominantly Jewish, and the man who ran the restaurant, though Chinese, had begun to look a little Jewish himself, in the odd way that people have of absorbing into themselves their surrounding atmosphere. (The most notable example is that of people who begin to resemble their dogs.) I cleared dishes, poured the remains of tea over the Formica-topped tables, swabbing the mess up with a damp cloth, and scraped off the dishes in the tumult of chopping, frying, and Chinese language in the kitchen. After the restaurant closed—during the middle of the week, roughly at 8:30— the staff could eat, limitlessly, anything they wished, with the exception of shrimp dishes. At that time—I was then fourteen —it was Chinese shrimp dishes almost exclusively that I liked, and so I ate scarcely anything at all. Through the mechanism psychologists call "overcompensation," I continue to try to make up for this youthful folly.

But that summer I began the best job of my life—that of ball boy for a nearby university tennis coach and teaching professional. My job was to tote out a large box of used balls, which the pro would use to demonstrate strokes—backhand, forehand, volley, and three kinds of serve—to his pupils. During the lesson I would shag the loose balls and return them to the box. I would also sometimes throw balls to the pro, a great gruff but very gentle fat man, who would thwack them back across the net. On occasion I would demonstrate a stroke or a serve. Mostly, though, I shagged balls.

The pay was poor—it barely covered the expenses of my travel and courtside soda pop intake—but the benefits bountiful. These included unlimited free court time and a modest discount on equipment. I would hang around the courts all day long, working two, at most three, hours a day, the remainder of the time playing with people whose partners didn't show up or were late, or filling in as a fourth for doubles. The courts were clay, of a light copperish color, from which loose clay dust turned one's shoes and tennis balls lightly beige. The sun shone down, the days stretched out. A taut tennis net, a clean white ball, and pow—and life, as Mr. Khayyám's *Rubáiyát* has it, was "paradise enow." The lesson this job taught, if on a very rudimentary level, was that work was best when it was combined with play.

This was a lesson reinforced by working with my father, which I began to do when I was sixteen years old and had acquired a driver's license. Although he then owned a business in partnership with another man, my father was this business's chief salesman, and my job was to drive him to cities anywhere from a hundred to four hundred miles away, where he would call on customers; I also lugged his sample cases, and sometimes wrote up his orders. My father, it occurs to me, was then exactly the age I am now as I write this.

I wish Arthur Miller had met my father before he wrote his lumpy and mawkish play about Willy Loman. My father was not only very good at what he did, but he seemed to enjoy it all immensely. "Now this is a very popular item," he would say to a customer. "I know a man who bought an enormous quantity of it—me!" Here was a man having a very good time while at work.

"What do you think," my father would ask, at six o'clock at the end of a day on which we had set out at four-thirty in the morning to drive two hundred miles. "What do you think —should we spend the night here or have a nice dinner and try to make it back home tonight?" For slow readers allow me to say that the correct answer was "have a nice dinner and try to make it back home tonight." And this we would do. Some days we would put in eighteen or twenty hours. I would usually sleep long the following morning. My father would be down at (as he called it) "the place" well before it opened for business. I love my work now, but I think my father must have loved his even more.

Love is not something one reads much about in connection with work. Quite the reverse, in fact. Studs Terkel once assembled a book of interviews that he called *Working*, which turned out to be a clanging best-seller and which begins on this cheery note:

This book, being about work, is, by its very nature, about violence—to the spirit as well as to the body. It is about ulcers as well as accidents, about shouting matches as well as fistfights, about nervous breakdowns as well as kicking the dog around. It is, above all (or beneath all), about daily humiliations. To survive the day is triumph enough for the walking wounded among the great many of us.

But then Studs Terkel's is the conventional anti-capitalist view of work. He is a man who sees capitalist conspiracies everywhere, the way the old John Birches used to see Communist conspiracies. He has a syndicated interview show on FM radio, and on this show his idea of a fine time is to interview someone who has written about some fresh piece of big-business skulduggery. It might be an interview with a man who has written a book about, say, IBM having recently acquired the Gerber baby food company, and he has discovered that the plumbing connected to the urinals in the executive washroom at IBM leads directly to the assembly line at the Gerber baby food factory, and . . . "That's right, Studs, it's as bad as you think."

Although there is much tough work in the world, some of it done under grueling and some of it under grinding conditions, I doubt that the picture of work conveyed by a tricked-up book like *Working* is anywhere near accurate as a picture of how most people regard their work. True, many people have been cornered by circumstances into work they would not have chosen if their freedom of choice had been wider; many people find themselves under bosses or supervisors who are stupid or petty tyrants; and many others long to work at something other than what they work at now. Yet many more people, my guess is, feel the need and the stimulus and the satisfaction of their work—and for these people not to work, quite apart from the money that work provides, is a kind of slow death. When on television one hears the unemployed interviewed, there is, naturally enough, much talk of bills piling up and of financial worry generally; but at another level one can grasp a deeper demoralization—their feeling, now that they are deprived of work, of uselessness.

Other people's work often looks fairly interesting to me, or seems to have oddly interesting virtues. Apart from jobs for which I am altogether unfitted—lion tamer, say, or brain surgeon, or ship's captain—there are only two jobs for which I feel a strong antipathy. One is working in a bank, which involves too much detail for my taste and the additional difficulty of spending my days handling other people's money, which would not exactly plant roses in my cheeks. The other job I should not like to have is that of clergyman, especially today when values are so scrumptiously scrambled and the prospects of making a dignified appeal for faith so slim. Yet T. S. Eliot, I note, much preferred working in the international department of Lloyd's Bank in London to teaching; and many women in almost all the modern Western religions feel somewhat put down because they are not permitted to work at the job I wouldn't touch with a ten-foot pulpit.

When I was an adolescent I never had the best jobs: these included construction worker, which paid very well, built up muscles, and withal seemed very manly; or copyboy on a major metropolitan daily, which put one on the periphery of interesting events; or lifeguard, which, along with giving one an opportunity to acquire that most ephemeral of the world's possessions, a nice tan, put one in a fine position to meet girls. But neither did I have the worst jobs: these included setting pins in a bowling alley, which in those days paid ten cents a line and gave one an opportunity for so many uninteresting and extremely painful injuries; and selling shoes, especially women's shoes, which could try the patience of a glacier and often paid no commission, except one percent on polish and laces.

I had middling jobs. My last two years in high school I sold costume jewelry on Saturdays and during Christmas holidays downtown in what must have been one of the first of this country's discount stores. During the time I was there, two veterans of carnival life worked the costume jewelry concession with me. The first was Art, a man in his late forties, with pomaded black hair, who sweated heavily in all seasons. "Hold down the fort, kid," he would say, ducking out for ten or fifteen minutes, his breath, on return, areek with booze. He was a fumbling man who had confident views, particularly on contemporary sexual mores, which, though often amusing, seemed to me even then wildly erroneous. Then there was Fritz, an Englishman who referred to all other Englishmen as limeys. He had the accent of a man of some cultivation, and on the cheap cigarette lighters, lockets, and identification bracelets we sold he engraved names and initials with a grand artistic flourish. He was a fine companion, filled with stories of traveling round the world, in all a decent sort, though at the time very much down on his uppers. He would sometimes borrow a few dollars from me, which he always repaid. Fritz, too, was a boozer, not a nipper but a binger. He would miss work for two or three days, then come in as if nothing were amiss, his same good, gentle self. For reasons never known to me, and perhaps not to himself, he was not to be one of the world's winners.

By the time I had my first factory job, I was in college, which is to say that I knew for certain, if I hadn't already known it earlier, that I would not work at a labor job permanently. I was a visitor there, a tourist on the payroll. The factory made phonograph needles. It had no assembly line; instead most of the people, the majority of them women, worked at long tables. I worked in the receiving department. My job was to unload trucks, but not enough trucks came in to merit my working full-time at this, so I put in part of my time organizing and filing boxes of labels, which was heartily boring. But I also sat around a lot, schmoozing away with the head of the receiving room, a middle-aged man named Steve, who was extremely efficient at covering over the fact that he was exceedingly lazy. We were often joined by two brothers-in-law, Italians of fine high spirits, who were the factory's maintenance crew. Both were small men, and one of them might technically have been a dwarf. Well under five-feet tall with a large head, long arms, and big hands, he was courageous in his mischief, sometimes ducking out to one of the factory's upper floors, where behind packing cases he might take a nap of two full hours' duration. The brothers-in-law appeared to use the factory as a place to hang out during the day. Their real life was elsewhere. Their true speciality was fixing up old cars, which they would sell for a few hundred bucks profit. Then they would buy another, and start fixing it up.

At the factory it was known that I was a college student, which was problematic. It was the first inkling I had of the separation between those whose lives revolve around books and those whose lives don't. I didn't want the separation made any greater than it needed to be, so instead of saying that I was studying such things as literature, history, and philosophy, I claimed I was thinking of going to medical school. This turned out to be a mistake. More than once the brothers-in-law wanted to know if I needed any dead cats for purposes of dissection, and I was sure that one day I would have to bring a dead cat home on the bus in a shopping bag. Worse still, Steve and other people round the plant came to me for medical advice, some of it, I fear, rather intimate in nature.

Many people at the factory told me to be sure to return to

school, saying that they regretted not having had the opportunity to go themselves. Yet their lives did not seem to me either dreary or dreadful. On coffee breaks in the lunchroom their talk was what most talk is about: the economy, the previous day's no-hitter or the pennant race, the bowling league being formed for the fall, their kids. I recall each afternoon standing in line to punch out. The working day did some people in; others, indomitable, were not in the least done in. Not at all. Work, I thought then, is neither intrinsically dignified nor undignified; it is the people doing the work who give it its character. There are people who can make the creation of poetry or leadership of a large university or corporation seem loathsome, and then there are people who can make the job of porter or waitress seem a good and useful thing.

The most impressive man I encountered in the army was a training sergeant named Andrew Atherton, who in private life had been a soda jerk in St. Louis; the most intelligent person in many academic departments in universities is the secretary. Nothing, really, so surprising in this. Nearly a century ago Henry James noted the common occurrence of "imbeciles in great places, people of sense in small." Although few people actually work in Henry James novels, James knew a great deal about work and its special benefits. After the rude failure of his play *Guy Domville* on the London stage, James, it will be recalled, lapsed into a dark blue funk. The only way out of it, as he himself recognized, was work. Writing to his friend William Dean Howells, James recounted his depression and its antidote:

The sense of being utterly out of it weighed me down, and I asked myself what the future would be. All these melancholies were qualified indeed by one redeeming reflection—the sense of how little, for a good while past (for reasons very logical, but accidental and temporary), I had been producing. I *did* say to myself, "Produce again—produce; produce better than ever, and all will yet be well.

And he did. And it was.

The restorative effects of work seem to be beyond doubt. Being out of work, for so many, is the surest path to self-loathing. The loss of work isn't only the loss of wages but the loss of an organizing principle in life. Blocked writers are but one example of the phenomenon. But one needn't turn to the arts for examples. Some years ago, when I had not yet produced enough work to be allowed to consider myself a writer, I underwent roughly a five-week period of unemployment. I was married and had children, and the sense of not producing for them diminished me in my own eyes, which is, I suppose, not surprising. What did surprise me, though, was that during this time jobs I would not formerly even have considered for myself suddenly came to seem highly possible, interesting, attractive even. Driving a bus, for one, or selling men's clothes, for another. Leisure enforced, I found, was no leisure at all, so I took no pleasure in my free time. At one point, just to be doing something, I attempted to sell newspaper subscriptions over the telephone; I rarely made more at this than seven or eight dollars for three hours' work—a figure so demoralizing that after less than a week of it, I quit. I walked around envying people who had jobs to go to. Unemployment had made me feel useless, utterly hopeless. I recognize that this doesn't compare with any sort of serious tragedy, or even with any sort of serious unemployment, but I nonetheless cannot recall when I felt quite so sorry for myself. At other difficult times in my life, at least I could throw myself into my work.

For a great many people TGIF (Thank God It's Friday) is a serious slogan, but then for a great many others so is TGIM

(Thank God It's Monday). As a TGIM man, I think work has gotten a bad rep—and a bum rap—in recent years. Consider the word "workaholic," whose implicit meaning is drunk on work. Or consider the term "Protestant ethic," which began as an explanation for the economic behavior of a historical people but which today exists almost solely as a pejorative term applied to people who are thought to take their work too much in earnest. Those Protestants Max Weber described in his famous essay may or may not have been welcome in heaven for their hard work, but they surely could have spent their days worse—pool-side, let us say, at Caesar's Palace or at Esalen. I am neither Protestant nor quite a workaholic, but I have known many moments when work seemed to me a more plea-surable prospect than being with very good friends. Toward the end of two or three weeks of even a splendid vacation, I have longed to read my mail, to sit at my desk, to slip into harness.

Once one has acquired skills, it seems a waste not to use them. Strike, I say, even when the iron is merely warm. A career passes so quickly. ("Careerist" is another pejorative word.) Someone once said, cleverly in my view, that every career has five stages, which may be denoted thus: (1) Who is Joseph Epstein? (2) Get me Joseph Epstein. (3) We need some-one like Joseph Epstein. (4) What we need is a young Joseph Epstein. (5) Who is Joseph Epstein? Am I now at stage 3, or getting close to stage 4? When I consider these stages, and how quickly one passes from one to the next, I think perhaps it is best to strike even before the iron is plugged in.

Life is short, and work life shorter. At many jobs, age works against one. Much work is, as the sociologists have it, age-specific. Certain jobs are more than a touch unseemly be-yond a certain age: lifeguard, movie reviewer, gigolo, televi-sion anchor-man or anchor-woman (unless you happen to have one of those granitic Cronkitic faces). The jobs I work at—writing, editing, teaching—though one can go at them for quite a spell, nonetheless all have about them a sense of a prime period, after which one does not figure to get better. Some writers, most famously Yeats, found their true prime in their old age, but most do not get better as they get older. Editors beyond a certain period tend to lose their touch and their passion. And teachers, perhaps from having been allowed to hold the floor for so long before a captive audience, not infrequently grow spiritually gaseous and mentally gaga. When I think of these possibilities, it occurs to me to strike even without an iron.

H. L. Mencken, himself a hard and highly efficient worker, says somewhere that it is probably a fine idea for a person to change jobs every ten or so years. Without consciously setting out to do so, I seem to have been following this plan. The last time I changed jobs was when, in my late thirties, I began teaching at a university. The chance to mold minds, the opportunity for lively exchanges of ideas, the pleasures of virtuous friendships with the young, all these are doubtless among the possible rewards of teaching. But what attracted me were the spacious margins of leisure—or, to put it less grandly, the time-off seemed terrific. My view of the job then coincides with that held by my barber now. Often, in order to beat the rush of customers that gathers in his shop in the afternoon, I will go in for a haircut at nine or nine-thirty in the morning. Flapping the sheet over me, he will usually say, with a barely perceptible smile in which I think I have espied envy mingling with the faintest contempt, "Through for the day, Professor?"

I still think the leisure offered by university teaching is impressive. Yet while working at it, the job often seems oddly enervating. Perhaps it has to do with the pressures of intellectual performance—of being "on," in several of the complicated senses of that simple word. Perhaps it has to do with working too exclusively among the young, which can be a sharp reminder that young is, most clearly, what one no longer is. Perhaps it is the element of repetition, for teaching is one of those jobs in which, as one grows older, one's responsibilities do not increase. Perhaps it has to do with the fact that, in teaching, the sense of intellectual progress, in one's students and in oneself, is often unclear, and teaching is never more tiring than when the sense of intellectual progress is absent.

Still, teaching has it moments, and these come in various forms: exhilaration, surprising intellectual discovery, appreciation for things one felt confident went unnoticed. Yet of the jobs I do, teaching is the one I approach with a tinge of fear. I shall hold back on a quotation from Kierkegaard here, but even after several years on the job I often walk into classrooms slightly tremulous. Colleagues have told me that they continue to do so after thirty or more years of teaching. What is there to be fearful of? Of being boring? Of seeming boobish? Of, somehow, blowing it? I do, after all, know more than my students—at least most of the time I do. Yet the touch of fear is still usually there, and the troubling thing is that I tend to teach worse when it isn't.

I imagine fear has salubrious effects on other kinds of work. The stage fright of actors is of course well enough known. So, too, are those butterflies in the stomachs of even the most fearsome athletes before games. Do trial lawyers feel fear? I should hope that airline pilots feel a bit of it. I should hope, too, that surgeons feel fear, but fear, in their case, that stops well short of trembling. I don't mean to exaggerate the benefits of fear; a little of it, I have found, goes a long way.

So, in connection with work, does play. Good work often involves play, an element of fooling around even while doing the most serious things. Fortunate are those people in a position to transform their work into play. Artists are often able to do so. But I have seen fine waitresses and businessmen do it, too. The most fortunate people of all, though, are those for whom the line between work and play gets rubbed out, for whom work is pleasure and pleasure is in work. I may be one of those people. Strange. When I was a child I never dreamed of doing any particular kind of work, for none especially attracted me. I wished merely to be rich and respected, in a general way. Rich I am not; whether I am respected is not for me to say; but, because of the joy I am able to take in my work, I feel myself luckier than any child could have dreamed. Now, if only I could shake this feeling that, comes another Depression, it's guys like me they fire first.

Joseph Epstein's
Lifetime Reading Plan

O NE DAY NOT LONG AGO, over coffee, an earnest
and likeable student about to graduate from the
university where I teach allowed as how he would like to do
a second draft on his education. There was so much he hadn't
read, he said, so many enormous gaps in his education. To
make up for all he had missed he was now going about asking
people whom he thought well-read to make lists of books that
he ought to read. I was pleased to have been asked. Being asked
meant that this young student took me to be an educated man.
Splendid. A little shallow learning lightly carried goes a long
way, at least with the young; my genial pose seems to have
worked yet again.

When someone asks you to make a list of books for him to
read he is, whether he knows it or not, really asking, "How do
I become an educated person?" Now that is a tricky question.
It presupposes that one knows what an educated person looks
like. While not for a moment claiming myself to be educated,
I do think I have an inkling—perhaps a touch more than an
inkling—of what this particular rare beast looks like. I say
"rare" because, even though I travel in intellectual circles (are

they called circles because so many of the people who travel in them usually end up back where they started?), I meet remarkably few people whom I consider educated.

I know a good many smart people, I know some highly intelligent people, I know a small number of people who know a vast amount about a few things, I am not sure I know anyone who is consistently wise, but I do know two beautifully educated men. I shall not go into semantical back flips about what constitutes an educated person. Of these two men I shall say merely that I think they are educated because they have read lots of books in lots of languages, and because they have kept their eyes open to the world around them, and because they have made lots of extremely interesting connections between books and the world. If one were to ask either of them to make a list of books for one to read, I cannot imagine them doing other than exclaiming, in a more refined way than I am now about to put it, "Whaddaya, kidding me?"

Yet my student was awaiting his list and, in his earnestness, was not to be put off. "Have you read the Greek philosophers?" I began, taking what seemed to me a safe road to start upon. "Plato, for example?" He answered that he hadn't, and here I inwardly sighed, recognizing that his university had let this young man down. I was luckier than he, for I had gone to a school—the University of Chicago in the middle 1950s—that had a firm idea of what the young should read, which was chiefly great writers. Aristotle and Plato were, in those days, most prominent among them. We also read Thucydides, Tacitus, Rousseau, Tocqueville, and Dostoyevsky; dribs of Marx and Freud and Max Weber; drabs of some contemporary writers, chiefly in the social sciences. If you weren't a clever student—and I wasn't, particularly—at eighteen or twenty years of age doubtless anywhere from 30 to 70 percent of what these great writers had to say sailed blithely over your head. Yet such reading did establish a few essential things: it taught you who the important writers are; it gave you some notion of what is important about them, which is chiefly the questions they deal with; and it lent you a certain animal confidence, so that you were never afraid of taking on the most serious of books. This, I have since come to think, is a great deal.

Not that anyone could claim to be educated in four years, even at the most serious of schools, which the young man sitting across from me knew. Still, one had to start somewhere; and where, he wanted to know, ought he to start? An obvious answer would have been to tell him to read the Bible straight through—something I myself have never done—and then proceed to read the *Iliad* and the *Odyssey* back to back. Yet this advice, I felt, would only have depressed him; and contemplating it briefly, sound though it was as advice, I had to admit that it depressed me a little too. Instead I said, "You know, Jim, the main thing is to have some time-tested and officially great book going at all times—Gibbon, perhaps, or Cervantes—alongside which you can read less thumpingly significant books." Checking to see if I was following my own sensible advice, I recalled that I at least had bookmarks currently in Montaigne's *Essays* and Tocqueville's *Old Regime and the French Revolution*, though I hadn't read in either one for a good while. "As for the rest," I continued, "the important books will come to you when you need them. Or so in my life I have always found." Even as I said it I felt that this piece of what must have sounded like mystical wisdom did not go down too well, so I availed myself of the prerogative available to teachers through the centuries—I quickly changed the subject.

Yet I felt sympathetic to this young man and his hunger for a list, for anyone even moderately aware of the vast number of books in the world and of the quite pitiful dent any man or woman can hope to make in it is likely, as a first response, to cry out for help. Small wonder that people feel they require a list, a map, a guide to find their way. Smaller wonder that so many other people over the years have been ready to supply lists catering to this demand. In this century alone, to cite only those lists and collections of books that come to mind, there have been the Harvard Classics, the Great Books of the Western World, *The Lifetime Reading Plan, The List of Books* (edited by Frederic Raphael and Kenneth McLeish), and, most recently, a listing of nine thousand books in a book entitled *Good Books* (edited by Steven Gilbar, who also produced *The Book Book*). When it comes to books, it becomes clear, one could make a list of lists.

When I was my student's age, I thought of books less in connection with a list than in connection with a menu. Or, more precisely, I tended to view the world's books as set out on a buffet, and the educated person as one who could eat his way farthest along the table. Books were to be devoured, to be got under one's belt, so that one might in effect say, "Ah, the Kafka (the smoked salmon), I've already read (eaten) it." I recall that, shortly after leaving college, I packed a suitcase that included some sixteen volumes, paperback and clothbound, by Joseph Conrad, whose collected works I planned to read in the order in which they were written. As it turned out, I managed to get only as far as *Lord Jim* (Conrad's fourth book), in which I bogged down; and today, twenty-odd years later, I have yet to read all of Conrad, in or out of sequence, whose work I still admire. In fact, now that I think of it, I have not yet finished *Lord Jim*.

In my youth I had planned to read systematically through all the important writers—Shakespeare, Tolstoy, Dostoyevsky, Dickens, George Eliot, Balzac, James, Mann, Proust, etc.—each in his or her full corpus. I would knock them off, one after another, and when I was finished there I would be

—*voilà!*—an educated fellow. It didn't quite work out that way, and I am able to stand here today and say that I have not read all the works of any of the above-mentioned writers, not to mention those of that prolific author Etc. I am embraced by shame, covered with the blush of my own inadequacy. When it comes to reading, though, nearly everyone feels, or ought to feel, inadequate in one way or another. For in one way or another, nearly everyone is inadequate. One simply cannot have read everything; if one tried to read most of the world's good books, there would be scarcely any time to read many of the world's interesting books, for, as any veteran reader will tell you, good and interesting books are sometimes but not always the same.

How much better just to relax in one's inadequacy, to enjoy it or, at any rate, to accept it. Yet this appears to be a difficult thing to do; it is difficult to admit one's own limitations to oneself and perhaps even more difficult to admit them to others. Among academics and intellectuals, one of the most troublesome sentences to pronounce is, "I haven't read it." I have not myself actually lied by claiming to have read a book I have not in fact read, but I have stood by allowing others to think I have. To make amends, and to reform through public confession, I should now like everyone to know that I have never read *The Brothers Karamazov*.

This abject confession reminds me of a game I heard about not long ago, one supposedly played at academic parties. In this game, academics—one has to imagine them slightly fried —admit to the great books they ought to have but indeed have not read. I gather that the rhythm of the game is such that it begins with small admissions, but soon a competitive edge cuts in—a kind of one-downmanship—and the admissions get larger and larger. At a party of English department academics, for example, someone might begin by confessing that he has

never read a novel by Norman Douglas. The next person
might claim never to have read, say, *The Autocrat of the Break-
fast-Table*. Someone then chimes in with the admission that
she has never read the poems of Gerard Manley Hopkins.
"Hopkins hell," someone else says, "I've never read a poem by
Yeats." Everyone agrees that this is fairly impressive, until a
full professor says, "Yeats, Schmeats, I've never read the *Faerie
Queene.* " A sucking in of breath is heard round the room. Then
a woman off in the corner, the department's resident Marxist,
admits that not only has she never read Chaucer, but she isn't
even certain of the century in which he lived. Suddenly a quiet
man, the head of the school's American studies program,
strides forth, obvious pride in his posture, to announce, "I hate
to break up these festivities, but I'm afraid that's just what I'm
about to do. You ready for this? I have never read a play by
Shakespeare—and that includes your bloody *Hamlet.* "

One of the reasons that most people feel inadequate about
reading is the ideal—an ideal that is difficult to shake off—of
well-roundedness. Being well-read generally implies being
well-roundedly-read. Well-roundedness remains an ideal, even
though taste and temperament make it an ideal impossible for
almost all of us to achieve. Thus the other day I almost bought
a ten-dollar paperback entitled *The Experience of Mathematics*.
It looked to me a fascinating book—so fascinating that I nearly
forgot that I barely have the mathematical concentration to do
long division. I need to read a longish book on mathematics the
way a couple living in a Manhattan high rise needs a Brahma
bull; and I have about as much chance of making headway in
such a book as that couple does of sneaking the Brahma bull
past the doorman. Yet, as the old pop tune has it, I can dream,
can't I?

Yet the dream of intellectual well-roundedness may be
chimerical, well-roundedness itself being considerably over-

rated. I have neither read nor met a polymath whose mind seemed to me very interesting. Still, most of us cannot quite get over our amazement at people who can do more than one thing at a fairly high level. A scientist such as Lewis Thomas, for example, who not only can do cancer research but also can write splendid English prose and has actually read Montaigne, seems, in our day, an astonishing creature. It is comforting, though, to note that Montaigne himself neither was intellectually well-rounded nor sought to be. "I should certainly like to have a more perfect knowledge of things," he wrote in his essay "Of Books," "but I do not want to buy it as dear as it costs. . . . I seek in books only to give myself pleasure by honest amusement; or if I study, I seek only the learning that treats of the knowledge of myself and instructs me in how to die well and live well."

Montaigne did not ask that books make him learned—"In general I ask for books that make use of learning, not those that build it up"—but that they make him wiser, which is what one needs "to die well and live well." Montaigne might be Everyman, but not every man is Montaigne. What makes the problem of choosing reading for other people so difficult is that, as Montaigne himself puts it in the essay entitled "Of the Inequality That Is Between Us," there "are as many degrees in minds as there are fathoms from here to heaven, and as innumerable." To learn the degree of one's own mind, let alone that of the minds of others, is not so simple. It is chiefly because he knew his own mind so wondrously well that Montaigne, among other reasons, shall always be honored.

Because minds do so differ in degree, it can be a bit hopeless to instruct people about what they ought to read. I, for example, have discovered in myself a powerful feeling for fantastical literature—this feeling is one of powerful apathy. A decade or so ago many friends advised me to read J. R. R. Tolkien's *Lord of the Rings,* but it was no go. Neither have I ever wished to read William Golding's *Lord of the Flies.* (Earlier I mentioned never having finished *Lord Jim;* is there a pattern emerging? Please make a note not to give me, on my next birthday, any books with the word Lord in the title.) The real is fantastical enough, and so I eschew fantastical books. Some quite intelligent people, similarly, have no taste for reading philosophy, and not only contemporary technical philosophy but philosophy of the kind Santayana and F. H. Bradley wrote. Others find nothing for themselves in even the most intelligible poetry. How many first-class physicists have had a serious interest in modern painting; and how many first-class modern painters have had a serious interest in physics? Would they have been better physicists and painters if they had? Or would they simply have gotten less physics and painting done?

One may be able to tell more about a person by what he doesn't read than by what he does. In *A Writer's Notebook,* Somerset Maugham offered an interesting catalogue of what he did not read, which included most modern novels, though he did read detective stories that he claimed he no sooner read than forgot. Maugham noted: "I have never cared to read books on subjects that were in no way my concern, and I still cannot bring myself to read books of entertainment or instruction about people or places that mean nothing to me. I do not want to know the history of Hungary or the manners and customs of the Eskimos, I do not want to read a life of Manzoni and my curiosity about stout Cortez is satisfied with the fact that he stood upon a peak in Darien." Maugham goes on to say that he can read "everything" that has to do with Dr. Johnson and "almost everything" about Coleridge, Byron, and Shelley. He also read "Plato, Aristotle (who they say is dry, but in whom if you have a sense of humor you can find quite a lot to amuse you), Plotinus, and Spinoza, with sundry modern

philosophers, among them Bradley. . . ." Maugham felt that
"old age robs one of the thrill one had when one first read the
great masterpieces of the world," adding that this "one can
never recapture." Yet he claimed that to read the philosophers
and the Greek tragedians was "to sail with a gentle breeze in
an inland sea studded with a thousand isles."

A most ungentle breeze—a small typhoon, really—on the
subject of what and what not to read blew in some years ago
in the form of a book entitled *Fifty Works of English and American Literature We Could Do Without* by Brigid Brophy, Michael Levey, and Charles Osborne. Sound advice on what not
to read would be a boon to humankind, or so one might think.
Every book one doesn't need to read, after all, represents one
book more one will have time to read. Few negative pleasures
are as exhilarating to the bookish as reading a persuasive review
whose gravamen is that one needn't bother reading a prolific
writer whose many works one has had a bad conscience about
not hitherto having read. But the authors of *Fifty Works* aren't
kidding around. Among the works they tell us they could do
without—and, by implication, so ought we to do without them
—are *Tom Jones, Moby-Dick, Leaves of Grass, Alice's Adventures
in Wonderland, Pickwick Papers,* and, yes, that old game-ender,
Hamlet, Prince of Denmark. Iconoclasm can be a fine thing;
many an icon is worth shattering; but *Fifty Works* is an attempt
to blow up the church. Reading down the list of classics con-
demned by the authors of *Fifty Works,* I can only report my
personal conclusion that here three people's poison more often
than not turns out to be another man's meat.

Behind the condemnation proceedings of *Fifty Works of
English and American Literature We Could Do Without* is the
charge that, in one way or another, these works are boring. I
do not happen to agree, for example, that *Pickwick Papers* is
boring. ("It does not develop," the authors write, "it simply

goes on. And on.") But a question that arises is, How many boring books need to be read by a person seeking to become educated? I should guess that the figure might be between two and three hundred. Such a book for me was John Locke's *Two Treatises on Civil Government*, which as a young man I read somewhere in the middle of Texas. Time never hung so heavy as when I clumped my way through that work. I have thought since that, were I given a limited time to live, I might return to Texas with the collected writings of John Locke. Under the Texas sun, with John Locke's text before me, each day would seem a decade.

Is it possible, though, that it is I and not John Locke who is boring? I don't think I care to answer that question, for I have noticed that people who are easily and therefore regularly bored are frequently themselves quite boring. What is boring and what is not boring is a question that puts one on tricky terrain. The ground often shifts with age. I have read many writers that, though they seemed to be dull when I was young, seem splendid in middle age (Matthew Arnold, for example). The reverse also sometimes obtains: books I adored when young I can barely read now that I am older. (When, a few years ago, I tried to reread Hemingway's *The Sun Also Rises*, I found myself, so hokey did much of this once-loved book seem to me, counting the drinks its characters imbibed.) Interest, in bookish matters, is all very well, but it seems to me that it cannot be allowed to count for everything, especially among the young. A freshman student, in a course I teach in American novels, recently told me that, so interesting has he found Arthur Hailey's *Airport*, he has now read it four times. As I heard this, I winced and hung a flag with a star on the window of my heart for all that killed time.

Boredom, like beauty, is in the mind of the beholder. Still, I wonder if the student who asked me for a list of books would

not be well-served with a category within that list entitled
"Perhaps Boring But Doubtless Essential Books," on which an
author such as John Locke might appear. So, too, might many
a work by Marx, a number by Rousseau, and no few by John
Dewey. A longer list would, of course, be one entitled "Doubtless Boring But Perhaps Inessential Books." But I forebear
naming authors here. Once I began, once I really got into the
swing of it, there might be no stopping me.

Unfortunately, giving people advice about what they
ought to read invariably makes the person giving the advice
sound stuffy. In his introduction to *The Lifetime Reading Plan*
Clifton Fadiman, who is very well-read indeed and who can
write well about books when he is criticizing or reviewing
them, sounds the dread note of stuffiness when extolling the
virtues of reading the most serious books: "They can be a major
experience, a source of continuous internal growth. . . . Once
part of you, they work in and on and with you until you die."
He is talking about books, I know, yet what he is describing
sounds curiously like fungus. Once you start talking about the
delights of reading, funny things happen. Some years ago,
discovering that a fairly bookish friend had never read any of
the books of Isaac Bashevis Singer, I said to him, in what I
thought was complete sincerity: "You're lucky, really. I envy
you all the pleasures in store for you." He looked at me
strangely. "You know," he said, "I never realized how damned
condescending you can be when you put your mind to it."

Since that little exchange I have been chary of offering
advice about books, except in print (when paid to do so) and
except to the occasional student who asks for it. Not only is
there the danger in doing so of sounding like a stuffed shirt,
but in my case there is the additional danger of hypocrisy.
When it comes to reading I am unable to follow any system
whatsoever; the word desultory may have been invented to

describe my reading habits. The phrase "full of fine but finally fickle intentions" would not be misapplied either. Thus on a recent Sunday I resolved to finish the last seventy or so pages of a book I had been reading in five- or ten-page snatches, Herbert R. Lottman's *The Left Bank,* a study of French literary intellectuals in the middle third of the current century. I didn't finish it, of course. Instead I began *Aunt Julia and the Scriptwriter* by the Peruvian novelist Mario Vargas Llosa and *Goodbye to All That* by Robert Graves, a book I should have read before now but for one reason or another haven't. This, if I may say so, is a typical performance. I have only to declare that I shall finish a book to be certain of starting two others.

In reading, my personal hero is Justice Holmes. His literary diet was always so nicely balanced between the classic and the contemporary, and his reading for pleasure and for his profession seemed to feed into each other with only the blurriest line of demarcation between them. He took proper delight in a solid book, and he could be properly ticked off when a book didn't deliver the goods, such as a work in French on the right of privacy, of more than six hundred pages "and not a damned word from start to finish that I don't know or disbelieve." Taking a book's measure for him meant calibrating the mind of its author, an activity at which he was generally quite accurate; and his opinions about writers, never predictable, are always provocative. "I am a long way off," he wrote to Harold Laski, "from believing that Thoreau was a thinker in any important sense." He knew what he wanted from reading and where to go to get it. He cited, for example, the *Letters of Horace Walpole* as perfect for "the moments between vacuity and thinking." He sought from his reading what any sensible person ought to seek from reading. "I seek improvement," he wrote, "without excessive *ennui.*"

In one of his letters Justice Holmes speaks of his inability *not* to finish reading a book once he has begun it—an inability that plagued him until his seventy-fifth year. Here is the one instance where I think of myself having the advantage over Justice Holmes. I learned not to finish books by the time I was forty. I do not, it is true, set out not to finish books but neatly accomplish this task all the same. I could put together an impressively long shelf of books with my bookmarks in them, which have had bookmarks in them for some time, and which in all likelihood will continue to have bookmarks in them. Many of these are books of the kind I think of as dippable— books not to be read straight through or even straight across but instead to be dipped into from time to time: collections of letters, books of stories or poems, an author's collected writings, diaries and journals, essays, an occasional ambitious novel begun in a fever of cultural ambition but put aside for more pressing business.

On the whole I seem to finish more novels than other kinds of books. Thus the Mario Vargas Llosa novel I mentioned a few paragraphs back has been read, but a bookmark now resides in the early pages of *Good-bye to All That.* My guess is that I may not say good-bye to *Good-bye to All That* for months and months. One of the especial pleasures of Anthony Powell's novel series, *A Dance to the Music of Time,* was that, once I had read three or four books in it, I found I could stop reading any of these novels almost in mid-sentence, then pick it up again three or four months later without the least sense of losing step. Mr. Powell's *Dance,* after all, is no boogaloo but something more on the order of a minuet. Again, I have been reading Abraham Joshua Heschel's book *Maimonides,* a work of fewer than three hundred pages, for nearly eight months now. It is not a difficult book, certainly nothing that needs to be swotted up; it is instead a book that gives pleasure, and I see no need to rip through it. I should as soon be a man who is reading

Abraham Joshua Heschel's *Maimonides* as a man who has read it.

But doubtless the oddest of all my current bookmarks is the one to be found on page 1048 of volume three of the new English translation of Marcel Proust's *Remembrance of Things Past*. That bookmark has been advanced only ten or so pages over the past year. The final page of this, the final volume in what I believe to be the world's greatest modern novel, is 1107. I have read more than three thousand pages of this novel; I am within sixty pages of completing it; I have adored it; and yet something in me does not want me to finish it. Psychological interpretations of this most extraordinary behavior will be welcome and read with passionate interest, though I cannot promise to finish reading any of them.

Because of such erratic behavior I am all the more hesitant to give advice to others about what they ought to read. The intellectual world is, besides, much divided on this question. I happen to be someone greedy to read all the world's interesting books. But there are other views. The students of the great yeshivas of Eastern Europe spent lifetimes poring over a few basic texts. The disciples of the political philosopher Leo Strauss read and teach the same twenty or twenty-five books to the exclusion of almost all others. Vladimir Nabokov had a similar diet of twenty-five or so main books, which he read over and over, though these were of course very different books from those Leo Strauss chose to concentrate on. But Strauss, I think, would have agreed with Nabokov when the latter wrote: "Curiously enough, one cannot read a book: one can only reread it."

Rereading presents yet another immense complication. Every serious reader knows that he has read significant books at the wrong times in his life—usually when he was too young and hence not prepared for them—and would like to have another go at them. Then there are those books that gave one so much pleasure that one wishes to recapture the pleasure by the only known way—by, that is, rereading them. The late Alexander Gerschenkron, acting on this impulse, read *War and Peace*, as he wrote in *The American Scholar*, "at least fifteen times." Yet when Somerset Maugham claimed that rereading masterworks did not give him the limitless delight one might expect, he blamed this in part on his own superior memory. Evelyn Waugh, on the other hand, writing to Anne Fleming, noted: "It is very pleasant losing one's memory. One can read old favorites with breathless curiosity."

Although theoretically I approve of rereading, I must confess that I have not done a great deal of it. The problem is my ardor to read at least once all the books I wish to read. What is more, I continue to buy books all the while: three books by F. H. Bradley; four of the five volumes of Osbert Sitwell's autobiography, *Left Hand, Right Hand!*; *The Letters of Gustave Flaubert*; *The Noël Coward Diaries*—in short, the usual mishmash. The likelihood of my finishing these books soon—or, possibly, ever—is not large, for I also have a good deal of reading to do in connection with my own writing and teaching. Yet I remain, like a man holding a quinella ticket at the racetrack, ever hopeful.

The hope is dampened a bit by age. There are so many things I already realize I shall never read in toto: Emerson's *Journals*, Sainte-Beuve's *Port-Royal*, Samuel Butler's *Notebooks*, Balzac's *La Comédie humaine*. There are so many things I should hate to think of not being able to reread: the novels of Tolstoy, Gibbon's *Decline and Fall of the Roman Empire*, Proust's *Remembrance of Things Past* (if I can bring myself to finish it the first time). When does a bookish person decide it is time to begin rereading? The decision is no minor one. It is akin to deciding that perhaps one has swum out as far as one can and that one must now head back to the shore.

What complicates this even further is the almost continuous discovery of new writers—or, more precisely, older writers who are new to me. I had thought, for example, that I had read nearly all the interesting Yiddish fiction that had been published in English, and therefore had that subject—to revert to a phrase I used earlier—under my belt. Alas (or Hurrah?), in a book entitled *Rabbis and Wives* by Chaim Grade I recently discovered another master in this line. Worse (better?) news: Grade has a chunky oeuvre. I am currently reading his two-volume novel, running to nearly eight-hundred pages, *The Yeshiva*. Worse (better?) news still: it knocks me out. How many more hidden Chaim Grades—fine writers I ought to have known about but didn't—are out there?

Quite a few, my guess is. Barbara Pym, another such writer, in her novel *No Fond Return of Love*, has a character who, in response to the statement of another character who has been doing research on an obscure eighteenth-century poet, says: "You were lucky to find one so obscure that not even the Americans had 'done' him. . . . It's quite serious, this shortage of obscure poets." Yet this shortage has not yet reached alarming proportions, I dare say, and neither has the supply of good books from the past diminished. "Of making many books there is no end," it is written in Ecclesiastes, and the fellow who wrote that line, even though he did not subscribe to *Publishers Weekly*, knew whereof he spoke.

All this could only have thoroughly depressed my student, who came to me for a little sensible advice about what he ought to read, and who, if I had gone through this megillah with him, would only have departed with a headache. What I did tell him, finally, was to read no junky books, to haunt used-book stores, and to let one book lead him to another. And I tried to make clear to him that amusement, beauty, and, with a bit of luck, wisdom are picked up along the way in a reading life. But there is no systematic way to go about it, no list, key to the kingdom of the educated. There is also a danger: once begun, there is no end. I myself would rather be well-read than dead, but I have a strong hunch about which will come first. Even that, though, is fair enough and fine with me. Meanwhile, if you hear of any good books, or writers whose works you think I ought to look into, I shall thank you, if you please, kindly to keep them to yourself.

Let Us Now Praise Famous Knuckleheads

"I DO NOT HAVE ULCERS, I give them," it was recently reported to me that a big-time New York lawyer is fond of saying. Always on the outlook for stealing if not a phrase then at least its rhythm, I thought, "I do not ask for recommendations, I write them." Mostly I write them for students seeking entry into graduate or professional schools, but occasionally I am called upon to do so for scholars seeking grants or writers looking for lodging in one or another literary hostelry. But in writing these recommendations I have often thought that, to return to the lawyer's bareknuckle phrase, I would prefer to have ulcers. Begun in insincerity and ending in doubt, these recommendations tend to give me a bad conscience—the ulcers, you might say, of the intellectual life.

I believe I have mastered the form all right. Of students I say that they are "intelligent, industrious, and imaginative." I note that they are "mature beyond their years." I salt my recommendations with pert phrases and happy buzz words: I refer to scholars as "creative" and to writers as "serious." This sort of thing is, I assume, what is wanted. Calm language and measured estimates, given the hyped-up atmosphere in which we now live, can only serve to squash a claimant's hopes in the minds of unthinking admissions officers and directors of endowments and grant boards. Imagine yourself a member of the admissions committee of the Stanford Business School starting to read a recommendation of mine, written with the difficult intent of accuracy, that begins: "Miss Carol Throckmorton, who has been a student of mine, is a reasonably intelligent young woman with a fairly clear mind." With a recommendation like that, and a good deal of luck, poor Miss Throckmorton may be able to get onto the waiting list of a mediocre beautician's school.

My small problem is of course part of a much larger problem—the problem of the inflation and subsequent debasement of praise, to the point where praise has lost almost all value and requires, if it is to be noticed at all, a great deal of pumping up. The general debasement of praise has been going on for a very long while. Raymond Chandler, in letters he wrote in the late 1930s, spoke of the depreciation of praise in his time. But so far has this debasement gone that praise must now be shouted to be heard. Not that in the world today there is any scarcity of megaphones. Thus, announcers on my local FM classical music station—men who regularly refer to the most sublime works of Bach, Mozart, and Beethoven in a tone of voice best described as "cultivated blasé"—in reading the advertising for a contemporary avant-garde play must abruptly shift the gears of their larynxes to claim that this play "kicks us in the guts and the soul and entertains us at the same time." Now a kick in the guts I can understand, though it is not my idea of a pleasant night on the town. But you would think a "kick in the soul" ought to be reserved for dramatists of the caliber of Sophocles and greater.

Not long ago I came up against the problem of praise when called upon to write about Marguerite Yourcenar, a novelist I greatly admire and whose books I feel have been inadequately appreciated. Should I describe Mme Yourcenar as "brilliant," which, as it happens, her books often are? Unfortunately, the word "brilliant" has been used up. Students are now called "brilliant"; Norman Mailer is "brilliant." What about "masterful," which, when she is writing well, she also can be? No, sorry, "masterful" has been pressed into service to describe every other scribbler, dauber, and fiddler of our day, and consequently must now be retired. What about cutting out all these middlemen words of praise and simply calling her a "genius," then knocking off for lunch? Problems here again, I fear. Not only have people such as Woody Allen, Leonard Bernstein, and the Beatles been wrongly called "geniuses," but Marguerite Yourcenar is not a genius. She is merely—some "merely" —a very considerable and highly learned literary artist. *Brilliant, masterful, genius*—all these words have lost their absorbency; they no longer, as Virginia Woolf once said good words and phrases ought to do, soak up much truth. So I decided not to use any of these words in connection with Mme Yourcenar. Instead, when I came to write about her, I attempted, as carefully as I was able, to say what I thought it was that made her novels so good—and hoped that no one would take my essay, shorn as it was of praise spelled out in neon, for a put-down.

Praise has been called the least palling of the pleasures, and it was doubtless owing to this that powerful ancient rulers kept panegyrists at court. Does praise never pall? On the occasions when praise has come my way, I have shown remarkable patience and stamina while listening to or reading it. Yet praise is also a very delicate literary art. "Fulsome" is probably the adjective most frequently linked to the noun "praise"; still, praise can be underdone, especially praise directed at oneself. I was recently introduced to a couple who, I was told beforehand, were great admirers of my writing. When I shook the

man's hand, he said, "You are so prolific," to which his wife
added, "How do you manage to turn out so much?" And
nothing further was said. Ah, thought I, but an unfixed female
alley cat is prolific; and the ample boutonniere that is my ego
sadly wilted.

The malicious would do well to learn the art of faint praise,
though most faint praise let loose in the world is, I am sure,
without malice aforethought. I recall coming across a book
bearing a blurb citing its author as "surely among the best
thirty or forty of our younger novelists." Do get back to me,
I thought to tell the writer of that blurb, when you think this
kid is among the best three or four of our older novelists. On
the back of James Gould Cozzens's *Guard of Honor* I read,
courtesy of a reviewer in the now-defunct *New York Herald-
Tribune,* that this book is "the most skillfully constructed novel
of 1948," and wonder if 1948 was a particularly good year for
well-constructed novels. Of a poet named Charles Edward
Eaton, author of a book of verse entitled *In the Land of the
Thing King,* the critic Robert Boyers writes, "Increasingly one
of our finest poets." Why is it I feel this blurb would have been
more convincing if Boyers had written, "Decreasingly one of
our worst poets"?

The passion for praise feeds upon itself. Praise may well be
a narcotic of the kind that, once imbibed, calls for larger and
larger doses. It has been said of a famous playwright and
memoirist, a woman who when it comes to praise has over the
years had a pretty good roll of the dice, that she was toward
the close of her life uninterested in anything less than a standing ovation. A still fairly young James Gould Cozzens, having
won the O. Henry Prize for his short story "Total Stranger,"
wrote to his mother to mock such prizes, jokingly adding that
"the reason I prefer to live as nearly like a recluse as possible
is that I subconsciously know that people, the world, never

would and never will greet my entrances into it with the reverent applause required for my pleasure and if I cannot have that I will not, in effect, play." But that reads to me like one of those jokes that, at bottom, just might be serious.

When one has had a little praise, the tendency is to get a bit sniffy about praise. A good friend not long ago wrote to praise some recent writings of mine, saying that I "must now be thought of as the Sammy Davis, Jr., of American letters." The praise was quite sincere, and meant to compliment me, I believe, for my energy and variety. I, however, wrote back to ask for an adjustment. Although Sammy Davis, Jr., is my co-religionist, I would be willing to pay anywhere from fifty to one hundred dollars on any given night simply *not* to see him perform. This being so, could he change his praise? A flexible man, my friend then dubbed me Sir John Max-Beer-bohm Squire, an honor I accepted with large-hearted graciousness.

The best single piece of praise I have ever had came from a businessman I much admire who once remarked that I handled a matter of some complexity in a way he thought "very business-like." Which is a reminder that the source of praise is of the utmost significance. Two dozen long-stemmed roses and a jeroboam of Piper-Heidsieck in recognition of one's achievements from the chairman of the American Nazi Party can scarcely bring satisfaction, unless of course one happens to be an American Nazi. Similarly, praise from people in no position to know the true nature of one's accomplishments, though better I suppose than contempt from the same quarter, isn't good enough to allay doubts about one's real worth, which is one of the things praise ought to do but seldom does.

Praise from one's peers is lovely, but praise from one's betters surpasses even it. Yet what if one doesn't have any betters? I can think of people who, in their respective fields, do

not. I should imagine the only altogether satisfactory praise for
I. I. Rabi, for example, would have to issue from Einstein or
Niels Bohr; for Arnaldo Momigliano from Theodor Mommsen;
for Edward Shils from Max Weber; for Oscar Peterson from
Art Tatum. But perhaps these men no longer require much in
the way of praise; perhaps by now they know their own worth.
Still, my guess is that it is not their worth they dwell on but
instead what they have not yet accomplished and still hope to.

Knowing one's own worth reminds me of a story I heard
about a literary critic, a woman in her seventies, who, in approaching a foundation for a large grant, balked at the requirement of sending out recommendation forms. "I have been
writing in public for nearly fifty years now," she is supposed
to have said, "and if my quality isn't apparent by now it never
will be." I think she is correct; her quality is apparent, and on
the basis of it, if I were an official of that foundation, I should
have turned down her application. But she has a point: she has
been at work too long to be asked to go out and organize praise
on her own behalf.

About this ingathering of one's own praise there is something more than a little unseemly. Yet in intellectual life it goes
on more and more. A student must find teachers to praise him
so that he may proceed to the next level of professional learning. A scholar in search of a grant must find fellow scholars to
praise him. A writer, when he publishes a new book, is asked
to submit the names of other writers who will supply praise for
him that can be used in the form of blurbs on the dust jacket
of his book. Thus, in the new praising era, one hand washes
itself. One of the nice things about being a philanthropist, I
should think, is that, when they come to honor you for your
good works, at least you don't have to go out and fetch your
own testimonials.

When the Kissing Had to Stop is the title of a novel by

Constantine FitzGibbon that I have never read but that often comes to mind as I prop myself up to my typewriter to tap out yet another student recommendation. If this need for recommendations doesn't let up soon, I sometimes think that I shall be driven to candor. "Michael Goodman is a solid, industrious, and so far as I know honest enough young man," I feel myself wanting to write. "He is a bit dull, perhaps, yet I can predict with fair confidence that, no matter what group young Mr. Goodman is in, he will go right to the middle." Now that ought to render Goody a gone goose.

Although it may be a true enough assessment of this student's abilities, I cannot bring myself to write it. Let us say that young Mr. Goodman is applying to law school, and not to any of the top five or six law schools. How do I know that he won't be a quite decent lawyer? And if he turns out to be a mediocre one, well, the world is filled with mediocre lawyers—also mediocre doctors, architects, teachers, writers, and cooks—and worse than mediocre ones, too. Why should this student suffer from my somewhat sniffy high standards? Perhaps in the next office a colleague with more relaxed (let us call them "laid-back") standards might, at the very moment I am disqualifying the Goodman kid, be lying monstrously about the merits of a young man or woman even more mediocre than he? I don't, after all, keep a sign on my desk that reads: "Mr. and Mrs. Goodman's aspirations for their son Michael stop here." Instead I toss off two paragraphs of light praise, the usual effluvia, and rate Michael Goodman somewhere around the top eightieth percentile in intellectual ability, creativity, responsibility, leadership, and a few other qualities at which I should probably rate myself somewhere near the fiftieth percentile. If one day he turns out to be a public prosecutor, and I am on trial—for dereliction of duty, no doubt—perhaps he will recommend a gentle work-release program for me.

When did we first lose our grip on standards in this country? With the spread of higher education? With the institution of the automatic standard-of-living raise in jobs? With the onset of the psychological concern that no one go unpraised, however meager his talents? Not all of these are bad things, in and of themselves. Nor can I with a clear conscience come out for implacably, irretrievably high standards. Because its standards are not rigidly high, the United States is the country of the second chance, and that, too, is not such a bad thing. As a boy who had a less than glittering academic adolescence, I know that, had I been born in England or France, where academic standards are set early in life, I should probably not have been permitted to go to university at all. Still, there is undeniably a problem here. The problem is how to give everyone a fair and decent chance without giving the game away.

The interim solution, and not a very successful one as far as I can determine, is to see to it that as many people as possible are passed through the portals—and praised on their way through. Praise has increasingly become one of the items on the lengthy list of modern entitlements, part of the revolution of rising psychological expectations. Yet at the same time that praise has become more widespread, it has become less good. There is, I suspect, a slightly snobbish element to praise: if everyone has it, who wants it? At Versailles, the duc de Saint-Simon informs us, the maréchal de Choiseul was so immensely pleased by being permitted by Louis XIV to become a member of the order that allowed him to wear a blue ribbon over his coat that, when wearing his ribbon, he could not refrain from gazing at himself in every mirror he passed. The maréchal continued to do so until the courtesan who called herself Mlle L'Enclos said to him one day, before a rather large gathering of courtiers, "Monsieur le Comte, if I catch you doing that again, I shall tell you the names of your fellow members." I was reminded of the poor maréchal when a small but highly pleasing honor came my way in the form of my having a story I wrote selected for the anthology entitled *The Best American Short Stories, 1983.* The rub came when I learned—and not from Mlle L'Enclos—that among my fellow contributors to this volume are a number of writers whose work I actively dislike.

As for the simultaneous spread and inflation of praise, perhaps no better indication of it is available than in the continual pumping up of job titles. I first noted this a few decades ago when banks began to bestow the title of "junior vice-president" on some of their employees. What this meant, I took it, was that not to be a vice-president of some kind in a bank was nearly disgraceful. A non-vice-president in a bank will soon be rarer than a German without a doctorate. Something similar has begun to take place in academic life. Anyone who is not a full professor by his early forties is clearly becoming someone left by the wayside; and not to be the Ralph and Rita Raffles Double Distinguished Service Professor of All Human Sciences by fifty probably means you are a bust. Soon academic titles will be awarded with oak-leaf clusters.

The need for praise is greatest among people who do not know their own worth. This includes all but the tiniest minority of human beings. It also includes whole large categories of people. High on the list of the thousand neediest categories are students, who cannot know their own worth except through the judgment of their teachers. Yet praise for students, as for the young generally, ought to be applied delicately, with a very fine brush, lest its recipients start out in life with too high a valuation of themselves. Edith Wharton, in her memoir *A Backward Glance,* remarks how fortunate she was never to have been considered, by her parents or such teachers as she had, promising. It allowed her to develop in her own fashion. Meanwhile, most of the young men with whom she had grown up who had been considered promising seemed to suffer greatly at not being able to live up to their own highly touted promise. Among the students that I see, I can fairly quickly make out those who have had the fires of their youthful egos well stoked and banked with praise, and they are, by and large, not the most pleasant or interesting.

Artists are famously hungry for praise, with writers pushing themselves away from the table last of all. Perhaps this is because writers—with the exception of dramatists—are not usually permitted to witness people actually partaking of their work, unlike actors, performing and composing musicians, and painters and sculptors, all of whom can watch people in the very midst of their enjoyment of their art. Writers have to take people's word for it. Even Proust, who seems to have known his own worth very well, liked his portion of praise. In her lovely memoir of Proust, Céleste Albaret, who served as his general factotum during Proust's last years, remarks that her employer was a keen connoisseur of praise. When she reported to him that the mother of the banker Gans said to her that Proust's book was "so rich, so dense," Proust replied: " 'Dense' —is that what she said? I like that, Céleste." Yet Proust also knew how to spot and deal with false praise. "I thank them, Céleste, and they think I'm taken in. If they knew! They have not read a word of what I have written. I see through them immediately!" Imagine trying to pull the wool over the toes— the phrase is e. e. cummings's—of someone as perceptive as Marcel Proust.

The word for exaggerated or false praise is of course flattery. Flattery is the pit in the plum of praise, and most of us are ready enough to swallow it. I not long ago met up with an old school chum, now a quite successful salesman, and flattery being among the weapons in the salesman's arsenal, he lobbed a few grenades my way by reminding me what a good athlete

I was (I wasn't), how smart I was (I wasn't), how youthful
looking I have remained (I haven't). No sale. Worse, though,
was an experience I had when giving a talk to a fairly large
group—a thing I do neither easily nor well. Afterward, a
woman in the audience took me aside to say, "You were brilliant!!!" So emphatically did she go on that before the last
exclamation point had faded from the air I wondered where,
exactly, I had botched it.

Occasions do present themselves in which praise of some
sort seems in order. Especially does praise seem in order on
meeting people whose work is of a public kind. It is here that,
if not exactly false praise, mis-aimed praise can come into play.
I recall hearing about a young writer, in his debut in London
literary society, who was introduced to the late Sir Herbert
Read. "Ah, Sir Herbert," said the young man, "I have derived
so very much pleasure from your books." And then, struggling
to remember something that Herbert Read had written, he
added: "I particularly enjoyed *The Nude.*" "Actually," Sir Herbert is said to have responded, "I didn't *quite* write that one."
I myself for more than a few years now have avoided meeting
a writer who teaches at the same university I do, because I feel
that on meeting him I probably ought to say something about
his writing, which in fact I find loathsome. If I were a more
combative fellow, I should shake his hand, look him in the eye,
and say: "I have of course been reading your work for years.
Terrible stuff. What do you suppose it would take to cause you
to stop writing? I mean, can you name a figure? I should be
only too glad to begin fund raising." In this regard I much
admire a friend of mine, an art critic of high standards, who
was asked if he were ever embarrassed to meet artists whose
works he had strongly criticized. "Not at all," he said. "They
ought to be embarrassed for producing such wretched art."

Awards and prizes are a species of formal recognition, and

hence of praise, and while winning them is, on the whole, to be preferred to not winning them, I wonder if they don't, in their own way, encourage doubt in their recipients. To begin with, given the public-relations atmosphere in which we now live, there are so many prizes and awards: Nobels, Pulitzers, Guggenheims, Rockefellers, MacArthurs, Tonys, Oscars, Emmys, Polks, Peabodys, and so on, into the dark night of the ego. Then there are the honorary degrees, honorific lectures, blue-ribbon commissions, critics awards, and other prizes so obscure that only their recipients and donors seem to know about them. The University of Chicago, for example, has an award inaptly named Communicator of the Year. I say inaptly because whenever I see mention of it I tend to think of programs to stamp out venereal disease, and the aforementioned Communicator sounds less like an honorand than someone who must be captured and cured—and quickly.

Two embarrassing questions that anyone who has just won an award might—even though he is unlikely to—ask himself are: Who before me has won this award? And who, of obvious great merit, has not won it? Perhaps a third question might be asked: Who has shunned it? In the modern era, for example, Proust, Gide, Sartre, and Camus have disregarded the French Academy. In literature it has to be a source of minor but persistent dubiety to anyone who has won the Nobel Prize that over the years various lunkheads in Stockholm have overlooked giving a Nobel Prize to Leo Tolstoy, Henry James, James Joyce, and Marcel Proust. As the valuable Mlle L'Enclos might put it, "Monsieur le Nobel laureate, if you don't stop preening, I shall tell you who your fellow laureates *aren't.*"

The fly backstroking in the soup of praise represented by prizes and awards is that it doesn't take long for any prize or award to besmirch itself. Give it to two or three of the wrong people, or fail to give it to one or two of the right people, and the job is done. One has to press to think of many prizes in the world today that have not been so besmirched. For intensity of besmirchment, no single award has so covered itself with the reverse of glory as the Pulitzer Prizes. Two examples will have to suffice. The Pulitzer Prize was awarded to Saul Bellow for fiction only after Bellow had won the Nobel Prize, which must have seemed like being given a cup of warmed-over instant coffee twenty minutes after having drunk the world's most expensive cognac; and it was never awarded to Hilton Kramer, whose criticism, with the possible exception only of Virgil Thomson's music criticism, for seriousness and general high quality has known no peer in the history of American newspaper journalism.

That prizes and awards have less and less significance does not for a moment mean that people yearn less and less for them. It may even be that when inferior people win awards, the merely mediocre become envious. Sometimes it is surprising to learn who considers himself a contender. I, at any rate, was surprised to learn—as I did from Burton Bernstein's biography —that James Thurber was sorely disappointed not to win the Nobel Prize. Do you suppose John Barth or Joyce Carol Oates or John Irving marks his or her calendar for the day on which Nobel Prizes in Literature are given and sleeps uneasily the night before? One can readily imagine an Edward Koren cartoon set in the house of a writer in which a mother says to her small child: "Do try to be quiet today, darling. Daddy didn't win the Nobel Prize again this year."

It might be a good idea if, during certain years, prizes were not awarded for want of prize-winning achievement. Yet once the prize-awarding machinery is set in motion, the process, like the huge furnaces at steel mills, cannot be snuffed out. Consider, for instance, honorary degrees, without which many universities feel no commencement exercise is complete. I realize that there are many secret motives and hidden agendas in the awarding of honorary degrees, and these may include inducing a rich man or woman to set down large lumps of legal tender in university coffers or getting a speech on the cheap from a famous person. Some highly comic meetings must take place in which university officials try to find someone to whom to give an honorary degree. Originality in this field cannot be easy. My guess is that a man such as Father Hesburgh can by now wallpaper his bathroom with his honorary degrees. Often a true scholar or scientist or artist is awarded a just honorary degree, but honorary degrees seem increasingly to belong less to the realm of cultural achievement than to that of publicity. How else to explain the awarding of honorary degrees in recent years to the housewife-comedienne Erma Bombeck (DePauw University), the pro basketball star Julius Erving (Temple University), and the actress Meryl Streep (Yale University) than by the hunger of these institutions for publicity? Henceforth all commencement programs ought to carry, along with the union bug, a single line from the Reverend Sydney Smith: "Among the smaller duties of life, I hardly know any one more important than that of not praising where praise is not due."

Some events do seem to cry out for praise, and the most common and saddest of these is death. Death fogs the mind, usually misting over the faults of the deceased, but a too-strong eulogy or an overwritten obituary can leave a coppery taste in the mouth. I once attended a party at which Edward Shils was presented with a Festschrift volume in his honor, and after listening to the laudatory speeches of some of his former students, the honorand remarked: "A Festschrift is much to be preferred to an obituary. Both, of course, figure to be filled with lies about one's merits, but the nice thing about a Festschrift is that, unlike an obituary, one still has a bit of time left to turn a few of these lies into truths."

The dead are owed kindness; whether they are also owed praise is another question. Who has not been to a funeral service in which a clergyman is called upon to eulogize a man or woman he has never known, the effect of which can be relied upon to come off as successfully as Bach played on a two-penny kazoo. A few years ago I attended, in an Episcopal church, a memorial service for an acquaintance who had badly flubbed his life. Alcoholism had brought him too many sad indignities and a fatal heart attack at fifty. I thought the priest who conducted the service was wise in scarcely speaking of the man, whom he didn't know—the service was held at the request of the man's mother, who was a member of the church —and instead emphasizing the mercifulness of death in the Christian religion.

At another memorial service, a secular service, this one for a man I knew rather better, three speakers arose to quote various great authors on the dead man's behalf, and all three praised him for his fine sense of humor. Now if this man had an abiding flaw, it was precisely his sense of humor, which tended to be fidgety, a screen for a painful sense of insecurity, and so overlaid with levels of irony that fully half the time one needed to be an archaeologist to get at the joke he was intending, which, when one did get at it, turned out to be not very good. The service—and our memory of the dead man—was only saved when a fourth speaker, one of the man's sons, arose to talk about what a good father he was.

A highly effective device so seldom called upon in speaking of the dead is truth. When the notebooks of the Englishman Geoffrey Madan were published not long ago, the editors, J. A. Gere and John Sparrow, after speaking of Madan's virtues, did not flinch at recalling his flaws, chief among them aloofness and great dispassion. They then cited the opening sentence of an obituary article meant for *The Times* of London but apparently never sent: "A genius for friendship with all and sundry, infectious enthusiasm, selfless devotion to progressive causes, a deep and touching love of animals and of natural beauty— he [Madan] would not have claimed for himself any of these so frequent attributes of the lately dead."

Skill at the obituarist's art is rare anywhere, but seems at especially low ebb in the United States. I cannot remember having read a single obituary in the *New York Times* that I consider close to being worth dying for. The great obituarist of our age is perhaps Isaiah Berlin. He always seems to hit exactly the right tone, not scanting weaknesses and flaws, yet making these issue in a finer appreciation. As an example of what I mean, here is a paragraph from the middle of Isaiah Berlin's obituary article on Maurice Bowra:

Bowra saw life as a series of hurdles, a succession of fences to take: there were books, articles, reviews to write; pupils to teach, lectures to deliver; committees, even social occasions, were so many challenges to be met, no less so than the real ordeals—attacks by hostile critics, or vicissitudes of personal relationships, or the hazards of health. In the company of a few familiar friends, on whose loyalty he could rely, he relaxed and often was easy, gentle and at peace. But the outer world was full of obstacles to be taken at a run; at times he stumbled, and was wounded: he took such reverses with a stiff upper lip; and then, at once, energetically moved forward to the next task. Hence, it may be, his need and craving for recognition, and the corresponding pleasure he took in the many honours he received. The flat, pedestrian, lucid, well-ordered, but, at times, conventional style and content of his published writings may also be due to this peculiar lack of faith in his own true and splendid gifts. His private letters, his private verse, and above all his conversation, were a very different matter. Those who know him solely through his published works can have no inkling of his genius.

That long and intellectually nutritious paragraph seems to me less praising than appreciative, yet at the same time it makes one recognize that solid appreciation, appreciation that does not scamp complexity, conduces to the highest, the most worthwhile, praise.

I have been reading a book entitled *To Absent Friends* by Red Smith, by all reckoning the best sportswriter in this country over the past half century, which strikes this appreciative note with quiet good grace. The book is composed of a series of commemorative articles about people whose athletic and sometimes simply human performances Red Smith felt enriched his own life; and here, in prose, he repays them. His article on Stanley Woodward, his editor at the *New York Herald-Tribune*, begins: "The best and kindest man I ever knew died yesterday." Of Grantland Rice, he writes: "I do not mourn for him, who welcomed peace. I mourn for us." What is finally very impressive about these articles is that someone —Red Smith, specifically—took the trouble to notice and record men acting better than we are accustomed to having men act. Thus, of Joe Louis, Smith writes: "Not once in sixty-six years was he known to utter a word of complaint or bitterness or offer an excuse for anything." One did not have to be a great figure to have Red Smith notice one's quality, and of a press agent named Harry Mendel he wrote: "He was the best [at what he did] partly because he worked at it and was unfailingly reliable and tirelessly considerate, and partly because he knew the game [of boxing] so well, but especially because he was such a dead-honest guy." How lovely to have a wreath like that draped over one's grave!

In appreciation, there is no substitute for genuine feeling, and even the blurbs on the dust jacket of *To Absent Friends* convey genuine feeling. Allow me to cite but one: "Red Smith was not only an outstanding sportswriter, he was a true gentleman. Over the years, he accumulated a multitude of friends. It was a privilege and a pleasure to be included among them."— Joe DiMaggio. The best of the other blurbs on *To Absent Friends* come from athletes and coaches, and they are a reminder of the degeneration of praise as it comes through most blurb writing in our day. Blurbissimo, I call it, hoping that this neologism will properly convey its Mussolini-like hollowness and pomposity.

Searching among my own books, the most handsome set of blurbs I have discovered decorates the back cover of *The Complete Poems of Marianne Moore*, whose blurbs come from W. H. Auden, Louise Bogan, T. S. Eliot, William Carlos Williams, and, tailing off some, Sir Herbert Read and John Ashbery. But generally blurbs are poor stuff. Peter Prescott, for example, is quoted in an advertisement for Norman Mailer's novel, *Ancient Evenings:* "Mailer remains the most talented writer we have just now." I especially like that "just now"; it makes me want to respond, If Mailer is the best we have just now, please wake me later. For a novel by Susan Fromberg Schaeffer, the various blurbifiers write: "Not written but breathed. . . ." "A riveting, intricate, and altogether astonishing novel. . . ." "A long, detailed, intelligent and moving novel . . . the result is a richly textured, engrossing narrative that at midpoint becomes impossible to put down." What is there about that last blurb that makes me think I would have no hope of getting to midpoint? There is something about this kind of writing that makes one feel its authors aren't really praising but imitating praise.

Perhaps there is simply too much praise in the world; perhaps praise itself has become too institutionalized, too much expected, altogether too much business as usual. Perhaps it has become time to follow the lead of the elderly friend whom Somerset Maugham describes visiting in his book *The Summing Up*. A religious man, he read prayers to the assembled household each morning, but crossed out all the passages in the *Book of Common Prayer* that praised God. "He said that there was nothing so vulgar as to praise people to their faces, and, himself a gentleman, he could not believe that God was so ungentlemanly as to like it. At the time it seemed to me a curious eccentricity. I think now that my friend showed very good sense." I do, too. However much the rest of us may need praise, surely God doesn't.

I have been judged in print on a number of occasions and, on some of these occasions, have been found praiseworthy. On too many of them, though, the praise—either because it was fulsome or ignorant or came from the wrong quarter—has seemed to me embarrassing. At such times I have been sharply reminded of Saint-Beuve's remark to the effect that if you tell me who admires you, I can tell you who you really are. I would add to this that today, when praise is so abundant, who you really are can perhaps be better told by the people who hate you. For this reason I have always felt gratified to have been compared, in print, by Gore Vidal to Hitler and by Alfred Kazin to Zhdanov. I hope that, in any obituary that is to be written about me, it will be noted that these things were said about me. After all, an intelligent reader will know that any man who has been compared to Hitler by Gore Vidal and to Zhdanov by Alfred Kazin can't, really, have been all bad.

Unwilling to Relocate

A T THE AGE OF FORTY, I resolved to stop complaining. This will seem rather less uplifting than it at first may sound when I go on to say that I was greatly aided in this resolve by having the ground for complaint swept out from under me by having almost everything in life I had ever hoped for. "I didn't have the two top things—great animal magnetism or money," F. Scott Fitzgerald once said. "I had the two second things, though, good looks and intelligence." I don't happen to agree with Fitzgerald's listing of the four top things. None of them in any case is listed among the assets I tote up as my own: a wife I adore, work that keeps me perpetually interested, good friends, good health, and (thus far along) supreme good luck. And, though this was not so easily admitted, I also like where I live.

I say that it was not so easy to admit liking to live where I do, chiefly because where I live is, well, a bit lacking in glamour, or so at least the world would judge. Not only do I not live in a world city; I don't even quite live in a city. I do not think myself a dull fellow, but I couldn't prove it by my address. One's address, as every clever real estate salesman knows, is an extension of oneself—partly for snobbish reasons, no doubt, but partly as well for quite valid ones. "Anywhere

you go," an old saying has it, "there you are." I take this saying
to mean that, drag your hide anywhere you like, the person
inside it will stay the same—you will remain, immitigably,
ineluctably, however reluctantly, you. Still, it is difficult to
think one would regard oneself quite the same from, say, the
terrace of an apartment in Rome overlooking the Spanish
Steps, or a house in Mayfair, London, SW1, or a duplex in the
sixteenth arrondissement in Paris as in, say again, my neighborhood in the southeastern part of Evanston, Illinois, the first
suburb to the north of the middle western, very American city
of Chicago.

I have been living in Evanston sixteen years. Working in
Chicago, I chose Evanston chiefly for its schools for my then
young children. These schools turned out to be vastly overrated, but then to be overrated is perhaps the fate of almost all
schools, while the rest are rated, correctly, as not very good.
My children are grown now and gone, but I am still here.
Thrice I have moved within the same neighborhood, and twice
within the same block. I have in fact lived in three different but
contiguous buildings on the same block. At one point during
this time I was offered a teaching job at Northwestern University, which is ten or so blocks from where I live. "That's nice,"
said my mother, in a line that has always seemed to me to call
for a Yiddish accent, which, owing perhaps to a mistake made
at central casting, my mother doesn't have. "That's nice," she
said, "a job in the neighborhood."

So far as I know no one very famous lives in Evanston. One
of former President Jimmy Carter's sons lives somewhere in
my neighborhood; but which son it is, what his name is, or
where exactly he lives, I haven't any notion and even less
curiosity. James T. Farrell does not live but is buried here, in
a Catholic cemetery about two blocks from my apartment, but
buried doesn't count. The Woman's Christian Temperance

Union still has its headquarters in this town, yet that organization scarcely even seems good for a few of the easy guffaws writers such as H. L. Mencken used to be able to ring out of it during Prohibition days. I don't find myself dropping in on the ladies very often—actually, never—though I imagine them to be a fairly frail, if still vigorously vigilant, lot; and I almost admire them as advocates of the most completely lost of all lost American causes. The town of Evanston puts in a cameo appearance in Saul Bellow's *The Adventures of Augie March,* where, in the 1930s setting of that novel, it is made to seem, as all indications lead one to believe it was, rather stuffy and WASPish. Until the past twenty years, if someone said Evanston, one thought of brigades of women with blue-rinsed hair and print dresses, many of them walking with canes, dowager biddies strolling on tree-shaded streets.

Evanston, and particularly the neighborhood within it in which I live, is nowadays much more various—so much so that, though the town has a population of only 80,000, I hesitate to generalize about it. (As is well known, generalizations only hold up for populations of more than five million.) Even on the most fundamental statistical level, I am pristinely ignorant. I don't, for example, know how many Jews now live in Evanston, or how large a percentage of the population—a third? a fourth?—is black. I cannot begin to give you, as the demographers say, an age profile, an occupational profile, or an economic profile of the town. Although I have strong and fairly precise views about the future of NATO, I cannot tell you the name of my local alderwoman, yet I seem to remember that she is smallish and that she has a winning smile and that I voted for her. Such, then, is the extent of my hard knowledge about where I live; as they used to say on the playgrounds on which I grew up, it comes to diddly. I only know this—I like it here.

What is it one wants from the place where one lives? Status? As a younger man I felt the pull of status as urgently as the next fellow, but today I don't believe I would give up one whit of comfort in exchange for it. Nor would I be willing to pay a penny extra in rent or taxes for it, as do so many young people who pay eight and ten and twelve hundred dollars a month to live in a one-room studio apartment on the east side of Manhattan. The higher the status the higher the price, of course. In this connection I not long ago heard a story about a couple who was being shown a one-million-dollar condominium apartment on Sutton Place in New York, when the wife noticed that the apartment had no dining room. She mentioned this to the real estate agent, who is supposed to have replied, "Lady, what do you expect for a million dollars?"

If physical comfort and convenience is wanted in the neighborhood where one lives—I know I want it—so is a certain social ease. By social ease I do not mean the opportunity for exuberant sociability with neighbors, but an atmosphere of tolerance sufficient to allow one to go pretty much one's own way. I once owned a house in a working-class neighborhood, and while I felt fairly comfortable there, in time it became clear that my neighbors were not altogether comfortable with me. Although I think myself a plain enough bird, they thought me rather an odd duck. What was I doing among them, they wondered; and when it came time for me to move on, they worried lest I sell my house to someone even odder than I. The pond on which I now live provides much more comfort, for it is loaded with odd ducks, though we all seem to swim around in it comfortably enough.

"I pity the man," writes Laurence Sterne in *A Sentimental Journey*, "who can travel from *Dan* to *Beersheba*, and cry, 'Tis all barren—and so it is; and so is all the world to him who will not cultivate the fruits it offers." I do not know about the

world, but most of the fruits I am likely to be offered will have
to come from orchards and vineyards in my own neighborhood, where, I estimate, I must spend something like 98 percent of my time. Of course, I go into the city of Chicago to visit
friends, to test the claims of restaurants, to contribute to the
upkeep of dentists, physicians, accountants, and other middlemen. I travel both to New York and to Washington a few times
each year on business; every second year or so I find myself in
San Francisco; and when time and purse permit, I appear in
Europe cleverly disguised as a tourist. But for the vast most
part, I am at my desk at home, or running an errand, or
teaching a class—carrying on my life within a space of roughly
ten square blocks. "That's nice," my mother might have said,
"a life in the neighborhood."

Not going to the city to work has made me, in a curious
way, into a combination child and pensioner—the two types
who also tend to stay in the neighborhood. Few housewives are
among the regular cast of neighborhood characters; women, at
least on my block, tend to go off to work, leaving children at
either day-care centers or school and the retired and me at
home. With the exception of a single house, my block is made
up of apartment buildings. (Blocks of large older houses lie to
the east.) The occupants of these apartment buildings change
fairly often. Younger people especially seem to move on, perhaps climbing upward in the world, perhaps going under. The
middle-aged seem to stay, and the older people appear to be in
for the duration. As things stand at the moment, I look to be
—in fact, I rather hope to be—in for the duration myself.

Since I attempt to take the measure of the people I see
regularly walking the streets in my neighborhood, I wonder
what other people, engaged on the same project, might make
of me. Do they think: He seems a healthy enough fellow;
what's he doing in the neighborhood during the working day?

Maybe he's a remittance man, and owing to some dark scandal, his family sends him money to keep him from returning home. Maybe he's a minor Mafia guy—nothing so exotic as a hit man, but more likely someone from the Mafia's bookkeeping department. Maybe he just works nights. Or, then again, maybe he's mad.

The smart money would be on the last-named possibility, for, even though in this instance the smart money would (I prefer to think) be mistaken, there are a number of certifiably mad people walking around my neighborhood. I don't know what the current modern euphemism for mad is—disturbed? a-rational? dis-sane?—but mad assuredly is what they are. They are not bad-mad but sad-mad, and they live in a former residence hotel that is now called, euphemistically, the Evanston Ridgeview, A Quality Health Care Center. They are men and women who have been dealt dreadful hands in life; some have been cheated by their body's chemistry, some by the conditions of their upbringing, and some by the fragility of their temperaments, which snapped and broke on them. In one way or another, they have been ill-equipped for life, which they cannot take neat but only with the aid of heavy chasers of tranquilizing drugs. Thirty or so years ago they would have been packed away; now zonked to the hairline, they walk the streets. Now is better, but still no bargain.

They are a pathetic but not unedifying spectacle. One small emaciated woman, always smoking a cigarette with one hand and clutching a pack of Pall Malls with the other, walks by my apartment building daily. For reasons known only to her, she walks on the three or four inches of pavement that separate the gutters from the lawns. Another man, young and heavyset, appears to trudge about the streets all day long, no matter how vile the weather, a look of bewildered determination on his face. Sometimes a shattered man and woman from the Evanston Ridgeview will walk the streets holding hands, as sure an illustration as one is likely to find of E. M. Cioran's aphorism that holds love to be "an agreement on the part of two people to overestimate each other." One man wears a hat with a feather that shoots at least a foot into the air, above a face permanently red with suppressed rage; another man rides a bicycle that must have something like sixty pounds of accessories—horns, carriers, baskets, lights—attached to it. The women seem most devastated of all. Madness has aged them, stripped them of all vanity, so that they walk about with clashing clothes, clean but not very carefully groomed, de-sexed and deracinated from life itself. One day I was walking past the Evanston Ridgeview when I saw a sign announcing that they were planning a Halloween party—a Halloween party for the insane!—and I thought, wait a minute, who is crazy around here anyway? Still, while no one asked me, I am glad that the Evanston Ridgeview is in the neighborhood; it is a sharp and salubrious reminder of how close along the edge we all walk.

Sometimes people from the Evanston Ridgeview stop for coffee or a sandwich at a luncheonette called the Sher-Main. Despite their drug-induced, muddled state, they are, I note, always treated courteously there. The owner of the luncheonette, a Greek in his early forties, is a performing genius; the instrument upon which he plays is a three-by-four-and-a-half-foot griddle. On it he often has what looks to me like as many as eighteen or twenty lunches going simultaneously. Sometimes, at the height of the lunch rush, I have heard him talk to himself, to the food, to the griddle, keeping straight the orders while keeping his own adrenaline flowing. It is quite a performance.

But then, in a different sense, the clientele of his luncheonette provides quite a performance of its own. Along with the mad folk from the Evanston Ridgeview, on any given lunch hour it might include a booth of young house-painters in be-speckled work clothes; two cops; a table of construction work-ers; a black criminal lawyer huddled in a booth with his client; a table of local merchants, at least one of whom (the owner of a huge and hugely successful fabric store) must be a millionaire many times over; while at the counter odd solitary diners perch, many of them reading newspapers over their cheese-burgers or fried-liver specials. The Sher-Main is distinctly not the sort of place into which Brooke Astor is likely to walk.

Over the years one picks up scraps of information about local merchants. One of the regular diners at the Sher-Main, who owns a shop across the street and down the block from it, once told me that he left his father's business when, in his middle thirties, he overheard his father, on the telephone, tell a business associate that he couldn't hope to go on vacation, for he had no one whom he felt he could trust to run the business in his absence. I know the exercising regimen of the man who runs the fish store. The barber, an Austrian, takes winter skiing vacations, and his son, an osteopath, married this past spring. The woman who runs the shop where I drop off my shirts survived the Nazi death camps. The man at the post office is a White Sox fan; the pharmacist has a bad case on the Cubs. One of the young men who works part-time at the newsstand is a playwright.

From the time I first moved into this neighborhood, I brought my dry cleaning to Jensen Dry Cleaners. For some-thing like ten years I exchanged greetings with its proprietor. "Morning, Mr. Jensen." "Friday will be fine, Mr. Jensen." "Merry Christmas, Mr. Jensen." For a decade at least I said, "Thank you, Mr. Jensen." "You have a pleasant weekend yourself, Mr. Jensen." "Happy New Year, Mr. Jensen." Then, about three years ago, a silk blouse of my wife's was scorched by the dry-cleaning process. When I reported this to Mr. Jen-

sen, he said he wanted to send it out to a place where they
might be able to fix it, but if it couldn't be done, he would of
course pay for the blouse. He would, he said, telephone in a
day or two. When I picked up the phone a few days later, I
heard Mr. Jensen's voice, except the voice said, "This is Sam
Phillips at Jensen Cleaners." *Sam Phillips?* You could have
knocked me over with a plastic bag. For ten years he had
allowed me to call him a name other than his own without
bothering to correct me. Why? What's the difference, did he
say to himself? If he wants to call me Jensen, let him call me
Jensen, just so long as he pays his bills. Had he—has he?—so
little in the way of ego that it didn't matter? Or, conversely,
is his ego so strong that it didn't matter? Ten years. I still
cannot quite get over it. It is one of those little shallow myster-
ies that life in the neighborhood is in the habit of providing.

Three doors up from Jensen Dry Cleaners is a launderette
where—once more to air my dirty linen in public—I drop off
our sheets and towels. It is run by a young Korean family,
judging from their English fairly recent immigrants to this
country, and run very efficiently. In fact, the shop scene is very
much looking up in the neighborhood. For a long spell we
were under the blight of boutiques. During this period you
couldn't travel twenty paces without tripping over a piece of
macrame, an adorable plant, or a sprout sandwich. The shops
in the neighborhood on the whole now seem rather more
serious—that is, rather more useful—and therefore more likely
to stay around for a while. I mark the end of the boutique era
with the closing a few years ago of a store called Space Savers.
It sold plastic kitchen shelving, collapsable file cabinets, and
cardboard dressers, all designed, as the name of the shop suggests, to save space. After a very brief go, it folded itself up and,
saving still more space, disappeared entirely.

A few quasi-antique, quasi-used-furniture stores have moved

into the neighborhood; so, too, have a resale shop and a shop whose proprietress does clothing alterations. In a more modern mode, a shop selling and renting video movie cassettes has moved in; and a block or so away from it we now have a store selling computer software. A few doors down from the latter is a shop selling running gear, for ours is a neighborhood in which the religion of the body finds many devotees. On the subject of religion, there is also a small headquarters for the Church of Scientology, which, my guess is, has many fewer followers than the Church of Joggology.

We have a new and quite good used-book store a block or so from my apartment, which I greet as mixed news. The town of Evanston has a number of good used-book stores and a superior academic bookstore called Great Expectations. I owe a great deal of my education to roaming about such stores, and I sometimes think that the institution of the used-book store may have contributed more to the general education of the populace than has the institution of the university. Yet I have come to think of these stores as the equivalent, for intellectuals, of pool halls. I at any rate find it difficult not to hang around them, looking not only for that important book at that perfect price but for the equivalent of a fast game—that is, a fast schmooze about books. I should, I tell myself, spend my days reading and writing books, not buying and certainly not talking about them. But I am weak. Oh, Lord, I plead, lead me not into Great Expectations.

I don't have to ask not to be led into Wulf's Grocery, for I am fearful of going in there. About Wulf's I have a bad conscience. I used to go into Wulf's at least once a day, picking up a head of lettuce, a carton of milk, a box of cereal—the odd item or two. Being a desk-bound man, I always look for an excuse, any excuse, to break away for a few moments. ("The great thing about the law," the writer and lawyer John Morti-

mer's father told him when he, John, was thinking about writing full-time for his living, "is that it gets you out of the
house.") Except for Mrs. Wulf, a very winning Irish-born
woman, the crew at Wulf's is not riotously chummy, and it
seems as if it took me about twelve years to get on friendly
terms with them. Then, once I did, once I learned about the
butcher's television-watching habits, the produce man's son
who plays second base for the University of Michigan, and
Mrs. Wulf's father in Ireland, I up and left them. An enormous
supermarket moved into the neighborhood, and I began to take
my custom there. True, the supermarket provided more varied
and better food than Wulf's and generally at better prices; true,
logic and good sense and sound financial management argue
for my shopping at the new supermarket. All true and too true
—and yet I still feel a betrayer. I have not gone into Wulf's for
nearly a year now, and clearly there's no going back. Hoping
that they assume I have moved, I walk most gingerly, stealth-
ily, guiltily past the store.

This neighborhood has ghosts. I speak of dead friends who
walked and drove its streets and whose presence I still sharply
feel. It is bittersweet to pass corners or walk into shops where
one habitually met them. I think of my friend Walter, for
example, whom I used to notice each Sunday morning walking
past my apartment on his way to buy his three or four pounds
of *New York Times*. I would also see him parked out in front
of Wulf's, awaiting his wife who was shopping within. Invariably, I would climb into the backseat, and a lovely talk would
be set out before me, a hardy stew of reminiscence, erudition,
and whimsy, in all three of which Walter specialized. When
he was alive, I liked, when coming home late, to drive past and
note the light in his window; it meant he was probably watching late night television, no doubt some talk show, and with
his deadly comical eye spotting pretension, fraud, and fifty-

seven other varieties of public phoniness. Walter, I used to think, is standing guard.

If Walter was witty and skeptical, my friend Nelly, who lived a block and a half away in the other direction, was lively and, in her seventies, committed to the cheerful view. She was an immensely gregarious woman who was forced, in violation of her nature, to live most of her life alone. She wore bright colors and drove a red car—on principle. She, too, worked at home. Nelly was a freelance editor. Although for her own good reasons she chose to keep it hidden, she was filled with learning. She had gone to Smith College in the 1920s, knew foreign languages, seemed to have read everything thirty years before, had perfect pitch, and she carried it all with a most gracious lightness. We were always running into each other in the neighborhood: in front of the newsstand, in one of the drugstores, in the post office, on street corners. She passed Tolstoy's test of a beautiful face: she was loveliest when smiling, which she did nearly all the time. Now, three years after her death, at certain corners, on certain streets, in certain shops, I recall my friend and neighbor Nelly and feel a tug of pleasure at the recollection and a twist of resentment at her absence.

A spectre of another kind haunts these streets. It is that of crime. Crime in the neighborhood comes and goes, in small waves. The worst was a few years ago, when the middle-aged man who ran the Main Street News Stand, while closing up for the night, was held up and ultimately murdered for the eighty or so dollars then in his till. A few nights later a young woman in the neighborhood was raped and murdered. Suddenly the neighborhood seemed a very frightening place, in which paranoia seemed the most sensible conduct. A year or so later, when silver prices were inordinately high, there were a number of burglaries, several of them committed by young kids, who then tried to sell the stolen silver to local dealers. Every so often one will hear about a mugging or a purse snatching, and once a rapist was loose in the neighborhood. The neighborhood newspaper has run stories about youth gangs, black and Spanish, hanging out at night along Main Street. More recently, in a building directly across the street from the one I live in, a man was stabbed thirty-one times— need I say "to death"—on a sunny Saturday afternoon. Speculation has it that it was a crime of passion, but, since the murderer hasn't been caught, no one except him knows for certain.

An acquaintance, a young man of some sophistication, recently told me that he, too, likes living in Evanston. Unlike other suburbs farther to the north of Chicago, he said, there was about Evanston a big city sense of danger, and this, he felt, wasn't altogether a bad thing. While I don't quite agree with him—I think it is a pretty damn bad thing—I know what he means: namely, that there is something urban, contemporary, *real* about crime, and that people who live in safe suburbs, somehow sealed off from it, are living in a most unreal dream world. Yet I wonder if there is much to choose from between an unreal dream world and a quite real nightmare one.

Crime is certainly not new, but then neither does one ever grow accustomed to it. Perhaps, though, it is at its most sinister when one nearly does grow accustomed to it—when one assumes that this is the way it is, this is the way we live now. A friend who lived for years on West End Avenue in Manhattan not long ago told me that it was only with his move to the East Side that he recognized how over the years he had conditioned himself to accept the cruddiness of crime all about him on the West Side—how he had acquired the almost instinctual moves enabling him to thread his way around gangs, addicts, and other menacing characters—and what a relief it was to unlearn these moves. They order these things worse in New York, and my neighborhood cannot compare to West End Avenue, but, nevertheless, returning home late at night, I look over my shoulder. Crime as a regular fact of life—as opposed to what it ought to be, an aberrant fact of life—is one of the great wicked sadnesses of our time. Along with cancer, heart attack, and stroke, one now has to consider death at the hands of a vicious young man or a crazed drug addict as one of the "natural causes" of death.

But it is the natural causes of living that interest me more and make me like this neighborhood so much. It is its variety, its jumble, that impresses me. My pleasure in it also proceeds from the nature of neighborhood life itself. People one is likely to pass without turning one's head on a crowded downtown street become of interest in a quiet neighborhood. Janitors, for example. When I first moved into the neighborhood the majority of the janitors were Belgians, with names such as Paul Tenard and Marcel Noorts. They worked very hard and, judging from the cars they drove, made quite good money. Russian émigrés then moved into some of these jobs. A father and son combination—Appalachians, my guess is—has taken over the janitorial work in a few of the local buildings. The janitor of the building in which I live is a young Pole. One day he asked me if I had any publishing connections, for he had written a book. The book, which I have read, is on martial arts training and has since been published. Janitors who are published authors—in the last fifth of the twentieth century you can no longer so easily tell a man by the cut of his clothes.

Many of the people whom I have watched walk up and down my block for more than a decade I have never spoken to, yet one learns something about them merely by noting them in the course of their comings and goings. There is the mild-mannered man, who looks to be approaching sixty, the story of whose life appears to be that he has stayed behind to care for his very elderly and quite deaf mother. There is the small man who at seventy or so wears his hair in bangs and, though he lives in a modest enough building with his wife, has a penchant for Cadillacs, especially Cadillac convertibles, which he buys in either white or cream color and parks in a garage behind my apartment. There is the man who each day chugs down the street in a motorized chair—because of a stroke? a weakened heart?—on his way to the supermarket, where each day he exchanges eight empty A & W Root Beer bottles for eight full ones. There is the scruffy but handsome man who hires out as a window washer and whose face on some days is scarlet—with anger? drink? poor health? I know not what. And there is the man who one day, quite drunk, put a most improper question to me and thus feels—quite rightly —that he can never speak to me again and consequently hasn't.

Joggers trot by this block, and men and women in helmets and black lycra shorts, members of bicycle clubs, pedal past in a whir. The neighborhood's young are keen to stay in shape. Early mornings, from my kitchen window, I see runners going through stretching exercises before setting off. At dusk, after a full day's work, others chug past, upon their faces looks of determination, exhaustion, and, when the run is over, sweaty bliss. Four blocks to the east, the paths beside Lake Michigan are jogger laden, especially on Sunday mornings, and some-times one can hear pairs of joggers discussing their major organs or the aerobic benefits they are acquiring while in the very act of acquiring them. All such talk I have come to think of as joggorrhea.

Live in a place long enough and you come to know not only the people but the livestock. This neighborhood has a hardy squirrel population, which roams about assured of the goodwill of all but the neighborhood cats. Edith Wharton once called cats snakes in furs; I am inclined to think of squirrels as rats with bushy tails, but then Rodentia is not my favorite taxonomic order. For a long spell large dogs seemed to be *à la mode*. So much was this so in the early 1970s that, if you lived in my neighborhood, you might have thought a basic nuclear family consisted of an unmarried young man and woman living together with an Irish setter. Neighborhood dogs now seem to be growing smaller. I note the resurgence of the cocker spaniel, which was very popular when I was a boy and came in black, beige, or auburn and was predictably named, respectively, Inky, Taffy, or Rusty. A kind-hearted woman named Florence, who always greets me most friendly, keeps a little white dog named Sammy on a long rope leash. A number of my neighbors have dogs of truly impressive inelegance; small black hairless dogs, hugely overweight Labradors, stub-legged dogs whose ears stand straight up—dogs that only their owners could (and apparently do) love. Seeing these owners standing out in below-zero weather, awaiting, with plastic bag or the instrument indelicately known as the pooper-scooper, their dogs' completion of their business is a tribute to—I am not sure what. Solzhenitsyn says that anyone who cannot be kind to an animal is unlikely to be kind to a human being. I admire these dog owners without in any way wishing to emulate them.

The center of the neighborhood, both geographically and spiritually, is the intersection of Chicago Avenue and Main Street. A bank occupies two of the corners of the intersection; a used-furniture store a third corner; and the Main Street News Stand the fourth. This intersection takes its character from the time of day: crisp and hurried in the morning, quiet for much of the middle of the day, tired yet rushed at day's end, slightly fearsome late at night. Of its four corners, easily the most interesting is the one that serves as the site of the Main Street News Stand, which is not precisely a stand but a small one-story building. Along with local papers and popular American magazines, it stocks out-of-town papers, foreign magazines, business and intellectual journals. It also sells lottery tickets, a large line of paperback books, and, off in a corner near the rear of the building, pornographic books and magazines. On a number of occasions I have watched a dark, expensively dressed, middle-aged man make his way to the porno section; he drives a luxe version of a BMW; he appears to be making something like a porno pit stop on his way to the richer suburbs to the north. I used to mark his appearances with some interest until I realized what my doing so made me—a voyeur of a voyeur —and then I knocked it off.

I seem to have stressed the oddity of the neighborhood, its freakishness and dramatic qualities. While I prize its oddity, true enough, I value above all its stability: its nice dull stretches, its long, quiet afternoons, the evenings on which nothing at all happens. I like the comfort and regularity it provides of dealing with the same mailmen, shopkeepers, bank clerks, barbers, and shoemakers I have dealt with now for years and years. These are important people to me; they see to those mundane things without which life could not go on—at least not anywhere near so smoothly. I delight in the small pleasures of greeting neighborhood friends, of nodding at nodding acquaintances. When I think of it—which I don't often do—I am immensely impressed at the complexity of arrangements required to lead even the simplest life.

And, being a trifle thick-headed perhaps, I am regularly surprised by the obvious. One hot day the young man who has our neighborhood as part of his route for one of the air express companies was in my apartment to pick up a manuscript. I asked him how he was holding up in this hot weather. A man in his middle twenties, with blond, longish hair, and a tattoo on each forearm, he replied: "I don't mind the heat. It's sum-

mer, and summer is supposed to be hot. I really love the spring
and the fall. Actually, I also dig the winter. I guess I like the
whole year. In fact, if you really want to know, I like it above
ground." That is nicely put, and a sentiment to which I wholly
subscribe. I, too, like it above ground, and, luckily for me,
above no piece of ground more than the one on which I spend
the better part of my life, this neighborhood.

New & Previously Owned
Books & Other Cream Puffs

I RATE THE FOUR MAIN AGENCIES of education in my life
—schools, libraries, magazines, and bookstores—in
the following order of importance: 1. bookstores, 2. magazines,
3. libraries, 4. schools. To consider the last first, I had better
own up right off that I was never other than a mediocre student, though mediocre may be overstating it. After acquiring
the rudiments of reading, writing, and arithmetic by about age
eight, I went into roughly a decade-long intellectual snooze,
from which I arose a trifle cranky but otherwise refreshed. By
the time I arrived at university, I was some two or three hundred furlongs behind the front-runners of my generation and
spent the better part of my time playing, to alter the sports
metaphor, catch-up ball. On various occasions since then I
have met professors who taught me, and not a single one
among them can remember me as a student. This is not so
surprising; I scarcely remember being there myself.

While I am thankful for libraries, the next of the educational agencies in my life, I have chiefly functioned in relation
to them as a small-time benefactor. I borrow their books, can
be relied upon to bring them back late, and consequently am

made to pay fair but nonetheless irritating fines. My record here isn't as impressive as that of a friend of mine who once kept a book on the Mexican revolutionary leader Emiliano Zapata out of his branch library for fourteen years and, when bringing it back, decided not to take advantage of his right to renew it, though, he tells me, he never did finish it. (I suppose that this qualifies for what is nowadays called a "slow read.") My style with libraries is steadier; I go in for lots of two- and three-dollar fines, and every so often, just to show them I am no cheapskate, I will lose a book and have to fork over fifteen or twenty dollars to replace it.

As for working in libraries, it is not for me. The sight of stacks turns me into instant Oblomov; I have only to enter a library to long for my pajamas and robe. The library at the university where I teach offers carrels—small monastic cells for study on the premises—to its faculty, but I would sooner serve time in a minimum-security prison than use them. I like a certain amount of distraction when I work: doorbells ringing, radios playing in the background, noise coming in from the street. Even as I finish this paragraph, I hope my telephone will ring.

Magazines are something else. Around the age of twenty I discovered the intellectual and literary magazines—*Partisan Review, Commentary, Encounter, The Hudson Review, The Kenyon Review, The American Scholar, The New Republic, The New Yorker*, the British weeklies—and I have read them ever since. They were especially helpful to me as a young man who himself one day wanted to write. This was during a time when second-rate books were not taught at universities. Reading great authors is the best method of education; but for someone who wishes to write, they can be discouraging. How, after all, at age twenty—or at age sixty—can one hope to write like Hazlitt, Macaulay, or T. S. Eliot, not to speak of Homer,

Dante, or Shakespeare? Maybe, though, with diligence, one could some day write for these magazines, or so I felt. The intellectual magazines gave me not only some sense of what the issues, questions, and problems of the day were but also a sense of a continuing tradition. I still read them—and, I hope, learn from them—for the same reasons. For the most part, my great teachers have not been professors but writers and editors.

I am, then, something of an autodidact, though *autodidact* is a word I have never completely understood. Apart from people who have trained for one or another of the professions, or have been taught by two or three professors in a field of fairly narrow specialization, who among us isn't an autodidact —that is, who among us isn't self-taught? And the place where most self-teaching begins, or at any rate has begun for me, is in bookstores. Books remain the essential tools of education and bookstores the shops where they are most commonly acquired. One learns something about books from teachers, and a good deal more from the toutings of friends and from articles about books in magazines, but it is in bookstores that one picks up most of all, by wandering among shelves, making discoveries, being serendipitous but with a purpose. A. J. Liebling used to say that the first thing he investigated when he visited a new city was the taste of its drinking water and the quality of its newspapers. For me one of the tests of a good city is the quality of its bookstores.

If there were any bookstores in the neighborhood in which I grew up, I do not remember them. Drugstores used to rent out popular novels for, as I recall, a nickel a day. Paperback books had not yet become widespread. I remember seeing an occasional western novel or detective story in a paperback edition, though at the time they were usually referred to as pocket books (Pocket Books, which has a kangaroo for its imprint, is also the name of a paperback publisher). Not being a reader, I had no reason to go into a bookstore. The Board of Education of the City of Chicago supplied our schoolbooks. In fact, I don't believe I set foot in a bookshop of any sort, new or used, before the age of eighteen.

Someone who scarcely set foot outside a bookshop before he was eighteen was Anatole France. Père France was the proprietor of the Librairie de France, one of the best of the nineteenth-century Parisian bookshops. Anatole France grew up in the apartment above and spent a great deal of time in his father's shops. In 1853 the Librairie de France moved from No. 15 quai Malaquais to No. 9 quai Voltaire, along which book-stalls were ranged, and this caused Anatole France to remark that, as a boy, he had the use of a library fully three-quarters of a mile long. As a child, he played at being a bookseller the way other children played at being a soldier or a doctor. He learned bookbinding and repair; and later in life, when he would see a "wounded" book, he would acquire it, return it to good condition, and give it to a friend who would, in effect, give it a good home. He was a great reader of books, but he was also aware of their physical attraction. In *La Vie littéraire* he wrote: "There is no true love without some sensuality. One can only find true happiness through books if one likes to caress them. [Here I pull on the cord to signal the driver to let me off, for this last statement of France's is rather further than I care to go.] I can recognize a true bibliophile by the way in which he handles a book. [Here I reboard the bus, for this seems to me true.]"

I wish I had had the young Anatole France with me when I had gone into my first bookstores. Entering a bookstore can be quite as bewildering, even scarifying for an unbookish nov-ice, as entering a bordello can be for a young divinity student. There are so many wrong moves, so many potential mistakes, one can make. One wants above all to seem at home, which in a bookstore means not to seem unlettered or otherwise give evidence of one's natural barbarity. My own great fears were mispronouncing an author's name or getting a title wrong. I recall especially worrying about the correct pronunciation of Truman Capote's last name—was that final *e* sounded or not? The chances for seeming oafish in a bookstore seemed to me very great. One didn't have to read many books to recognize that bookstores could be minefields of potential snobbishness; and above all one didn't wish to come off as *nouveau intellectuel*, the mental equivalent of seeming *nouveau riche*.

Bookstores could also be centers for some very strange behavior. One of the first bookstores I frequented, a small but obviously highbrow shop in the neighborhood of the university I attended, was run by a man whom I wouldn't exactly called irascible since he seemed permanently irasced. He scowled, he growled, he was in a perpetual pet. But his shop contained some awfully fine books, including a large stock of English Penguins marked "Not for Sale in the U.S.A." I was in his shop one evening when a tall man wearing a beret asked where he kept his books on mathematics. "Over there," the owner grunted, pointing toward the far wall but scarcely looking up. When the man in the beret returned two or three minutes later to ask if he had any other mathematics titles in the shop, the owner rose to his feet, curtly announced "Shop's closed," pulled a cord that extinguished the one large fluorescent lighting fixture that lit the place, and plunged us all into darkness. I returned to the shop many times after this incident, but I made a mental note, in italics, never to ask him a question. When I bought a book, I even went out of my way to pay him in exact change.

Traditionally, booksellers have differed from other shopkeepers by their interest in, and in many instances possession of, culture. But culture, as those of us who have for any length of time sojourned in its purlieus have discovered, does not necessarily, all advertisements to the contrary notwithstanding, sweeten a person's temper. Sweet-tempered people—most famously, Sylvia Beach and Adrienne Monnier in Paris in the twenties—have been booksellers; and I have met a number of kindly and extremely helpful booksellers in my own time. Yet, even though running a good bookshop seems to me one of the finest things a man or woman can do—for it involves transmitting knowledge and thereby serving the cause of civilization— among many booksellers I have known I note an edge of disappointment. Many would rather produce books than sell them; some are, for one complex reason or another, unfulfilled scholars; and a few may feel too keenly their own marginality.

Certainly the range of types who work in bookshops is various. Some booksellers have a specialty. The owner of one bookshop I go to regularly knows a great deal about philosophy; once, when a customer asked him where his books on the philosophy of religion were, he was heard to reply: "Sir, there is no philosophy of religion. Religion has been the death of philosophy," which is probably more information than the customer bargained for. I have a friend who asked a clerk at Scribner's Book Store in New York if he had in stock *The Courage of Turtles,* to which he responded, "Lady, I ain't got the strength of a rabbit." A young black man at the Strand Book Store of whom I once inquired about the novels of Chaim Grade proved not only to have known about them but to have read all of them. The owner of a quite good used-book store in a neighborhood adjoining my own has never shown the least trace of a hint of a fog of a clue of having read a single book. Then there is the owner of a really superior used-book store I know whose owner, a Yale Ph.D. in history, is at first meetings a most taciturn New Englander. I was myself only able to break the ice with him when one day, after selling me three fairly thick volumes, he asked if I wanted them wrapped. "No," I said. "That's all right. I'll just read them here." This provoked a very small, a very quick smile. As I say, a wide range of types.

Owning a bookshop appears to be a fairly common fantasy. (Owning a successful bar is another such fantasy.) The attraction is not difficult to understand. To be surrounded by books —and books, as has been said often enough, do furnish a room —and to make one's living from people who are interested in books sound a pleasing way to pass one's days. Such a fantasy must have been the origin of another used-book store in my neighborhood, one run by a man of middle years who was formerly an advertising executive. At least I espy the origins of a fantasy in the tone and tenor of his establishment. Couches and chairs are deployed about the shop; at different places dishes of mints or hard candies have been set out; on occasional Sundays amateur chamber music ensembles perform there. The hope, clearly, is to make the bookshop a comfortable place where like-minded people can gather to talk about things they love. Surely there have been less destructive fantasies.

Still, if an antidote to the bookshop fantasy is wanted, perhaps no stronger potion is available than a gloomy little essay of George Orwell's entitled "Bookshop Memories." Orwell goes right to work on the fantasy; his first sentence reads: "When I worked in a second-hand bookshop—so easily pictured, if you don't work in one, as a kind of paradise where charming old gentlemen browse eternally among calf-bound folios—the thing that chiefly struck me was the rarity of really bookish people." Orwell goes on from here to attack the clientele of the bookshops of his day: the vague-minded women looking for birthday presents for their nephews or for invalids; the people looking for another copy of a book they had read forty years before whose title or author they cannot remember;

the sad people who try to sell you books no bookseller could possibly use; the people who place large orders and never arrive to pick them up; the "not quite certifiable lunatics" who "tend to gravitate towards bookshops, because a bookshop is one of the few places where you can hang about for a long time without spending any money." Orwell's description of the atmosphere in bookshops is no less gloomy. Bookshops are, according to Orwell, "horribly cold in winter," and "books give off more and nastier dust than any other class of objects yet invented"; more cheery news still, "the top of a book is the place where every bluebottle [fly] prefers to die." Finally, Orwell assures us, in that impressively confident manner he had, that working in a bookshop will eventually result in one's learning to dislike books. "Seen in the mass, five or ten thousand at a time, books were boring and even slightly sickening." Ah, that George, always a million laughs.

I don't say that what Orwell wrote was untrue, but, his having written his essay in 1936 during a time when London was perhaps never scruffier, its truth has certain limitations. Bookshops can be dreary places—the one Orwell worked in doubtless was—but they needn't be, and most, in my experience, aren't. Orwell remarked that "on the whole" he wouldn't care to be a "bookseller *de métier*," which is a negligible loss for bookselling and a considerable gain for literature. Neither, I must own, would I care to be a bookseller—not only because I like what I do at present but because I have an aversion to anything having to do with an inventory. My grandfather used to say that one of the nice things about doing intellectual work is that at least it doesn't tie you to an inventory. He ought to have known; he himself, who longed so to devote his days to teaching and writing and intellectual things, was for the better part of his life hostage to the inventories of several not very successful businesses. But let me tell you a tragicomic story about an inventory and our family's one brief undistinguished fling at being booksellers.

When my grandfather retired, freed at last from his wretched businesses, he devoted himself to things of the mind, not least among them a book of discursive learning in which, in Hebrew and in Yiddish, he commented on Biblical passages and on other Judaical matters. This book was published by subscription in my grandfather's home city of Montreal, with my father paying a goodly share of the publication costs. My father also helped his father out in his retirement with a modest monthly stipend; and once my grandfather's book was printed, my father suggested that he, who was out in the business world, could perhaps sell some copies for him. The copies were sent and stored in our basement. Each month, when my father sent his father his stipend, he would append a postscript: "Sold three copies of the book this month—an additional $15 enclosed." "Five copies of the book sold—all to a single customer—check for $25 enclosed." "An unusually good month for book sales—nine copies sold, an extra $45 added to check."

Of course, my father never actually sold a single copy of his father's book; nor did he try. The market for such a book was scarcely teeming. Whenever we had a visitor at our house who read Yiddish or Hebrew, which wasn't very frequently, my father would send me down to the basement to fetch a copy to give to the visitor. Meanwhile, his letters to his father continued to contain the inevitable postscripts: "The check for $35 represents seven copies of the book sold." "The check for $30 is for book sales." "Book sold briskly this month—extra added." Then one day a United Parcel Service truck dropped off two heavy boxes at our house. These were followed by a letter that arrived the next day from my grandfather. "My dear son, I assume your stock of my book must by now be running quite low. I have therefore sent, by United Parcel, an additional fifty copies. Let me know when you need more."

Does one have to be a writer to find pathos hidden in the crevices of that largely comic story? Perhaps not. Perhaps, too, I can make plain why it is that, whenever I have recently published a book, I make it a point never to go into, or indeed even gaze at the window of, a store selling new books. Having a recently published book changes the nature of one's relation to bookstores. One is no longer a customer, a browser, a disinterested flaneur seeking a slender volume that might capture one's fancy—one is instead all too interested. When a recently published author passes a bookstore, the first question he asks is, Why isn't my book displayed prominently in the window? As he enters the store, the second question he asks is, Why isn't my book on the best-seller table? (Do you suppose the fact that it isn't a best-seller could have anything to do with it?) The third question is, Why is it shelved under Sociology or under Self-Help? The fourth question, when it isn't found there, is, Why isn't it at least shelved under Sociology or under Self-Help—why, that is, isn't it even in the store? The fifth question is, Why do I have the publisher I do, since he obviously doesn't go in for distributing books? (Here I am reminded of the avant-garde publisher who, when his authors used to complain that they could never find their books in bookstores, used to reply: "Well, great gods, you don't want just anyone to read your book, do you?") The sixth question is, Is it too late in life for me to find another line of work?

When my first book was published, I frequently found myself going into bookstores to see how the little gem was doing. "What's your name again?" was not an infrequent response to my queries. "What's the title of your book again?" was another popular response. Of a later book, I recall a particularly painful telephone call. "Joe, it's Stan. I'm out here at the Old Orchard Shopping Center Kroch & Brentano's trying to buy a copy of your new book. They never heard of it. They called the main store downtown. Nobody there ever heard of it either. They're going to call me later about it. I'll get back to you on this." "Stan," I said, trying like mad to repress the rising tremolo in my voice, "please, don't get back to me on it." Some things in life are better not known, and the fate of one's own books in bookstores, at least for the non-best-selling author, is one of them.

Not that I go into as many new bookstores nowadays as I used to. Someone once said that you can either read books or write them, and that you can't do both. I would take this a step further and say that you can either buy books or read them. I utter this profundity upon making a rough estimate that I have probably not read fully 20 to 25 percent of the books I now own. Then, too, new bookstores do not seem quite so interesting to me as they once did. I came along too late for the time when bookstores were suitable hangouts for writers, such as the old A. C. McClurg Bookstore on Wabash Avenue in Chicago was during the early decades of this century. I know some very intelligent booksellers with whom it is a pleasure to talk, but a sense of community is not something I seek in a bookshop. Apart from the company of three or four good friends, I haven't found a sense of community anywhere else either— and this vaunted quality of community, I am beginning to feel, may be even more elusive than Jimmy Durante's famous lost chord.

What I have found is some extraordinary behavior on the part of bookstore clientele. I recall a scene in a plush bookshop in Chicago in which an older woman, one Mrs. Thompson by name, apparently a regular customer, informed a clerk that she and her husband were soon to be off for a three-week holiday to St. Croix. "While on holiday with Dr. Thompson," she announced, in a voice that sounded as if it ought to have belonged to one of those older women in a Peter Arno cartoon, "I generally read three books a week. Could you, then, send round nine books to our apartment sometime before Friday?" After she left, I hung back to watch the clerk gather up the books for her, at least four of which were very expensive, fully caffeinated, coffee-table tomes. In his place, I am not sure I should have done any differently. *Caveat lector.*

New bookstores have become less interesting owing to circumstances not entirely within their control. Chief among these is their relentless contemporaneity, which can be mildly depressing. Because of the vast number of books being published, because of a contractual arrangement that allows booksellers to return unsold books to their publishers, new books have an increasingly short shelf life. Stock in new bookstores is regularly returned and replenished by new stock. Try, for example, to obtain a clothbound edition of a respectably good book published as recently as two years ago. It is an extremely difficult thing to do. With the fairly fast turnover of goods now the rule of the day in publishing, such a book may not even be available from the publisher, for it could well have gone off to the pulpery—the equivalent, for books, of the glue factory to which old horses were sent.

In the essay "Bookshop Memories," from which I quoted earlier, George Orwell called the book business "a human trade which is not capable of being vulgarized beyond a certain point." He also said that "the combines can never squeeze the small independent bookseller out of existence." It may be impolite to find the prophetic George Orwell guilty of faulty prophecy, but neither statement holds up nowadays. We know bookselling is capable of being extravagantly vulgarized, and we know that the combines have squeezed many a small bookseller out of existence. Being against such combines as B. Dalton, Waldenbooks, and others may seem snobbish, even perversely archaic, on my part. I know that these supermarket book chains do get more books sold, and, by implication, as a result of their being in business, more books do get read; in many instances, they even get the books to their readers at cheaper prices. This may all be so; let us grant that it is. What I dislike about these supermarket booksellers is that their stores, devoid as they are of surprise, are devoid as well of pleasure. I also dislike their blasted efficiency.

Efficiency, so much to be valued in so many phases of life, ought not to be a primary value in others. Efficiency has no place in friendship, in love, in raising children, in the creation of much art, and it may have a limited utility, too, in the selling of books. Not that I, that raging beast, an author, don't mutter a vicious and highly rhythmic Spanish curse (in English) against the inefficiency of the book business when I learn that not a single copy of a newly published book of mine has made its way to such not entirely obscure cities as San Diego or Minneapolis; in fact, I do. Still, I think that a bookstore ought to have a certain disarray, a jumble, room for the odd and even largely unwanted item. "A bookshop, in order to be good," writes Edward Shils in an essay entitled "The Bookshop in America," "must have a large stock of books for which there is not likely to be a great demand but for which there will be an occasional demand." I could not agree more. If you are going to call it a bookshop, there ought at least to be a copy of, say, Ruskin around the joint.

Some new bookstores partially make up for their depressing quality of too strict contemporaneity by carrying a gorgeous array of paperback books. This helps. But, especially given the price of so-called quality paperbacks nowadays, I almost always prefer to have the same book in a cloth-bound edition. (Forgive me if I don't say "hardback"; turtles and armadillos have hardbacks, not books.) It is for this reason, among others, that to me used-book stores are so much more enticing. One never knows quite what one will find in a used-book store, which is what makes them, to the book-crazed, such exciting places.

I was extremely lucky when, in my early twenties, I worked in New York on a magazine whose offices were just off Union Square and hence only a few blocks from the great used-book stores of Fourth Avenue and University Place. I was then coming into my passion for literature and here, set out before me, were these vast emporiums of books. Each day on my lunch hour I would rush off to these shops; each day I would make a fresh discovery of some book I had not hitherto known about. I was in the splendid position of a young sailor whose ship has just pulled into the most exotic of ports—except that, figuratively speaking, my ship pulled into port fully five days a week. A married man with infant children, knowing myself not entirely in control, I would leave my wallet in my desk and usually not allow myself to take more than ten dollars along with me.

Fourth Avenue and University Place were then ideal locations for used-book stores. The economics of the used-book business is such that these shops require locations where there is high traffic and low rent. You will find no used-book stores on Rodeo Drive, nor on Fifth Avenue in the Fifties, nor on Michigan Boulevard in Chicago; nor will you find any in glittering suburban shopping centers. The ideal location for a used-book shop is a neighborhood gone slightly to decay—"a marginal area of a central business district," as Professor Shils has written, "or the university community." Himself a relentless and intercontinental forager in bookshops, Professor Shils knows whereof he speaks. Of his own bookish sojourning, he writes: "My case is an extreme one, and there are perhaps few people in my generation, more or less in their right minds and heavily engaged with all sorts of duties, who have spent so much time in bookshops as I have. I have talked with booksellers of every kind, angular Brahmins, mad *Ostjuden,* motherly widows, elegant patricians, sweet mice, and cagey and distrustful touts." Spoken like a man with true book fever.

Unless one goes in search of a specific title, one enters a used-book shop in the quiet but perpetual hope of being pleasantly surprised. One hopes to find that extraordinary book, long out of print, that one long ago all but despaired of ever finding (Ronald Knox's *Enthusiasm*); or to discover a book whose existence one hadn't even known about (Mark Pattison's book on Milton in the English Men of Letters series); or to come upon a book one had heard of but never really expected to have a chance to own (Max Beerbohm's book of drawings, *Rossetti and His Circle*); or to fill in volumes that are missing from sets of books one already owns (Élie Halévy's *History of the English People in the Nineteenth Century*). Of course it nearly goes without saying that one hopes to find these things at laughably low prices.

One is always making odd, sometimes touching discoveries in used-book stores. Not infrequently I have come across a book, usually some classic work in an edition republished in the teens or twenties of this century—the poems of Keats, say, or the essays of Montaigne—inscribed as a gift from a father to his daughter and evidently given away by the grandchildren. More embarrassingly, I have found books signed by the author to a friend (not, apparently, as good a friend as the author thought, or he wouldn't have sold the book). When I haunted the used-book shops of lower Manhattan, I often used to inquire after the books of A. J. Liebling. (All of them, I believe, are now available in paperback.) I never found any of them, and after a while I was told by more than one bookseller that Liebling himself used to come round and buy them up, no

doubt wishing to ensure that these books found a good home
—his own. The poet L. E. Sissman wrote a brief poem about
finding copies of his own book, *Dying: An Introduction*, re-
maindered for one shilling at Foyle's, the London bookshop.
The last four lines of Sissman's poem run:

> And there, a snip under a blackleg sign,
> "These books reduced to 1s.," there is mine,
> *Dying: An Introduction*. Well, if you
> Preach about dying, you must practice, too.

I occasionally see a book of my own in a used-book shop. The
sight of it is a bit discouraging, even though, on the shelf, it will
sometimes have a book by Ralph Ellison or T. S. Eliot for
company. I take its presence in a used-book shop to mean that
someone has decided that he can do quite nicely without owning my book, thank you all the same. Recently I noted a copy
of my last book on the shelves of a used-book shop three weeks
before the book was to be officially published. Talk about bad
omens; talk about intimations of mortality.

For all the potential delights they provide, there is nonetheless something a little sad about a used-book store. The sadness
has to do with the shattered fantasies, the broken dreams, of
writers who, while writing their books, certainly never intended them to end up on the shelves of used-book stores.
Doubtless many among these writers hoped their books would
garner for them fame, money, and the love of beautiful women.
(It was Freud who said that the artist gives up the pursuit of
fame, money, and the love of beautiful women for the sake of
his art, through which he hopes to win fame, money, and the
love of beautiful women.) Instead these books are now gathering dust and—in the case of those books unfortunate enough
to have wound up in the bookshop in which George Orwell

worked—dead bluebottle flies. Of course, many of the books
in used-book stores were best-sellers in their day and may well
have realized their authors' fantasies, but their appearance in
these shops is a clear signal that that day is done. Used-book
stores, then, function in part as a retirement home for authorly
hopes.

While being sold off at cut-rate may be dismaying to authors, buying books at cut-rate has always been one of the great
lures of used-book shops for normally greedy book buyers.
Harold Laski, in many of his letters to Justice Holmes, reported fantastic book bargains acquired in the shops of London
and New York. Laski's relationship with the truth was not
strictly constant on his part, to put the matter somewhat delicately, but here is one such report he made to Justice Holmes:

I have had some fine luck here this last week. Item, Roger (sic)
Wiseman, *The Excellency of the Civil Law* (1656). . . . Item, also a *Parte
of a Register* (1590). This is very rare. . . . Item, a volume of pamphlets
on the Wilkes controversy which belonged originally to Woodfall,
Wilkes' printer and has some notes in by him. . . . But my best find
is really more interesting than anything I have come across in the last
few years. It was a bundle containing thirty unprinted speeches
delivered by John Stuart Mill to the London Debating Society in his
own autograph.

How much of this is true it would be difficult to say, but
I hope you will believe me when I say that I first acquired the
two handsome Harvard University Press volumes of *The
Holmes-Laski Letters* at the Strand Book Store in 1963 for five
dollars. At that time, five dollars seemed a heavy outlay. Most
novels in used-book stores could be acquired, in cloth-bound
editions, for a dollar or two, and many for less than that; a
serious biography or historical work tended to go for three or
four dollars. I remember being greatly miffed at having to pay
seven bucks for *A Pushcart at the Curb*, a collection of the

poems of John Dos Passos, because it was a first edition. (I had not then, nor have I now, the least interest in first editions.) But there were great bargains to be had. A young man walking into a used-book shop with twenty dollars in his pocket cut a fine figure.

Palmy days, those, but, like most palmy days, they are now gone. The best seller of used books I know has a single but major flaw—he knows exactly what his books are worth and gets it. His stock, rich and handsomely arrayed, loses some of its piquancy for me through my knowledge that I shall not be able, in effect, to steal anything from him. Today a few used-book sellers I know have begun to mark the inside flap of their books, where they list the price, either "First Edition" or "Out of Print," both labels entitling them to anywhere from two to five dollars extra for the book, which in some cases is a very recent and rather poor one. (How fine to own a first edition of, say, Joseph Heller's *Good as Gold!*) This trend of marking the flap of a book seems to me to bode ill; it reminds me of nothing so much as those cars on used-car lots that have marked across their windshields, "One Owner" or "Low Mileage." Can we look forward to the day when one will be greeted at the entrance to a used-book store by a man in a red blazer, a toothpick in his mouth, who tells you he has a real cream puff of an edition of Epictetus, owned by a little old lady who only read it after church on Sundays? Will used books one day, as used cars are currently, be referred to as "previously owned" books?

Perhaps I go too far. But then I worry about the fate of bookstores, rather like a grumbling elderly alumnus who is unhappy about the turn his beloved school is taking. Bookstores are my alma mater, and I hate to see them lose the character that gave them their lovely traditional quality. Like everyone who reads and writes, I feel I have a further stake in them. They are the retirement home for much of what I and a great many other people write and, eventually, the cemetery as well—but a cemetery from which at least partial, or occasional, resurrection is possible. If writing and reading are to survive in roughly the form we know them now, so must bookstores, new and used. R.I.P.: Read in Peace.

Your Basic Language Snob

I DON'T MEAN to make anyone tense or otherwise edgy, but perhaps it is best you know at the outset that in me you are dealing with your basic language snob. Mention to me that when you were young your parents were very "supportive," tell me that before "finalizing" your plans you would like my "input," remark that the job in which you are "presently" employed provides you with a "nurturing environment"—say all or any of these things and you will not, I hope, see a muscle in my face move. I shall appear to show a genial interest in all you say, but beneath the geniality, make no mistake, I shall be judging you—and not altogether kindly. "Hmm," I shall be thinking, "I see that I am dealing here with someone who has a taste for psychobabble and trashy corporate and computer talk and misuses the word *presently* into the bargain." I shall, of course, say nothing about it to you; I certainly won't attempt to reform you. In fact, I rather prefer you stay the way that you are, for in using language as you do you are a source of real comfort to me. You allow me to feel that, in the realm of language at least, I am vastly superior to you; and the feeling of superiority—need I say it?—is what puts the lovely curl in the snob's smile.

As a language snob, one finds no shortage of playgrounds

upon which to exercise one's snobbery. Hegel reports that we learn from the study of history that no one learns from the study of history. So, we learn from the careful study of language that not many people have ever used language very carefully. Permit me to bring in an old adversary on this subject, that linguist of populist tendency, Professor Bernard Strawman.

"Arguably, you have a case," Strawman, trying to be polite, says.

"Wherever did you find so weak and weakly positioned an adverb as *arguably*, Bernie?" I reply.

"Perhaps," he says, "you don't allow enough leeway for societal pressures on language use."

"In the home of what woebegone sociologist did you ever find so ugly a word as *societal?*" I inquire.

"At this point in time," he replies, "*societal* is a very popular word. What do you have against it?"

"What I have against it, Bernie," I respond, "is that it tends to be used by so many people who also use such phrases as 'at this point in time.' "

Even Bernie Strawman, normally a model of conversational good manners, now sounds a touch petulant: "Wait a minute," he says. "Which are you against: the words or the people who use them? If the former, perhaps you are a man of principle; if the latter, it seems to me you are merely a snob."

To which I reply: "In this matter of language I view myself as a highly principled snob. May I take a moment—an essay, in fact—to explain?"

Let us look more closely at the word *supportive*. (Here you must imagine me picking up the word between my thumb and index finger, holding it as far from my body as possible, a disapproving pucker upon my lips.) At first glance, *supportive* seems harmless enough. At second glance, though, it strikes me as a fake. It is no more than the old words *supporting* or *supported* got up with a new suffix that gives it a psychological and hence high-flown air, rather like getting a letter from someone you used to know from the old neighborhood who, on his stationery, has had Ph.D. printed after his name. To use the word *supportive* is to take a sound enough old word and drag it from the solid ground of common usage into the marshlands of abstraction. The net result of this transfer, it seems to me, is not a gain in clarity but only an increase in pretension.

Richard Nixon has made it impossible ever again to say "Let me make one thing perfectly clear," so let me instead be as clear as I can be here and announce that I am not against all new words. While I have the mike, let me also announce that I am of course aware that language is almost ceaselessly changing. Some changes—such as the word "breathalyzer" to measure the drunkenness of drivers—are necessary to accommodate new inventions. Some changes I like just for their rhythm and sound. *Rip-off*, which has been in the language for roughly twenty years now, seems to me to have earned its way. *Shuck*, a rip-off with an element of bunko to it, seems to me a fine fresh minting. I am all for invention, asking only that it be useful, describe something that really exists, and, if possible (which it often isn't), be fun. For this reason I find myself partial to the recent neologism *wimp*. It seems to me a word in the family of those fine Yiddishisms *nebbish* and *nebbekle* and their spin-off *nerd*. I think of a wimp, in fact, as a Gentile nebbish.

I trust that by now I have established myself as not your run-of-the-mill snob; I prefer, in fact, to think myself a custom-tailored snob. I like what I deem to be good new words. I like to toss in a neologism of my own every now and then, and I like what the linguistically prudish used to call Americanisms. One of the few things I have ever disagreed with Henry James about is his fear, set forth in *The American Scene*, that immigrant groups in the United States would pollute the pure stream of the English language. I think the current in this stream is stronger than James knew. It can carry a great deal before it and still remain fresh. It was, after all, the grandson of an immigrant, H. L. Mencken, who made the English language do one-and-a-half gainers, back flips, and triple somersaults. A. J. Liebling, another scion of the immigranti, as Mencken might have put it, for my money didn't do too shabbily either. But then I have a weakness for people who know how to play language for laughs. I have a taste for the concrete, the colorful, the comic (also, I see, for the alliterative). When the pro-basketball player Kareem Abdul-Jabbar, after dining at the home of a colleague, Julius Erving, was asked by the press if Mrs. Turquoise Erving was a good cook, Mr. Jabbar replied: "Yeah, man, Turquoise can burn." Henry James, I think, was too good-humored not to have enjoyed that.

As a snob, the people I like to lord it over are the quasi-semi-demi-ostensibly educated, B.A., M.S., Ph.D. and degrees beyond. Few things please me more, for example, than to see the novelists Norman Mailer and Joan Didion misuse the word *disinterested*. Or to notice the well-known scholar, George F. Kennan, use the word *transpire* as if it were nothing more than a high-toned synonym for *happen*. Or to hear more degreed people than I care to count use *intriguing* as if it meant nothing other than *fascinating*. (Take the verb to *intrigue* away from spies and you leave these fellows practically unemployed.) To give you some notion of how far gone I am, now that it has caught on with the putatively educated classes, I have stopped using the phrase "early on"; when I hear it from others, I think, "Whatsamatter, baby, *early* standing alone not good enough for a swell like you?" And of course I am death on people who use the term "bottom line."

Few things please me more than when to my language snobbery I can join my economic jealousy—I am practically ecstatic, that is, when I hear a highly paid broadcasting journalist commit an egregious error. I watch television news ready to pounce; it is good exercise, for, as a language snob, I get to pounce rather a lot. One of the local anchormen hereabouts—about a $300,000-a-year man, I would estimate—made my day not long ago when, in connection with the Libyan embassy crisis in London, he asked a visiting expert whether this might spell the possibility of a *tête à tête* for Qaddafi. "Coup d'etat, you overpaid moron," I roared, leaping from my couch, "not tête à tête." Or when, during the NCAA basketball tournament, the former coach and current announcer Billy Packer referred to "three or four Achilles' heels" that De Paul University's team had. "Ah, dear boy," I whispered to myself, "one Achilles' heel was quite enough—even for Achilles." But I don't always require major screw-ups such as these. I am satisfied when one of the truly high-priced boys—Dan Rather, Tom Brokaw, or Peter Jennings—misuses *decimate*, which means to kill a tenth, or calls something "rather unique," which is akin to being rather pregnant. Do you take my point? Do you also think that what I have written thus far makes for "a good read?" If you do, please clean out your locker, for you're through—I hate the phrase "a good read."

One of the things a language snob learns early in his training is that there is probably no word or phrase that someone of stature doesn't despise. Edward Shils has kept up a running attack against the phrase "check out," as in "check it out." I know many people who hate *authored* as a verb, but I recently read that E. B. White didn't even like the word *author*. I can never hear or see the word *workshop*, referring to a management seminar or creative writing course, without thinking of Kingsley Amis's line, from his novel *Jake's Thing*, which runs:

"If there's one word that sums up everything that's gone wrong since the war, it's Workshop." Legion are the people who loathe the phrase "pick your brain," and I am among their number.

"I'd like to pick your brain," is a phrase my friend Dottie uses quite often. Dottie and I go way back. She is a good soul, large-hearted in so many ways. But Dottie is one of those people who seems to absorb whatever language is in the air, and the language that has been in the air in recent years has, I fear, driven my friend Dottie a bit, well, dotty. (Perfectly lovely people sometimes use the most awful language; that they do is, alas, the pebble in the caviar of language snobbery.) Because of language, Dottie's life reminds me of a man whom Keats, in his letters, records meeting at Robert Burns's cottage, whose life, Keats notes, is "fuz, fuzzy, fuzziest."

Dottie has been going through a rough patch in recent years. Among other crises in her life, she has had a painful divorce and two job changes. She explained her divorce to me in something like the following terms. Her husband, she feels, "seemed just to want to do his thing." She no longer knew quite "where he was coming from." He used to be so steady, but, suddenly, he was so "off the wall." She supposed it was in part "a question of life-style," or maybe a "mid-life crisis." When I pressed her for greater clarity, she said: "Whatever." On her last trip to my apartment to pick my brain, her subject was a new prospective boss. She had had three interviews with him and found him rather "flakey."

"What do you mean by 'flakey'?" I asked.

"You know," she said, "he's a bit spacey."

"Spacey?" I asked.

"You know," she said, "like a real flake. I couldn't make out where exactly he was coming from."

Dottie comes ostensibly to pick my brain, but in fact she

usually succeeds in scrambling it. When I left her at the door of my apartment, I suggested that she try to get a clearer picture of this man for whom she might soon be working by asking other people in her industry about him. She kissed me on the cheek and, turning to leave, announced, "Whatever."

Whatever!

I have never seen what I think of as the all-purpose, flying "whatever" used as a transition before, as I have just used it above, but then that is what makes it all-purpose. "I love you, I need you, whatever," or so I imagine young men nowadays proposing to their wives-to-be. "Yes, darling, I love you too. I want to have your children, to live out my life with you, whatever," the young woman replies, at which point they fall into each other's arms while across the screen appears not The End but Whatever. Used in this way, *whatever* is simply the word *etcetera* carried to the highest power. But it can also be used in the following way: "I suppose what I really mean is that, given society's current setup, it appears unlikely that one can find fulfilling work as long as the structure of employment is likely to, you know, whatever." Here *whatever* really means "Oh, the hell with it; I can't formulate exactly what I wish to say, but you know what I mean." My problem is that I usually don't know what the person means. What I do know is the utility of a word such as *whatever* to a confused mind, or at any rate a mind that chooses not to struggle with its confusions. It is a very useful word, *whatever*. You can even end paragraphs with it. Whatever.

Whatever may also qualify for the category that the sainted H. W. Fowler, blessed be his name, called "meaningless words." Of meaningless words, Fowler wrote:

Words and phrases are often used in conversation, especially by the young, not as significant terms but rather, so far as they have any purpose at all, as aids of the same kind as are given in writing by punctuation, inverted commas, and underlining. It is a phenomenon perhaps more suitable for the psychologist than for the philologist. Words and phrases so employed change frequently, for they are soon worn out by overwork. Between the wars the most popular were DEFINITELY and *sort of thing.* One may suppose that they originated in a subconscious feeling that there was a need in the one case to emphasize a right word and in the other to apologize for a possibly wrong one. But any meaning they ever had was soon rubbed off them, and they became noises automatically produced.

Fowler also mentions *actually* and *you know* among the crop of meaningless words. (*Incidentally* is another meaningless word Fowler mentions, which, incidentally, reminds me that, a while back, I had a long bout of beginning most of my sentences, at least in conversation, with the phrase "By the way." Everything, in those days, seemed to me "by the way." It takes a big-hearted snob, don't you think, to admit to a small-gauge error.) A few years ago, *basically* was having a good run. "Care for dessert?" "Basically, I don't think I do," is a ridiculous but not unreal example. *You know* has had very long innings, and flourishes today, particularly among athletes. Of Patrick Ewing, the center for the New York Knicks basketball team, it has been said that last year he led the nation in *you knows.* It was said, obviously, by someone like me, a language snob.

A language snob's work is never done. Natural feelings of superiority being fleeting, he must maintain his vigilance, staying almost perpetually on the lookout for fresh signs of solecisms and lapsed standards, if only to maintain his desired state of self-elevation. As infantrymen are sent out on missions known as search and destroy, so the language snob is regularly on missions to search and enjoy—to find and delight in the linguistic fatuities and faux pas of his fellows. While there is no shortage of these in the contemporary world, some of course are better than others and provide more profound delight. I wasn't there to hear it, but a friend informs me that he once heard a Chicago politician claim that he "wasn't one to cast asparagus at his opponent." It is not every day that one comes upon such treasure.

Still, the language snob must take his pleasures where he finds them. In bureaucratic prose, for example. Few samples of bureaucratic prose fail to include the verb *implement*, which generally causes me to want to reach for an implement to smash the person who has used it. *Guidelines*, too, has brought many a twinkle to these crowfooted and pouchy eyes. "*Guidelines* is a bastardization," I cry out to the walls. "It comes from *guy lines*, you idiot." No question about it, bureaucratic prose writers need to prioritize, dichotomize, and finalize, at least if they are to be responsive and people-oriented. Is what I say here of any ongoing interest? If so, I shall keep on going.

A language snob must not fear descending to pedantry. I know this language snob doesn't. I have had a good deal of fun, in this regard, watching people misuse the word *whence*, turning it into a tautology by saying or writing "from whence." But I have suffered minor setbacks here. Recently I noted "from whence" in both Shakespeare and Edmund Burke. More recently still, I discovered T. S. Eliot—T. S. bloody Eliot, for God's sake—misusing *presently* to mean "now" or "currently." Shock and dismay is the language snob's lot. Believe me, I don't enjoy feeling superior to Shakespeare, Burke, and Eliot, yet what is a man of serious standards to do?

But a language snob need not confine himself to pedantry. Euphemism always yields a full crop for his scythe—and, like cauliflower, euphemism is available all year round. My very favorite euphemism over the past twenty or so years has been, without doubt, "student unrest." It was used to refer to the activities of radical students in the late sixties and early seventies. "Student unrest" implies a mild crankiness, the antidote for which was perhaps a few good afternoon naps. I like, too, "Due to mature theme viewer discretion advised," which I take to mean "simulated fornication, extreme violence, and filthy language follow—get the kids the hell out of the room." This may seem an idiosyncratic reading, but I understand the word *interdisciplinary*, used by academics, to mean "I deserve a grant." I recall reading a grant proposal for the National Endowment for the Humanities a few years back in which the author wanted a grant for a course that would not only be "cross-curricular" but "interdisciplinary" and "interuniversity" as well. I suggested that NEH turn it down because it wasn't interplanetary. None of this parochial stuff for me.

A language snob must also be ready to outlaw words because the wrong people use them. *Charisma* is such a word. It once had a significant meaning, but no longer. "He has charisma," I not long ago heard Bucky Walters, the basketball announcer, say of a player. "He's got that smile." *Gnostic*, at least as used by literary critics, is another word I should like to ban. I have never read a sentence by a literary critic with the word *Gnostic* in it that I have ever understood (except this one). *Syndrome*, too, must go. "This is a syndrome he had foisted on him," I recently heard one politician say of another. *Structure* is another gone goose. On television the other day I heard another politician, one of the zinc-throated orators of our day, affirm: "I have invested in activities that have gone to enhance this total city's overall structure." Does everyone out there know how to enhance a structure? You add a touch of tarragon and soak it in lime juice. While we are cleaning the linguistic closet, let's toss out *learning experience*, which was never any good to begin with. Besides, I have noticed that people who say "learning experience" tend never to learn from experience.

On the subject of experience, it was Walter Pater who invoked us to live intensely for the moment, to seek "not the fruit of experience, but experience itself." But Pater didn't live to see the word *experience* turned into a verb, lucky chap. What would he have made of recent advertisements that ask us to "Experience Yoplait Yogurt," "Experience the St. Regis," "Experience Our 9.6 Interest Rates"? Walter Pater was not notably—how to say it?—a fun person. I am not at all sure he could "wrap his mind around" what has happened to the word *experience*. Nor is he likely to turn up in a restaurant I noted the other day called The Corned Beef Experience. Although in the passage of his I quoted above he seems to be inviting us to "get in touch with our feelings," he scarcely seems a man to whom one could say, as the people who use *experience* as a verb also tend to say, "Go for it!"

As a language snob, I judge a person less by the cut of his jib than by the grab of his gab. Where the gab has no grab I see a certain mental—not moral—flab. When a prospective buyer of *The London Observer* remarks that he intends to make that paper's editor "toe the line of viability," I make a judgment that is not charitable to him. When I read the phrase, in a book by Alvin Toffler, "decisional environment," not one but both my eyebrows fly up just beyond my receding hairline. When I read, in *The New Yorker*, about a Harvard Law School professor who refers to "a societal role not perceived as particularly helpful," to myself I exclaim, "Et tu, Harvard!" Can you identify with or relate to this? If you can—"identify," "relate"— I want you to draw a final paycheck and be out of here by five o'clock this afternoon. I loathe those words and phrases. You're fired.

"I have never seen a word derive," says the heroine of Renata Adler's novel *Speedboat*. I believe I have seen a word derive, and that word is *life-style*. I recall first coming across

the word *life-style* (from the German *Lebensstil*) in Max
Weber's essays on social class, some of which I read as an
undergraduate. I was immensely impressed with it; on Max
Weber, an authentic genius, all words looked good. In those
days, I used it myself, slipping it into term papers and conversation whenever possible. (Those were also the days of *ambiva-
lence* and *love-hate*—not the condition and the relationships
but the cheap phrases.) Soon I saw *life-style* taken up by advertising agencies and low-grade sociologists. College students
next took the word up in the most flyblown way: "Queen
Victoria lived a very different life-style than most of her subjects." The word fell into more and more common—and more
and more confused—use. Today the word carries something
of a philosophical freight: implicit in it is the notion, which
I, for one, don't believe, that life has an almost infinite plasti-
city—change your life-style, change your life, it's as easy as
that.

I have come to feel a fine invigorating hatred for the word.
Where I could fight against it, I have done so. I have abused
authors who use it when I have written about their books. My
poor students always receive a slightly squinty-eyed query
when the word pops up in their conversation: "*Life-style*—
what do you suppose you mean when you say *life-style?*" I ask.
But then a few years ago, in the course of editing a manuscript
by the late Nobel-Prize-winning biologist Max Delbrück, who
was a fluent and careful writer of English prose, I came across
a reference to "the life-style of the cell." Over the telephone I
explained to Professor Delbrück that *life-style* was a word that
drove me beyond the confines of distraction and into the country of apoplexy and asked him if I couldn't persuade him to
remove it from his manuscript. "I don't like it much myself,"
he replied, "but I am afraid that it is the word that scientists

have given to the patterning of certain cellular activity and that we are stuck with it." So there you have it—living testimony of a word deriving.

Do I, I wonder, begin to seem to you—to put it ever so gently—a touch crazed? Has the cheerful snob that I advertise myself as being begun to seem the beady-eyed fanatic? There is something about caring for language that does not allow for moderation. How can you tell if you care about language? You care, I should say, if it grates upon you to hear the word *impact* used as a verb. Next you begin to care if you see *impact* used to describe anything other than ballistics, car crashes, and wisdom teeth. You care if you find yourself wishing to flee the company of anyone who uses such words as *parenting, coupling, cohabing, husbanding,* or *wiving.* You care if it turns your stomach to see or hear a reference to "the caring professions." You know for certain that you care if the last thing in the world you care to be called is "a caring person."

In recent years language snobbery has suffered a real setback by having become institutionalized. There have always been writers who worried and complained about the state of the English language. Swift, Hazlitt, and Orwell have been among their number. But of late a great many books have been published on the subject. Magazines—*The New York Times Magazine, Esquire, Gentlemen's Quarterly*—have instituted regular columns on the state of the language. Such journalists as Edwin Newman, John Simon, and William Safire—a bit of a falling off here from Swift, Hazlitt, and Orwell—have set up shop as state-of-the-language pundits. By now there are even reverse language snobs loose in the land. Thus Professor Robert Pattison, in *On Literacy,* remarks upon "the dull, pragmatic rationale of established literacy" and writes:

The same students who resolutely remain in darkness about the niceties of correct English grammar are as capable of intelligence as any previous generation. . . . Months of exercises will not shake their nonchalance about commas, but few are likely to misspell the name Led Zeppelin.

What a shame that there isn't an antonym for the phrase "Right on!"

Mention of the state-of-the-language pundits brings to mind Lionel Trilling, who once wrote: "I find righteous denunciations of the present state of language no less dismaying than the present state of the language." Yet, I have to wonder, is what I have been doing here not also righteous? Perhaps it is, but there does remain the less than cheery state of the language. Then, too, I take some small pride in the fact that I am for the most part attacking my own class. More than thirty years ago, in *Noblesse Oblige* (1956), Nancy Mitford caused a great stir by pointing out the distinction in their use of language between U and non-U people—U people being those who had gone to university. This distinction, as I recall, had to do almost exclusively with social class, and spoke very little, if at all, to the quality of language used by either group. Today, though, it is people who have been to university who make the most gnawing depredations into the clarity and cleanliness of language. I cannot, for example, imagine any supposedly uneducated person using the word *supportive,* except possibly about his jockstrap. Who but a university student or graduate would refer to her mother as a "role model," or talk about "the gender gap," or say she wishes "to dialogue" with me? (I make it a rule never "to dialogue"; I find it gets in the way of serious conversation.) Who but a U person would fall back on so foggy a word as *values?* Wesleyan University, I note, has a course entitled "Touchstones of Western Values," and Jesse Jackson has said, "Values lead to values." See ya later, obfuscator.

With the possible exception of politicians, bureaucrats, professors with weak ideas, and those in other professions and trades where charlatanry is requisite, few are the people who have a real taste for obfuscatory language. Doubtless Nietzsche was correct when he said that "general is the need for new jingling words, which shall make life noisy and festive." Yet language is still far and away the best tool we have for deceiving ourselves. When a famous ecologist writes that, if we are to save the earth, "we must enter into a creative association with our environment," I don't think the man is a knave or even a liar; I do, though, think, perhaps unbeknownst to himself, that he is embarked on the mental equivalent of whistling Dixie. When a young mother takes an active hand in a political campaign because she wants "this country to be a positive experience for my son," I do not impugn her sincerity, only her clarity. Was Russia a positive experience for Tolstoy, Germany for Bismarck, France for Proust? Do countries supply "positive experience"? The thought makes one wonder whether this young mother isn't searching for something that is not available.

So the language snob persists, lorgnette held high. Sometimes he looks quite as much at the people who use them as at the words themselves. I have never, for instance, met a professor in the humanities who called himself or herself a "humanist," without irony, whom I didn't dislike. I am extremely wary of people who go in for botanical metaphors in a big way to describe psychological states. "I feel myself growing," they will say. Or: "It has been a growthful experience." To the basic botanical metaphor of growth, further metaphors are stitched in. Abra Anderson, a Rockefeller granddaughter and a millionairess who lives in Chicago, recently told a journalist:

Right now I don't know where I am, except that I feel everything else is finished. The apartment's finished, I've got a wonderful man, my kids are fine, the bills are paid, the charities are OK. And I'm just repotting myself.

Repotting? Hmm. Sounds like a lot of fertilizer to me.

Certain words such as *growth* seem to have a built-in squishiness; they grow soft at the touch. But, as any language snob will be pleased to tell you, good solid words, if sedulously misused, can lose their solidity, too. The word *honest* applied to art—and for a long stretch it was the key word of praise for works of architecture—always merits suspicion. *Excellence* is nowadays all but drained of meaning, so often has it been applied to things that are scarcely mediocre. The word *complete*, when used to describe collections of one or another kind of writing, usually turns out to mean merely "quite a bit of." *Literally*, in so many current usages, doesn't mean "literally"; it's literally a scandal, so to speak. "Ballpark figure" is a nice fairly new phrase meaning "rough approximation" (such as the estimates of attendance at a ball game), but it sometimes seems, to this language snob at any rate, as if we are entering the era of ballpark language, where words are used approximately; they mean only roughly what we think they mean.

My biases ought by now to be clear; so, too, my snobbery. But I earlier referred to myself as a principled snob. Wherein, you may about now be wondering, lie my principles? All right, turn down the houselights, boys, give me the strong spotlight and a drumroll, here they are: take out after all language that is pretentious and imprecise, under-educated and over-intellectualized. Question all language that says more than it means, that leaves the ground but does not really fly. Question authority only after you have first seriously consulted it; it isn't always as stupid as it looks. Never forget that today's hot new phrase becomes tomorrow's cold dead cliché. (What will we do, a writer in the *Chronicle of Higher Education* asks, "when the Baby Boomers get to Golden Pond?") Know in advance that the fight for careful language is probably a losing one, but at the same time don't allow this knowledge to take the edge off your appetite for battle. The war may be lost, yet the skirmishes are still worth waging. Recall the words of that grand snob, Proust's Baron de Charlus: "I have always honored the defenders of grammar and logic. We realize fifty years later that they have averted serious dangers."

Hey, you know, I guess that some of you think I'm doing a number on you. If you do, check it out. C'mon over. I'd like your input. The old lady'll put out some peanuts, pretzels maybe—you know, fun food. We'll break out a few tall cool ones. Hey, no problem. See if you think I've really gone flakey on this language thing. I think you'll find I'm pretty viable and am playing well within myself. We'll do some zero-based thinking, look at it in terms of worst-case and in terms of best-case thinking—in terms of the process itself. Maybe, when you come right down to it, it's a policy question. It's an intriguing bit. Arguably, it's worth arguing about. I haven't gone so far beyond the wall as to be above a little insightful feedback. But I'd better knock off, you know, because I've come, as they used to say in the bad old days, to the bottom line—and when I say bottom line, daddy, I mean bottom line.

What's So Funny?

ONE OF THE TRICKIEST QUESTIONS on the Stanford-Epstein Personality Profile is the following: Which of these statements would you be least willing to own up to? (1) Good taste is clearly not my long suit. (2) I never have been much good at judging people. (3) I guess I'm pretty much a humorless person. I don't know about you, but I would be more ready to admit to bad taste and poor judgment than humorlessness any day. Yet why? Is it possible that having a good sense of humor is overrated? What can be said against it? For one thing, humor is anti-erotic; it is extremely difficult to be passionate while laughing. For another, a strong sense of humor may well be an obstacle to achievement on the grand scale. Among great statesmen, only Disraeli and Churchill had notably fine senses of humor. Not many laughs are to be found in the works of Aristotle, Newton, Goethe. Animals have no sense of humor; nor do they feel the want of any. Only human beings laugh.

When I was younger and not so profound as I am today —"That's a joke, son," as Senator Claghorn used to say—I thought that a sense of humor was an absolute requirement in anyone I would care to call my friend. As it happens, most of my friends do have a sense of humor; perhaps it is required if they are to tolerate me. But I have since met many men and women with superior humor who seem to me otherwise inferior people. A sense of humor is an ornament to character but no replacement for it. In certain lines of work I can do nicely, thank you very much, with workers whose sense of humor is not too spirited. I shouldn't want a surgeon who too greatly enjoys jokes, lest one occurs to him while one or another of my vitals is under his blade. I prefer my accountants without mordancy, my dentists without wit, my clergymen altogether unribald. I used to go to a barber named Felix who caused me to laugh so much and so hard in the chair that getting haircut from him became unsafe. "As funny as a theologian" (or undertaker, or physical therapist, or plumber) is not a phrase one often hears or, with luck, ever will.

Despite all this, most of us highly value a sense of humor; and among those of us who do so value it, few things are funnier than a humorless person. "Only man has dignity," Ronald Knox has said, "only man, therefore, can be funny." Excessive dignity can be excessively funny. The story is told of a dinner given by Prime Minister and Mrs. Harold Macmillan for General and Mme de Gaulle, at which Mrs. Macmillan is supposed to have said to Mme de Gaulle: "Your husband has accomplished so much. You have both lived such rich and full lives. Is there anything left for you? Is there anything you still desire?" To which Mme de Gaulle is said to have replied, "Yes, one thing: a penis." After a brief stunned silence, General de Gaulle interjected: *"Non, non, ma chérie,* the word is pronounced *Happiness."* No doubt that story is apocryphal, and while it is about the international comedy of trying to speak foreign languages, it wouldn't be as good with a less dignified cast of characters. With M. and Mme François Mauriac, it would be only mildly amusing. With M. and Mme André Gide, it becomes too complicated to be funny at all.

If there were a pantheon of the humorless, who would be in it? Some American names leap to mind: Ralph Waldo Emerson, Douglas MacArthur, Walter Cronkite. A place would surely have to be reserved for D. H. Lawrence. Wordsworth would get in on the first ballot. So would Wagner. What about the reigning Queen of England? Or Fidel Castro? Or General Jaruzelski? Has there, in fact, ever been a witty Communist? Milan Kundera, the Czech novelist, has remarked of his life during the early days of the Communist regime in his country: "I could always recognize a person who was not a Stalinist, a person whom I needn't fear, by the way he smiled. A sense of humor was a trustworthy sign of recognition."

A sense of humor is not, thus far at least, one of the items that the Japanese have chosen to export. Henry James once wrote of the Italians: "The more I see of them, the more struck I am with their having no sense of the ridiculous." The Germans have not been notable for their rip-roaring, rollicking sense of humor either, to put it very gently, yet there have been supremely funny German writers, among them Heinrich Heine and, perhaps surprisingly, Thomas Mann. (Mann's *Confessions of Felix Krull* is a comic masterpiece.) Mark Twain, during his days as a comic lecturer, always preferred not to work his act in churches, commenting: "People are afraid to laugh in a church. They can't be made to do it in any possible way." Yet the current Pope has a sense of humor. So, too, must God; after all, he created the world.

Then, for me, there is that special category of people who are supposed to be funny, but whom I have never quite found so. I have never found Art Buchwald funny. P. G. Wodehouse I find only mildly funny. Peter De Vries, whose humor knocks so many people out, has always left me sturdily on my feet. I find Ogden Nash funny only in flashes. And here is a confession that may land me in the pantheon of the humorless: Mark

Twain doesn't do it for me either. I know he is reputed to be very funny; I know about the rich tradition of Southwestern humor and all that; but for me Mark Twain's humor falls into that saddest of all comic categories, the faintly amusing. Dickens breaks me up, but Twain leaves me, alas, in one stolid piece.

What do I find funny? I have lately been reading the letters of Henry James, and find much cause in them, as James himself might put it, for high risibility. When James, in the midst of his great dining-out period in London (in the 1878–79 social season he dined out no fewer than 107 times), remarks that he cannot face "yet another inscrutable entrée," I laugh. When, after his disastrous attempt to lower his artistic sights by writing for the London stage, James caps the horrendous experience by noting that "you can't make a sow's ear out of a silk purse," I laugh again. I find Proust I won't say a scream but pretty damn funny when portraying his pedants, his snobs, his malapropistic headwaiters. The Baron de Charlus I believe to be one of the great comic creatures of all time, and when he returns to Proust's page a clapping sound goes off in my heart of the kind one makes to greet the appearance on stage of only the greatest actors. Kafka, in some of the details that appear in the midst of his nightmare stories, can also make my laugh-meter jump.

Kafka, I recognize, is not normally thought sidesplitting, but then humor turns up in odd places. That is part of its charm —its unexpectedness. I not long ago read a lovely but not notably funny book entitled *West with the Night* by Beryl Markham. Mrs. Markham was an aviatrix in East Africa in the 1930s. (When the gender gap finally closes—*clunk!*—I hope we don't have to surrender the word *aviatrix,* which has always seemed to me to combine adventure with beauty.) At one point in her book Mrs. Markham describes the perpetually busy Hindu telegraph operators she encountered along the Uganda

Railway. Whenever she came upon them, she comments, they seemed always to be tapping away. What, in desolate East Africa, could have kept the forefingers of these Babus, as Hindus in Africa were then called, so endlessly occupied? "I have no idea of what they really talked about," Mrs. Markham writes. "Possibly I do the Babus an injustice, but I think at best they used to read the novels of Anthony Trollope to each other over the wire." Pardon my giggle, but I find that very funny.

I think W. C. Fields very funny, too. Chaplin's charm is undeniable, Buster Keaton can put me on the floor, the Marx Brothers frequently have my number, but in my opinion W. C. Fields was the best of all movie comedians because his movies conveyed the most complete expression of a comic personality. A story is told about Fields's last words on his deathbed in a hospital in New York. His doctor, his mistress, a few close friends are in the room. Outside it is cold and snowing, the newsboys, hawking their papers, are crying out "Wuxtry! Wuxtry!" Fields, who has been dozing, on the edge of death, opens his eyes and signals the people in the room to gather round his bed. In a barely audible whisper, he says: "Poor little urchins out there. No doubt improperly clad and ill-nourished. Something's got to be done about them! Something's got to be done!" Fields closes his eyes. His friends return to their chairs. Twenty seconds later, he opens his eyes, signaling his company back to his bedside. They lean in to hear what he now has to say. "On second thought," Fields whispers, "screw 'em!" Now this story, too, may well be apocryphal, but if it is the man or woman who made it up is a small comic genius, for one cannot imagine a deathbed scene for the great comic that is more Fieldsian.

I am perfectly ready to accept that not everyone will find this anecdote funny. Those newsboys wouldn't have. Nor would Jane Addams. Nor would an ardent socialist, however otherwise good-natured he might be. The first condition of humor is its un-universality. If music be a universal language, humor is a quite particular one. "What is it like for people not to have the same sense of humor?" Wittgenstein asks. "They do not react properly to each other. It's as though there were a custom amongst certain people for one person to throw another a ball which he is supposed to catch and throw back; but some people, instead of throwing it back, put it in their pocket." Too true. Different jokes for different folks.

Which is why no useful all-purpose definition of humor can ever quite hold up. Such definitions as we have of humor are all right as far as they go, which is never far enough. Henri Bergson, in his exceedingly humorless essay *On Laughter*, defined humor as the release from inhibitions. Arthur Koestler, in *The Act of Creation*, defined humor as "the perceiving of a situation or idea in two self-consistent but mutually incompatible frames of reference or associative contexts," adding, with great Koestlerian confidence, "This formula can be shown to have a general validity for all forms of humor and wit." Freud, rather depressingly in my view, considered most humor to be secret aggression that often hid sexual motives.

> Sex and aggression, sex and aggression,
> My God, my dear Dr. Freud,
> Can there be no other use for expression?

The reason all definitions of humor are disappointing is that the motives for laughter are too diverse, contradictory, paradoxical. Humor may well be a reflex, a release, an act of aggression, the joining together of incompatible frames of reference—it may well be all of these things, and yet it is none of them alone. Humor is, as Wittgenstein (himself not a famously funny fellow) once said, "a way of looking at the world." Not everyone looks at it in the same way. "To explain the nature of laughter and tears," wrote Hazlitt, "is to account for the condition of human life; for it is in a manner compounded of these two!"

Although I should know better than to enter the definition-of-humor sweepstakes, here nonetheless are a few soft definitions. Humor is the element missing from most bores. (I exclude those bores who are always insisting upon their own humorousness.) Humor is any extremely well-phrased comment on yet another, hitherto unrevealed aspect of the bizarreness of life. Humor is what is funny to the humorous; it can include mots, puns, witticisms, and sheer whimsicality. Comedy, as Santayana put it, "is life caught in the act"; to which I would add, it is especially people caught in the act, which is why pretension is always such a fine target for humor.

"You know, Dottie," Robert Benchley said to Dorothy Parker after her third or fourth attempt at suicide, "you keep this up, you're going to make yourself very sick." Listening to a sonorous lecture on the subject of the importance of the humanities, I recall a friend, sitting next to me, say of the lecturer, "I'd like this guy better if his name were Moe." Of William Morris, Max Beerbohm once said: "Of course we all know that Morris was a wonderful all-round man, but the act of walking round him has always tired me." Still on the subject of pretension, Oliver Goldsmith once said of David Garrick: "On the stage he was natural, simple, affectionate. 'Twas only that when he was off he was acting."

Pricking pretension, letting the air out of the balloon tires of pomposity, belongs to that department of humor known as the put-down. Another name for it is creative abuse. Not everyone has a taste for this; I do. A little richly deserved and well-aimed malice seems to me a fine thing. Creative abuse involves the art of establishing a feeling of hopelessness in the next fellow. Some people specialize in it. Stephen Potter, in such books as *One-upmanship, Lifemanship,* and *Gamesmanship,* wrote instructional manuals on how to go about it. But many people require no such instruction. A. E. Housman, for example, is said to have jotted down acidulous phrases as they occurred to him and then later inserted these phrases in reviews of books by fellow Latinists. Subtle creative abuse is better than blatant abuse. An excellent example is Sydney Smith's remark about Macaulay, who was a famous nonstop talker: "He has occasional flashes of silence, that make his conversation perfectly delightful." In the modern era, none surpasses Evelyn Waugh's comment after learning that a benign tumor was removed from the lung of his friend Randolph Churchill: "It was a typical triumph of modern science to find the only part of Randolph that was not malignant and remove it."

A distinction has to be made between before-the-face and behind-the-back put-downs. (Maurice Bowra is supposed to have said of another Oxford don: "He is the kind of man who will stab you in the front.") I had a friend who once told me that when people he scarcely knew addressed him by his first name, he responded by saying, "My friends call me Mr. Young. Won't you do likewise?" That seems to me extremely good, but, though I have more than once thought of pressing it into service myself, I have yet to find the nerve to do so. When it comes to comic put-downs, I fear that I am largely a behind-the-back or, at best, an in-front-of-the-typewriter man. So apparently was Herman Melville, who wrote of Emerson that he had a gaping flaw: "It was the insinuation that had he lived in those days when the world was made, he might have offered some valuable suggestions."

Gentle put-downs can be lovely in their own quiet way. A friend and his wife were dining at the Russian Tea Room, when up to their table strode a well-known drama critic in a formidable, almost armored double-breasted suit, a shirt of nearly neon stripes, and a necktie that Louis Quatorze might well have rejected as too lavish. After he left, my friend's wife quietly exclaimed, "Dear me, I didn't realize that James went in so for haberdashery." I once attended an editorial board meeting at which one of the members asked if in fact the role of the board wasn't merely to supply window dressing. Edward Shils, who was also at the meeting, responded: "Window dressing," he said, rolling the phrase thoughtfully over his tongue. "Window dressing. Let us consider this fenestral metaphor. Assume we have a window. We might wish to set drapes around it. A cornice perhaps to surround it. A shade might be wanted. Perhaps a curtain. The window, so to speak, is dressed. But, really, just because one has a window in a room doesn't mean one has to look out of it all the time." I have never before, or since, seen wit, whimsy, and a sense of the absurd quite so neatly and spontaneously packed into so ornate a metaphor. I cannot report what the reaction to this extraordinary riposte was on the part of the person who had raised the question of window dressing, for I had to turn my head aside, lest the contortions in my face from suppressed laughter give me away. A sense of humor can sometimes be terribly inconvenient.

If pitched at a sufficiently high level, insults can also be very funny. What is funny about them is usually not the insulted but the insulter. There is something about the rage of a serious insult, if that rage is held under control, that can be hilarious. Frederick Rolfe, the writer who called himself Baron Corvo, was excellent at this sort of insult. And here he is, writing to his publisher, who has been instructed not to forward any letters to him:

Sir,
   I am weary of repeating that you are to accept *no* communications for me. I leave you no discretion. As for the infernally familiar

style in which you have presumed to address me, I beg to inform you
that I regard it as a fresh outrage committed by an impenitent thief.

By all, to whom I name your name, you are despised or hated;
but I doubt whether you ever made a more ruthless or persequent
enemy than—

> Your obedient servant—
> Frederick William Rolfe

I find funny a man who can deliver himself of such an outburst
yet keep it within the bounds of careful syntax and punctuation and even, for good measure, call up so arcane a word as
persequent.

But then I have a special weakness for insult as a form of
humor, for I went to a high school where insult was the chief
form that humor took. It wasn't called insult, though; it was
called "bugging." Under the auspices of bugging, everyone
went after everyone else for any weakness, physical deformity,
or psychological infirmity he could find. It was not insult that
came from on high, à la Frederick Rolfe, but it could nonetheless be highly inventive. Adolescent acne—"spots," as the English call it—was termed "tweed," and whoever had the rough-
est case of it at any particular time was designated, after the
Tammany Hall figure, "Boss Tweed." Being underweight or
overweight, having slightly squinty or slightly hyperthyroid
eyes, failing with girls or being too successful with them, anything and everything was fair game for bugging—including,
it needs to be added, the defects of one's parents. The father
of one of our circle had served in North Africa during World
War II, for example, and about him it was soon bruited that
he had spent the better part of the war playing gin rummy with
Field Marshal Rommel. ("I'm knocking on two, Desert Fox.")
It was an atmosphere, in short, that called not only for wit but
for quickness of wit. Around this same time, the early 1950s, the
professional insult comedians, Jackie Leonard and Don Rickles

chief among them, began turning up. I recall seeing Jackie
Leonard, on a television talk show, congratulate the then-
young comic Shelley Berman on his recent successful emer-
gence into big-time show business, then, without missing a
beat, suggesting the fly-blown quality of show-business success, inquire: "Tell me, kid, where d'ya rent your watch?"
Leonard would have done well at our high school, where nice
guys didn't finish last; they scarcely finished at all.

Ours is not, I think, a great age of comedians. Television
wears them out as do too-quickly-thrown-together movies.
Bob Hope I find no longer funny, but a man who has for years
been living off comic capital first gathered thirty and forty
years ago. Johnny Carson's humor has mostly to do with snig-
gling sex jokes; his idea of a good laugh is a woman with
enormous breasts; and he is funniest when attempting to recover from a badly misfired joke. Jerry Lewis I have never
found funny, though there is a joke about him I rather like.
This joke has it that the reason he works so hard on behalf of
muscular dystrophy is that, owing to all those years he imitated
spastics, he probably caused a lot of it.

Of the current crop of big-name comedians, the three who
have had the strongest and longest run are Richard Pryor,
Woody Allen, and Mel Brooks. (Eddie Murphy, Gilda Rad-
ner, Dan Aykroyd, and other comedians from *Saturday Night
Live*, though capable of wonderful comic bits, have not yet
established complete comic personalities.) Much of Pryor's
humor is built around the great touchy subject of race, and
such pleasure as derives from it comes from his joking, often
very well, about the unjokeable. Woody Allen's is largely the
humor of self-debasement—what at my high school would
have been known as "self-bugging." Fine though it seemed for
a while, it now seems rather tired and predictable: all those
analysand jokes, those Jewish family-life jokes, those food jokes

—one can hear them coming from several hundred versts off. Allen's own great success in the world has undermined his comedy of self-debasement; one cannot, after all, continue to joke about one's sexual ineptitude while living with beautiful movie stars. Mel Brooks is the purest funny man of the three. He is inventive; he has a charming sense of the absurd; he has been given a wonderful prop in his expressive, utterly urban Jewish face, which is itself a delightful affront to pomposity or even sustained seriousness. He is—I use the word as an honorific—silly. Yet I find if I see Mel Brooks roughly once a year, either on television or in a movie, that is sufficient. (Here I must add that he has apparently been able to survive by seeing me even less frequently.)

Great though the gift of comedy is, hopeless though life would seem without it, it is also fragile and can soon become cloying. To be under the burden of always having to be funny is to carry a heavy cross indeed. Charles Lamb—of whom Hazlitt said, "He always made the best pun, and the best remark of the evening"—felt that to be accused of always aiming at wit was a kind of libel, for one shouldn't set out to be witty but instead should allow wit to arise out of natural settings and situations. Professional comedians must be funny every night, must be funny on demand, and this is no laughing matter: few spectacles are sadder than watching a comedian "die" on stage. Nor is the spectacle any jollier of watching those amateur comedians, of whom I know too many, who feel they must come up with a quip or a witticism every thirty or so seconds. It has more than once occurred to me to ask some among them, "What would you take to smother your turgid little ironies? Quote me a monthly figure." One of the monumental self-deceptions is that of someone who thinks he is funny when he isn't. Unlike so many other self-deceptions, there isn't anything in the least funny about it.

In the category of the obviously-not-funny, a cornucopia of items must be included. Chimpanzees aren't funny—at least not to me, for when seeing them, I am too vividly reminded of human evolution. Dogs in skirts or jackets aren't funny. Neither are men dressed as women. Most jokes about parrots aren't funny, except the one whose punch line is, "Don't worry, we'll double our money on Yom Kippur." Off-color greeting cards aren't funny. Only two bumper stickers have struck me as funny among the hundreds I have seen: one, written over a few bars of musical composition, read, "Get Off My Bach!"; the other, a variation on "If You Love Jesus, Honk!," read, "If You Are Jesus, Honk!" I have an acquaintance who, knowing my penchant for jokes, regularly tells me the most unfunny ones imaginable, which are almost invariably about the most hopelessly unfunny subjects: crucifixion, bestiality, masturbation. When he tells them to me, I laugh falsely and try—as it turns out, with an impressive measure of success—to forget them as quickly as I can.

Entire books devoted to humor usually aren't funny. Light verse, for example, can be winning, but a full-blown 540-page collection such as *The Oxford Book of American Light Verse* can make light quickly seem heavy. I recently read a posthumous collection of the comic pieces of Robert Benchley, a man I always think of as very funny indeed, and was disappointed to discover how little of it holds up. In part, this is because time is hell on humor; in greater part, though, it is better to read Benchley—or S. J. Perelman or James Thurber—in short takes. I was not long ago sent a wide and thick volume entitled *The Big Book of Jewish Humor*, and found myself growing bored with it fairly quickly. Jokes tend to fade on paper, where voice and gesture do not accompany them. A book such as *The Big Book of Jewish Humor* is all right, I suppose, but the truth is that I prefer my Jewish humor delivered to me by individual

Jews at generous intervals. Reading joke after joke, comic piece after comic piece, is like eating a cookie that is all chocolate chips—it doesn't take long for one's teeth to begin aching and one's lips to purse like those of a bank loan officer greeting a couple who has missed their last eleven mortgage payments.

I used to find slapstick funny but now do so decreasingly. Perhaps my imagination for pain has grown more vivid. A short while ago I saw a Bugs Bunny cartoon, and found my heart going out to Elmer Fudd, that nasty rabbit's victim. The films of The Three Stooges, which cause much mirth in small children, I can no longer bear to watch, for I find myself wincing much more than laughing. The gentler slapstick of Laurel and Hardy, though, still gets to me; watching those two charming men attempting to settle down for the night in a malfunctioning in-a-door bed unfailingly touches my laugh button.

What, then, is so funny? Sex is funny—always, of course, excluding one's own endeavors in this line. One of the things that make pornography so damnable, in my view, is its humorlessness. (Must remember to save a niche in the pantheon of the humorless for Hugh Hefner.) Henry Miller writing about sex can make one laugh; Norman Mailer writing about it can make one cringe. What is funny about sex is its bizarreness, the wide range of appetites it can show, its sharp reminder (for all its glories) of our animality. The best sex jokes demonstrate a tasteful perversity, such as the joke about the nonagenarian who reports to his physician that he notices himself beginning to slow down sexually. "When did you first begin to notice this?" asks the physician, amazed that a nonagenarian is still sexually active at all. "Last night," the man says, "and then again this morning." Or the joke about the two homosexual men sitting at an outdoor cafe, when a voluptuous woman walks past. "Did you ever," one of the men asks the other with a sigh, "wish you were a lesbian?" Such jokes seem to me to hover, skirt, and play around bad taste without quite falling into it, though I am sure they will offend someone—a still-sexually-active nonagenarian homosexual, perhaps.

Jews are funny, Jews are very funny—not individual Jews, but Jews as a comic subject. If you wish to know why this is so, ask History. Having been kicked in the pants so often by History, Jews bring a certain comic preparedness to life. No people, Freud noted, has told so many jokes about itself as the Jews. ("I'm tired of hearing jokes about Jews," one man says to another. "Don't you know any jokes that aren't about Jews?" "All right," the other says. "One Passover these two Japanese gentlemen, Rabinowitz and Ginsburg. . . .") Perhaps, too, Jews bear out the not-uncommon notion that great humorists are, at bottom, people who have been driven to despair by the conduct of mankind. (This, as Peter DeVries has recently said, is "the tale that dogs the wag.") A man in a bar, quite drunk, offers to buy a round of drinks for everyone in the place, excepting only, as he puts it, "my Jewish friend there at the end of the bar." Twenty minutes later, he offers to buy another round, adding, "but none for my Israelite pal down there." Fifteen minutes more and he offers to buy yet a third round, "excluding of course my Hebrew buddy." Finally, the Jew stands up to say: "Look, I have never met you. We haven't exchanged a word. What do you have against me anyhow?" "I'll tell you what I have against you," the drunk replies, "you sunk the *Titanic.*" "What do you mean?" the Jew answers. "I didn't sink the *Titanic;* an iceberg sunk the *Titanic.*" The drunk, hiccupping, replies: "Iceberg, Greenberg, Goldberg— you're all no damn good!"

Tyranny is funny; not actual tyranny but the attempts of tyrants to cover up their tyrannousness. How else explain that the strongest flow of jokes right now comes out of Eastern

Europe. Andrei Sinyavsky, the Russian émigré writer, reports that the joke "is the only contemporary folk genre in Soviet Russia." For one thing, under tyranny humor is perhaps the only form of emotional outlet; for another, humor, by mocking official falsity and fantasy, brings reality back into focus and serves as a reminder that there is still something in the world known as reason. When one or another tyranny stamps down its heel, jokes squiggle out. During one of the harshest suppressions of the Solidarity movement in Poland, the joke went round the streets of all Polish cities about General Jaruzelski flying to Moscow where he asks for an audience with the corpse of Lenin. This is duly arranged, and Jaruzelski, alone at the bier of Lenin, pours out his heart about the terrible problems he is encountering in Poland. While he is doing so, he notices, through the glass covering Lenin's head, Lenin's lips move. He leans down, placing his ear against the glass, and hears Lenin say, "Arm the workers!"

"We discern in the joke," Andrei Sinyavsky writes, "an indulgent and superior vision of life." Bitter though jokes can be, they nonetheless can become, as Sinyavsky says, "an advisor and helper, an explanation and comfort in the most critical situations, as well as for all occasions." Here I recall the one occasion upon which I met Andrei Sinyavsky. Knowing his love of jokes, I told him one. I do not remember what the joke was, but only that, he having no English and I no Russian, I told the joke to him through a translator. After I told a line or two, the translator translated the lines. Finally, after delivering the punch line, I waited while the translator re-delivered it for me in Russian. It was greeted by Sinyavsky not with explosive but with appreciative laughter, after which Sinyavsky spoke a few words in Russian. "That is quite good, Mr. Sinyavsky thinks," the translator reported. I was pleased, though telling jokes around the corner of translation does dreadful things to one's timing. Still, a human transaction had been completed, as it is whenever a decent joke is told. "The joke," as Andrei Sinyavsky reports about the Soviet Union, "is alive and well. God grant it good health."

But apparently the joke is not everywhere in good health. The other day I came upon a story in the *Chronicle of Higher Education* that carried the headline, "Use of Humor by College Teachers Found to Stir Suspicion and Hostility." The story began: "Teachers who try to be funny in the classroom probably aren't doing themselves or their students any favors, according to a study at the University of New Mexico. Indeed, the study found a teacher's use of humor is 'likely to be perceived with suspicion and hostility,' causing students to react defensively and thus damaging the climate for communication." The story goes on to report that the researchers found that not only ridiculing humor, which one would expect to have bad results, but even "non-tendentious humor," such as puns and other forms of innocent joking, discouraged what the researchers call "supportive classroom interactions," no matter whether the humor issues from a male or female teacher. The lesson appears clear enough: if he starts joking around, give the professor the hook.

Clear though it may be, the lesson does not go down easily with me. I fear I am one of those jokey professors who— though I had not been aware of it—set up defensive reactions (through non-tendentious humor, I trust) and thus cannot expect much in the way of "supportive classroom interactions." But what am I to do? I teach classes of ninety minutes' duration, and usually I find I cannot keep a straight face for that length of time. I am frequently amused at the pomposity of teaching, into which I myself often lapse. I try to keep the "as it weres" and "if you wills" down to a bare minimum, but not long ago I found myself, about to interject an opinion, prefacing it by the phrase. "If I may say so," which instantly caused me to add: "I may after all say so, mayn't I? I mean, I see no one out there among you ready to stop me. Of course I may say so." Not that this is so very funny—it isn't—yet I need these little asides and cannot quite imagine functioning without them. Do they cause suspicion and hostility?

I know sometimes they cause confusion. Once, in assigning a paper to a class of freshmen, I said that this paper must be no fewer than five pages with the margins no wider than my necktie. (This was during the wide-tie era in the middle seventies.) A student, bringing her paper to my office, while explaining her reasons for its tardiness, kept staring at my chest. "May I ask what it is you are looking at, Miss Simpson?" I asked. "Your necktie, sir," she answered. "I wanted to make sure I got my margins right." Enough of these dopey little jokes, I said to myself at the time. Yet I have not been able to stop. I am too far gone.

"The world is a comedy to those that think," Horace Walpole said, "a tragedy to those that feel." That is very well put together, but is it true? Can't one both think and feel? Is it appropriate to laugh at serious things? I, for one, think it is not only appropriate but often necessary. "The one serious conviction that a man should have," according to Samuel Butler, "is that nothing is to be taken too seriously." I am reminded here, too, of Henry James's comment upon John Addington Symonds's treatise on homosexuality, "A Problem in Modern Ethics": "I think one ought to wish him more *humour*—it really is *the* saving salt."

One can understand if not altogether sympathize with those undergraduates who react with suspicion and hostility to professorial humor. Much of that humor, given the level of academic jokes, may be quite poor; and the better jokes, my hostile suspicion is, may well go over their young heads. There are few worse feelings than sensing yet missing a joke. To be in that position—and who among us has not been—is to feel excluded, ignorant, somehow put down. Still, must one suppress laughter to accommodate the humorless? This is a piece of reform that is doomed to failure. Those undergraduates who react to humor with suspicion and hostility might do well to read a brief piece by John Donne, who is not exactly everyone's idea of a madcap comic, entitled "That A Wise Man Is Known by Much Laughing," in which Donne remarks that one shows oneself "a Man because he can *laugh*, a *wise Man* that he knows at *what* to laugh, and a *valiant Man* that he *dares* laugh." To the undergraduates at the University of New Mexico I also offer the advice of Henry James: try to be a young man or woman upon whom nothing is lost—to which I would only add, especially the laughs.

This Sporting Life

Time, how do I waste thee? Let me count the ways: In lengthy telephone conversations with friends, chatting and laughing, schmoozing away the irreplaceable substance in fifteen-, thirty-, and forty-five-minute chunks. In reading bland and mostly biased accounts of terrible troubles in Gdansk and Damascus, Beirut and Bombay, then watching it served up yet again, this time with audiovisual aids, by creamy-cheeked men and women whom we call anchor-persons, the English call newsreaders, and the French call *speakerines*—the news, which as soon as it is written or said isn't new anymore, much time dropped down the drink here. In dreaming while awake, casting my mind back over its increasingly lengthy past, sliding it forward over its increasingly shortened future, lolling about in time past and time future while effectively obliterating time present. In other innumerable small ways—the little detour into the used bookshop, the false start on yet another intellectual venture, the empty social evening —I have devised no shortage of efficient methods of smothering time. I am someone who knows very well what T. S. Eliot meant when he spoke of the "necessary laziness" of the poet. I only wish a person equally distinguished had come forth to speak on behalf of my condition—the unnecessary laziness of the non-poet.

But I seem to have left out my most impressive achievement in wasting time. Far and away my most serious work as a time-waster is in watching men—sometimes but less often women—in various costumes running or jumping or hitting each other, smacking, kicking, shooting, or stroking balls of different sizes into cylinders, goals, gloves, or nets. With the sole exception of auto racing, there is no game, match, contest, or race I will not watch. "Dear Boy," wrote Lord Chesterfield to his illegitimate son, Philip Stanhope, "There is nothing which I more wish that you should know, and which fewer people do know, than the true use and value of time. It is in everybody's mouth; but in few people's practice." In this same letter, Chesterfield tells the boy, "I knew a gentleman, who was so good a manager of his time, that he would not even lose that small portion of it, which the calls of nature obliged him to pass in the necessary-house; but gradually went through all the Latin poets, in those moments." I tremble to think what, were I Chesterfield's son, his reaction would be to his learning that I, over the past year, have spent time watching men with permanents and blow-dry hair-dos bowling, other men in lavender and yellow trousers hitting golf balls, and stout women arm wrestling. "Dear Boy," I imagine him writing to me, "You seem to be making a necessary-house of your entire life."

From time to time I tell myself that I am going to stop, I am going to knock off watching all these games and useless competitions. Enough is enough, I say, quit now, while you're well behind; go cold turkey, put paid to it, be done, write finis, mutter kaput—enough is too much. The prospect dangling deliciously before me if I were to stop watching so much sports is that of regaining ample hunks of time that I might otherwise, and oh so much more wisely, spend. What might I do with the time not spent watching sports? Ah, what might I not do? Listen to opera, acquire a foreign language, learn to play the flute, go into the commodities market, actually play a sport. The possibilities, while not precisely limitless, are nonetheless very grand. Perhaps I shall one day do it. Wait, as loyal fans in cities with losing teams say, until next year.

If it were actually to come about, if next year I were to free myself of my bondage to watching sports, it would be a year like no other I can recall in my life. From earliest boyhood I have been a games man, passionately interested in playing games and in everything to do with them. In the neighborhoods in which I grew up, being a good athlete was the crowning achievement; not being good at sports was permitted, though not caring at all about sports, for a boy, was a certain road to unpopularity. Ours was strictly a meritocracy, with merit measured in coordination and agility and knowledge about sports.

The best-loved kid in our neighborhood was a boy named Marty Summerfield, whose father had pitched briefly for the Chicago White Sox. Marty was smallish, but he combined very high athletic prowess with absolutely astonishing physical courage. Still in grade school, I can recall him at least twice having to be carried off football fields with a concussion; in baseball, he would chase a foul pop-up off the playground into the street, where he would catch it to the screech of car brakes and the angry honking of horns; in later years I saw him refuse to back away from fights with young men six inches taller than and fifty or so pounds heavier than he. There was no brag to him or any meanness. He had a smile that made *you* happy. He was our Billy Budd, but, thank goodness, there was never any need to hang him.

Although Marty Summerfield was very intelligent—he went off to college on a Westinghouse science scholarship—

I do not recall his showing much interest in the statistics, lore, or other of the spectatorial aspects of sports; certainly not as much as I and others of us who were not anywhere near so good at sports as he. I have noted this phenomenon repeat itself in later years. Truly good athletes, men and women who can or once could really do it, seem not all that interested in talking about it. (Please allow for many exceptions here, chief among them the former athletes hired by television networks and stations to do "color" or to report sports news.) Ernest Hemingway's endless talk about sports—about baseball and boxing and hunting—has always made me think that he was merely passable as an athlete. As with sex, so with sports: too much talk about it tends to leave one a bit dubious.

Somehow it seems unlikely that a great writer would also be a very good athlete, almost as if the two forms of grace— verbal and physical—were in their nature necessarily contradictory. William Hazlitt was very earnest about the game called "fives," but how good he was at it I do not know. Orwell played a version of rugby football at Eton, though, unlike Hazlitt, never, as far as I know, wrote about sports. Vladimir Nabokov played soccer at Cambridge and is said to have been a very respectable tennis player, yet his pleasure in any game was greatly exceeded by his pleasure in lepidopterology. F. Scott Fitzgerald claimed that not playing football at Princeton was one of the great disappointments in his life. Evelyn Waugh played field hockey for his college (Hertford) at Oxford, noting of it, rather Waughfully, "There is a pleasant old world violence about the game which appeals to one strongly." This makes Waugh seem the possessor of greater athletic aplomb than he apparently had. A former student of Waugh's during his teaching days in the early 1920s remembers otherwise:

In the matter of games he was in fact so undistinguished a performer that after a few humorous episodes it was thought better that he should not exercise with the senior boys. He was issued with a whistle and allowed to amble harmlessly around the football field with the ten-year-olds. In the summer term, still wearing his plus fours, he was a reluctant umpire at the cricket games of novices.

It would be a monumental surprise, not to say an outright astonishment, to learn that Henry James was a superior athlete, but the facts hold no such surprise in store. Yet throughout his adult life Henry James, in his ultimately losing battle against corpulence, had recourse to one or another athletic activity as a form of exercise. He rode horses in Rome, took fencing lessons in London, cycled round Sussex after he had moved to Rye; at one point he lifted dumbbells, difficult as it may be to picture Henry James, as we now say, "pumping iron." There is a lovely letter in the fourth volume of the *Henry James Letters,* from James to his godson Guy Hoyer Millar, in which he writes to the boy: "I learned from your mother, by pressing her hard, some time ago that it would be a convenience to you and a great help in your career to possess an Association football—whereupon, in my desire that you should receive the precious object from no hand but mine I cast about me for the proper place to procure it." In the course of the letter, in which James informs the boy that the football is on its way to him in a separate parcel, he allows that "I'm an awful muff, too, at games—except at times I am not a bad cyclist, I think—and I fear I am only rather decent at playing at godfather."

As a boy, I was not an awful muff at games, but neither was I awfully good at them either. I was quick and well-coordinated, but insufficiently aggressive and too much concerned with form. I don't believe I was ever deceived, even as a small boy, about my being able to play a sport in college or professionally, although I should have loved to have been good enough to be able to do so. To attempt to take my own athletic measure, I would say that, for a writer, I am a fair athlete, while among serious athletes I am, as an athlete, a fair writer. I think here again of poor Hemingway, of self-deceived Hemingway, always quick with the inapposite sports metaphor, who, in a *New Yorker* profile written by Lillian Ross, talked about his quality as a writer in boxing terms:

I started out very quiet and I beat Mr. Turgenev. Then I trained hard and I beat Mr. de Maupassant. I've fought two draws with Mr. Stendhal, and I think I had an edge in the last one. But nobody's going to get me in any ring with Mr. Tolstoy unless I'm crazy or I keep getting better.

This rather famous passage makes me want to talk, in something like the same terms, not of my writing but of my athletic abilities. Let me put it this way: I'm ready anytime to play Ping-Pong with Mr. Balzac. And if Mr. Dostoyevsky ever cares to go one-on-one half court with me or to shoot a little game of "Horse," I'm ready to take him on, too. If either Miss Austen or Mrs. Woolf wishes to go head-to-head with me in an arm wrestling match, I think they both know where I can be reached. As for boxing, whenever he's ready to put on the gloves, tell Mr. Proust all he has to do is give me a jingle.

Until such time as any of these writers accepts my challenge, I can almost certainly be found seated on the south end of a couch, in a book-lined room, eight or so feet from a nineteen-inch Sony color television. There—you can count on it—I shall doubtless be watching exceedingly tall men slamming balls into baskets, or lumpily muscular men in helmets slamming themselves against one another. Then again I might be watching adolescent girls figure skating or doing gymnastics, or extremely wealthy young men and women thwacking fuzzy balls across a net, or slender men and women almost any of whom might easily qualify as the centerfold for Gray's *Anatomy* running distances far greater than the human body was ever intended to run. But if I were a betting man—which, as it happens, I am—I would bet that I would most likely be found watching a baseball game, for this game, which I never played very well as a boy, has become the game I more and more enjoy watching. Coaches speak of "benching" athletes, but I have been "couched." I don't want to know with any exactitude how much time I have spent over the years watching games from my couch, but my guess is that the amount of time would be—this is, as they say, a ballpark figure—roughly twice that which Penelope spent waiting for the return of Odysseus.

Booze and drugs, gambling and tobacco do not begin to exhaust the list of life's potential addictions. Some people cannot get through the day without a newspaper. Others take their fix in chocolate. I have been told that there are people who wig out on pasta. *The Concise Oxford Dictionary* defines *addict* colloquially as "enthusiastic devotee of sport or pastime." That's me—a colloquial addict. I don't require my fix every day, although I somehow feel rather cheerier if I know a game is coming up later in the day or during the evening. And if too many days pass without one, I do tend to get a touch edgy. I had my first serious intimation of this some eight or so years ago while on a two-week holiday in England, where, one evening in Bath, I realized that I hadn't watched a sports event for fully ten days and strongly felt the craving to do so. I turned on the television set in the hotel room to listen to the news. Then, suddenly, the BBC news-reader began to intone —it sounded like music to me—"East Birmingham 6, Brighton 4; Leeds 3, West Manchester 2; Bournemouth 4, Winchester 1." These were scores from soccer matches. I have almost no interest in soccer; I have certainly seen none of these teams. Yet I found the mere recitation of these scores soothing, and for the remainder of the holiday I looked forward to hearing soccer scores each evening. I believe this strange little anecdote establishes my bona fides as an addict—or, in the harsher term, "sports nut."

I have described some of the symptoms and labeled the disease, but you would be gravely mistaken if you are anticipating a cure. I have not found one and do not expect to. Instead of a cure, which is apparently unavailable, I seek a justification. What can be said on behalf of all the time I have put in watching games? Does it come to nothing more than—in the most literal sense of the word—a pastime, or passing time? Have my many hours spent watching games, either before my television or "live" (what a word!), been without any redeeming value? Am I doing nothing more than killing time? Enough questions. Stop stalling. Justify yourself or get off the couch. All right, since I have a few hours on my hands while awaiting a football game from the West Coast, let me try.

Although I scarcely watch sports for this reason, one of the benefits of watching them is that it keeps me in rather close touch with great numbers of my countrymen in a way that, without sports, I might otherwise have no hope to be. If you haven't a clue to what I mean here, please cast your eyes back over my previous sentence. What kind of person uses words such as *scarcely* or *rather* in the way that they are used in that sentence? Allow me to tell you what kind of person does—a bookish person. Without actually setting out to do so, I have become bookish. I am undeniably marked by the possession of general culture. I first noted this a few years ago when, after dining with a friend at an Italian restaurant in a lower-middle-class neighborhood, a woman waiting to be seated asked, "Where do you fellas teach?" "What do you mean 'teach'?" I asked. "My friend is the defensive line coach for the Miami Dolphins and I have a Buick agency in Terre Haute." This earned mild laughter, of the kind that follows enunciation of the phrase "Fat chance." In fact, my friend looked to me very much like a professor, which he is, but I had hoped I wasn't myself so readily identifiable. I guess I was still hopeful of passing for a not very successful lawyer, or perhaps a chemist, someone at any rate a little more in the world.

Not only do I apparently look to be what I am, but I also sound to be what I have become. A year or so ago, in connection with a book I had written, I agreed to do a radio interview. The interview was taped, and four or five weeks later, on a Saturday morning, I listened to it play over the local public radio station. As I did so, I thought, My God, I have somehow acquired one of those FM classical music station voices—a voice better adapted to saying words such as *Köchel, thematic, Hindemith,* and *motif* than to saying words such as "Yes, a hamburger sounds great to me." I sounded to myself a bit pretentious, not to say a mite snooty. Could it be locutions like "not to say" that did it? Or could I be imagining the entire thing? Any hope that I might be imagining it was ended when, last month, the six-year-old daughter of friends asked my wife about me, "Why does he speak English instead of American?"

The point of all this is that I believe there is a major division in this country between a small group composed of people who care a great deal about language and ideas and art, and another, vastly larger group for whom such concerns are considerably less than central. The problem, in my experience, is that this first group, even when it does not intend to, has a way of putting the second group off, making its members feel uncomfortable, slightly inferior, as if their lives were brutish and their pursuits trivial. It may well be that many members of the first group are truly contemptuous of the second group. Often,

though, the contempt works the other way round. It isn't for
no reason, after all, that piano players in whorehouses used to
be called "professor." Anyone who has belonged to the first
group must at one time have felt the sting of the division I have
in mind. I recall being about four hours into a poker game with
a number of printers, and, when the deal passed to me, I said,
"OK gents, ante up for five-card draw." At which point the
guy sitting to my left, who was losing about eighty dollars,
said, "Whaddya, some kind of goddamn Englishman?" Ah,
me, as Turgenev's nihilist Bazarov says, "That's what comes
of being educated people."

Not that I am displeased with being what I am—a man,
that is, marked by the possession of general culture. I talk as
I talk; I think as I think; I am what I am. My mind, such as
it is, remains my greatest stay against boredom. Still, I find this
division between the two groups sad. As a member of the first
of these groups, I know I do not feel any contempt for the
members of the second group. (Sorry to have to proclaim my
own virtue here, but apparently no one else will come forth to
proclaim it for me.) In fact, I tend to feel rather more contempt
for members of my own group, the culturati, with whom I am
more familiar—contempt, after all, being one of the items fa-
miliarity breeds.

Yet one of the things that make it possible to jump the
barrier and cut across this division, at least in masculine society,
is sports—more specifically, knowledge and talk about sports.
(Here I must add that I have met many intellectuals, scholars,
novelists, and poets whose addiction to sports is not less than
my own. "Closet sports fans" is the way I think of them. Yet
how easily they are flushed out of the closet. All one has to do
is offer a strong opinion about one or another team or player
in their presence and out they come.) For a bookish fellow in

a democracy, knowledge about sports seems to me essential. But not for the bookish alone; not even for a fellow alone. A friend tells me about a woman he knows who operates at a fairly high level in the real estate business and who began to study the morning sports pages in the hope of making lunches with male colleagues and clients easier. The hope, as it turned out, was justified, for sports talk is the closest thing we have in this country to a lingua franca, though I wouldn't use that phrase in, say, a bowling alley or pool hall.

Sports talk is easier for me than for the woman in the real estate business, I suspect, for I have grown up with sports, played at them as a kid, know them, and love to talk about them. I also know how inexhaustible sports can be as a subject; it sometimes seems, in fact, that there is more to say about yesterday's baseball game than about *Hamlet.* Nor do I think there is anything the least phony about using sports this way. As a conversational icebreaker, sports is very useful. It can rub away artificial distinctions. While sports may well be the toy department of life, not of towering intrinsic importance in itself, it can lead in and on to other, more intrinsically important subjects. Start with sports and before you know it you are talking economics, sociology, philosophy, personal hopes and fears. Socially, sports talk can be a fine lubricant.

I know I have often pressed sports into service, usually with decent results. I say "usually" and use the modest word "decent" because I think I may sometimes have gone too far. A few decades ago, for example, I found myself working in an urban renewal agency in the South. My fellow workers were mostly country boys. What they made of me I do not know. There was much to divide us: region, religion, politics. Asking them what they thought of the merits of the fiction of Jorge Luis Borges did not strike me as a happy way to glide over our differences. What did was sports. We talked Southwest Conference football, we talked baseball, we talked basketball. We got along.

I may have talked sports a little too well, for after a few weeks I was invited to play on the agency's basketball team in the local YMCA league. I showed up for the first game and learned that there were six members on the team, one of whom was in his early fifties. I was, in other words, a starter. Our opponents were made up of lean eighteen- and nineteen-year-olds of considerable height with, I remember thinking, rather menacing angularity of elbow. I had trained for this game by never smoking fewer than two packs of cigarettes daily for the previous ten years. Five or six times up and down the floor and I recall wondering if my life-insurance premiums were paid. Evidently time-outs had not yet been discovered in the South, for during the first ten minutes none was called. I had somehow managed to score three points, on a free throw and a crip lay-up. At the buzzer marking the end of the quarter, I walked over to the drinking fountain, into which I suavely vomited. Four or five games later, I went up for a rebound and, as good luck would have it, came down on my wrist, which was badly sprained. This excused me from further athletic combat. But the games I did play allowed me permanently to climb the barrier; in the eyes of the men I worked with I was OK and not a carpetbag intellectual.

But I don't want to push too hard the social advantages of knowing about sports. I don't watch them for social advantages. I watch them because most of the time they give pleasure. Nor do I believe that the reasons for my pleasure have much to do with personal psychology; I don't believe, in other words, that in watching sports I am attempting to regain my youth, or finding an outlet for violent emotions, or living vicariously through the physical exploits of others. No, part

of the pleasure for me in watching sports is that of witnessing men and women do supremely well what may not be
worth doing at all. It is the craft of superior athletes that is so
impressive, and that seems all the more impressive at a time
when standards of craftsmanship seem badly tattered. Literary
awards, academic chairs, political power, journalistic eminence
—all frequently seem to be awarded to people whose claims
upon them appear so thin, and sometimes even actually fraudulent. But when a sixteen-year-old girl gymnast needs a perfect
ten-point performance to win an Olympic gold medal, or a
twenty-year-old college basketball player has to sink two free
throws to win a game while fifteen thousand people are
screaming at him and a few million more are watching him
over television, or a golfer has to sink a tricky twelve-foot,
slightly uphill putt—none of them, in these moments, can call
on public relations, or social connections, or small corruptions,
or fast talk. All they can call on is their craft, which they either
have or don't have.

Sports also supply the pleasures of craft under pressure. I
find I respond extremely well to pressure—to other people
under pressure, that is. It excites me; I marvel at it. Much of
sports is pressure organized. At any rate, the great moments in
sports are those when athletes play through and win out under
immense pressure. I am all the more admiring of people who
are able to do this because, in the few moments of athletic
pressure I felt as a boy, I have known something of its crushing
weight. "Clutching," "choking," "the lump" are but a few of
the descriptions for people whose athletic craft is reduced as a
result of pressure. "Coming through," two of the loveliest
words an athlete hopes to hear, is the phrase reserved for those
whose craft is not impaired—is sometimes, in fact, heightened
—by the presence of pressure. The grand spectacle of people
coming through is one of the keenest pleasures of watching

sports—and it is a spectacle not usually on display elsewhere with such shining clarity.

The spectacle of athletes not coming through, though not at all grand, is nonetheless much more moving. While we may admire the winners, most of us tend to side with the losers. Sports, it has been said, is about losing. There is a great deal to this, certainly when it comes to team sports. Coaches with preponderantly winning records exist in plenty, yet few are the teams that over the years seem to be able to repeat championship seasons. In professional sports, I can think of only three: the Montreal Canadiens, the New York Yankees, and the Boston Celtics. I have never cared enough about hockey to have passionate feelings about it, but I have liberally despised —"hated" is too passive a word—both the Yankees and the Celtics. What I have despised about them is that they won too frequently. I have discovered many people have similar feelings. Unless they happen to be one of your hometown teams, too-frequent winners in sports tend not to be appreciated. "Everybody loves a winner" is a truism that, in sports, doesn't hold up.

Of course, I speak as a fan, and a fan, it is well to remember, is short for a fanatic. Sports in America may well be the opiate of the people, but, as opiates go, it isn't a bad one. Often when watching a game on television, I will note the television camera focus on the crowd, whose members are to be found, index fingers raised aloft, screaming, "We're number one! We're number one!" and think how easily, in another country, similar faces might be screaming, "Perón! Perón!" or "Khomeini! Khomeini!" I have never seen an adequate explanation for the passion of the fan. Roger Angell, who writes about baseball for the *New Yorker*, has written that "belonging and caring" is what being a fan is about. But I have encountered too many instances of behavior on the part of fans that go beyond mere belonging and caring. I have a cousin with ulcers whose doctor advised him, unsuccessfully, to stop listening to Chicago Cubs games. Of fans of the same team, I recently read about a widow who each spring places a Cubs pennant on her husband's grave, and of a man, a Cubs fan for more than fifty years, whose deathbed words, his son claims, were, "We gotta get rid of Kingman" (a high-salaried player notable for not coming through). A Chicago Cubs fan myself, when that team in 1984 lost its first chance to appear in a World Series in thirty-nine years by dropping its final play-off game to the San Diego Padres, I found I was mired in a slough of glumness that lasted fully a week. Fan-tastic. Such behavior cannot be explained to anyone who is not interested in sports; I cannot quite explain it to myself.

If we tend to idolize our athletes more than our politicians, I do not think that altogether a bad thing. I myself have not idolized an athlete since I was a small boy, but I have enjoyed the hell out of the really superior ones. *Dumb* appears before the word *jock* as frequently as *wily* before the name *Ho Chi Minh* and *untimely* before *death*, but I, for one, don't think athletes are unintelligent. They are unbookish, certainly; inarticulate, frequently; but dumb, scarcely ever, at least not at high levels of play. Instead their intelligence is concentrated upon their craft, and this they know in a way I can only hope I know mine. The only place I have ever seen the intelligence of athletes recognized is in the novel *Guard of Honor,* by James Gould Cozzens, where one of the book's protagonists assigns a military mission of importance to a young officer partly on the basis of his having played Big Ten football and thus being used to exerting his intelligence under real pressure.

While I do not idolize athletes, neither do I envy them. I consider them privileged human beings, men and women who have drawn lucky numbers in life's lottery. They are in the condition of someone born beautiful or to extremely wealthy parents. Lucky indeed. Professional athletes play games they love for salaries that take them effectively out of the financial wars that the rest of us must go on fighting our lives long. For a time the huge salaries that athletes have in recent years begun to earn bothered me. They are, in fact, immensely overpaid. Yet, as the economist Sherwin Rosen has explained, in an essay entitled "The Economics of Superstars," owing to television and now cable television revenues, the money is there, and I myself would just as soon that Julius Erving, or Dave Winfield, or Walter Payton have ample hunks of it than that even more of it go to some real estate or insurance millionaire who owns a sports franchise chiefly to soothe his own itch for publicity. Some say that athletes are too privileged, that they garner too many rewards too soon. I recall once watching an interview with Wayne Gretzky, the great young hockey player of the Edmonton Oilers. One of the television broadcasters pointed out to him that he, Gretzky, was at twenty-three already a millionaire many times over, that he had broken most of the records in his sport, that he would go down in history as one of the greatest hockey players the world has known. "Well, Wayne," the broadcaster said, "what can you possibly have to look forward to?" Gretzky, not a fiercely articulate fellow, paused, then said, "Tonight's game."

Addict and fanatic that I am, I must also confess that few of the supposed "issues" having to do with sports in its contemporary settings greatly trouble me. Amateurism, for one, is an issue upon which much false piety has been expended. In college athletics violations having to do with recruiting athletes do occur, and are punished when discovered. But everyone—excepting perhaps the officials of the National Collegiate Athletic Association—assumes that a great many others go undiscovered. I once heard a radio announcer, a former pro football player covering a Chicago Bears-Detroit Lions game, ask where a tackle on the Lions had gone to college. "Notre Dame," said his companion in the broadcast booth. "He went from Notre Dame to Detroit?" the first announcer responded. "Hmm. He must have taken quite a cut in pay." The next week the announcer himself took quite a cut in pay, for he was fired. Perhaps rightly. Violations in amateur sports are like adultery: everyone knows it goes on; still, it will not do to talk about it too openly.

Tennis has now all but dispensed with amateurism, and nearly all involved in the sport feel better for having done so. Track and field looks as if it might be the next sport to do so. In Eastern European and other Communist countries there is no hypocrisy about amateurism because there isn't any amateurism; in this regard one may say about them what Randall Jarrell said about the college president in his novel *Pictures from an Institution:* "He had not evolved to the stage of moral development at which hypocrisy is possible." Most universities and colleges that have big-time football and basketball programs have arrived at that requisite stage of moral development —and, hence, at hypocrisy, too. With millions and millions of dollars involved in gate receipts and television revenues and millions more for those teams that get to bowl games and postseason tournaments, college athletics aren't what they used to be.

But, then, neither is college. And because it is not, because so much of the prestige of college has been dissipated and the quality of education degraded, it becomes more and more difficult to think of the majority of college athletes at schools with big-time programs as anything other than young men serving out their athletic apprenticeships in the hope of one day becoming professionals. When such basketball players as Magic Johnson and Isaiah Thomas leave school at the end of their second or third year, or when a young man skips college altogether to make a run at a baseball career, one no longer exclaims, sadly, "But their education! What a shame!" Education is good, after all, only if it is really education. What is impressive to me is a young man who plays a major sport at a major school and is still able to find time to devote himself to serious studies, let alone excel in them. My guess is that the number of such young men is not legion.

At this point I believe I am scheduled to deliver a political rant, bemoaning the rise of the power of money and the fall of the prestige of education. But sports fans, when it comes to sports, are curiously apolitical. They tend to take the world of sports pretty much as they find it. Within the realm of sports itself, they tend to be purist conservative—that is, they want the sports world forever to remain as they found it. Innovation is anathema. Apart from improvements in equipment, almost all changes that affect the games themselves are regarded as regrettable. This at any rate is my view. I dislike the advent of Astro Turf in baseball and football; I dislike both the three-point play in pro and the shot clock in college basketball and the new dominance of the slam dunk in both; I dislike the designated hitter in baseball; I dislike the tie-breaker in tennis. . . . Some sports seem less sacrosanct than others: gradual changes in the game of pro football are permissible, yet alter baseball and you are fooling with the liturgy. To paraphrase the old and long-dead Chicago alderman Paddy Bauler, "Sports ain't ready for reform."

As much pleasure as sports have given me over the years, I am sure I do not want to have more to do with them than I now do. True, before I hang up my couch, I should like to see, in person, "live," a few World Series games, a Super Bowl, a Kentucky Derby, a Wimbledon final. But I shouldn't want to be a sportswriter or broadcaster. I once wrote an article about an elegant pro basketball player named Bob Love; in preparation for it I went to eight or ten of his team's practice sessions; I interviewed him and his coach and his teammates. Along with the fee for the article, I was given a press pass for a full season's games. It was good fun, superior jock-sniffing, in the locker-room phrase. Somehow, though, I felt too much like a camp follower, which is the true relation of the press to the actions they cover. One such article is all I ever care to write. Visiting the toy department is nice, but who wants to live there?

In watching sports, I seek not so much a golden mean or even a silver one but will settle for something akin to a tarnished bronze mean. Achieving anything like real moderation here is now well beyond me. If I never watch another game, I have already seen many more than my share. But I fully intend to watch another game, and another and another and another. My justification is that doing so gives me great delight; my defense is that it causes no known harm, and, on occasion, I learn a thing or two from it. Yet a number of years ago I recall hearing that Eric Sevareid, who was then reading the Sunday evening news on CBS, complained that it was demeaning to as serious a man as he to have to give the day's sports scores on his news show. I hope that this is true, for if it isn't I owe Mr. Sevareid an apology for thinking of him, ever after, as a starter on my All-American Pomposity team, along with William Jennings Bryan, Daniel Ellsberg, Barbara Walters, and the older Orson Welles. I don't know about anyone else, but I would rather have those sports scores than Eric

Sevareid's opinions about NATO, the Sino-Soviet dispute, and the balance of payments. Not that I don't think about such things. I do, but I can't say that I look forward to them. What do I look forward to? Among other things, along with Wayne Gretzky, to tonight's game.

A Former Good Guy and
His Friends

I RECENTLY SAW A COPY of the high-school newspaper
that appeared the week of my class's graduation and
found myself a bit miffed to discover that I was not voted Most
Popular or Best Liked or Most Friendly or Best Personality or
any other of the categories that speak to the ideal, vivid in the
days of my youth, of being a Good Guy. It may seem immod-
est of me to talk about myself in this way, and normally I
should refrain from doing so, but the plain fact is that I worked
sedulously at being thought not merely a Good Guy but an
extraordinarily Good Guy and felt that I had greatly succeeded. Whence this interest on my part in being such a devi-
lishly Good Guy, you may ask. I suppose it came about as a
matter of elimination. Since I was neither a first-rate athlete,
nor a notably successful Lothario, nor even a half-serious student, all that was left on the buffet of roles for me to choose
from was Good Guy or thug, and since I hadn't the wardrobe
for thug I went for Good Guy—and I went for it in a big way.
Almost anyone who attended Nicholas Senn High School in
Chicago when I did will, I feel confident, tell you, "Sure, I
remember Epstein. He was a Good Guy."

What a Good Guy is turns out not to be so simple a question. If Aristotle had gone to Nicholas Senn High School —a notion it gives me much delight to contemplate—he would doubtless have been able to posit no fewer than eleven kinds of Good Guy and compose an ample disquisition on the nature of the Good Guy, or Good-Guyness. Perhaps a disquisition is required, for there is apparently some disagreement about what constitutes a Good Guy. Not long ago, for example, when I remarked to a friend from my high-school days that I thought I used to be a fine specimen of the type known as Good Guy, he replied that he thought I had not quite made it. I was very popular, he allowed, but I wasn't bland enough. The pure Good Guy, he argued, should be very bland. Your true Good Guy should never give offense, or even hint at the potentiality for giving offense, and I, who was locally famous for an above-average sharpness of tongue, was considered verbally too dangerous to qualify as a pure Good Guy. Very well. I can accept that. Let me, then, revise my earlier statement: Almost anyone who attended Nicholas Senn High School when I did will, I feel confident, tell you, "Sure, I remember Epstein. He was a Good Guy—only don't cross him."

Does the ideal of the Good Guy still exist? For all I know, it may have gone the way of the Cute Girl, which, I gather, no self-respecting female above the age of ten nowadays cares to be thought. But as I construed it then, a Good Guy was someone whom vast numbers of people felt to be a Good Guy. I thus set out to convince vast numbers of people. It proved no very complex task. Ben Franklin, whom I did not read until years later, remarks in his autobiography that, if you wish to insinuate yourself in the good graces of another person, the trick is not to do that person a favor but to have him do one for you. So the trick of making many friends, at least on the superficial level on which the Good Guy operates, is not to charm them but to let them charm you.

It was many friends I wanted: multitudes, large assemblages, whole hordes. To acquire them I was ready to turn off the charm. I was, in those days, the reverse of a snob; I looked up my nose at everyone. No one was too lowly for me to court. I became a boredom-proof listener, a full-time dispenser of bonhomie. Sashaying through the halls of our high school, greeting my innumerable conquests in the Good Guy sweepstakes, I uttered a stream of babblesome salutations not to be equaled for inanity outside a major league infield: "Hi babes," "What say," "How're you makin' it," "Take it easy," "Hang in there," "How's it goin'," "Be good," "Yo!" and fifteen or twenty other utterances of equal profundity that I have since forgotten.

In cultivating friends, I was calculating but not altogether insincere. If one way to make friends is to show a great interest in other people, showing such an interest, however artificial it might be at the outset, can before long issue in genuine interest. Besides, I not only collected but liked people; I liked their oddness and idiosyncrasy. As a good listener, I was taken into many a confidence and vouchsafed many a glance into secret desires, passions, fears—all of which the incipient if still quite unknown writer in me found fascinating. As a Good Guy, I knew how to keep a secret, never to betray a trust, and was, withal, a ready and reliable confidant. "Kids say the darndest things," a smarmy radio "personality" named Art Linkletter used to remark. They do indeed, and I like their saying many of them to me, which was one of the minor fringe benefits of being thought such a corking Good Guy. A larger benefit was the small number of people who, initially captured by my Good Guy maneuvers, have thus far remained lifelong friends.

Still, I may have exulted too much, albeit secretly, in this knack I had for making friends easily. Sometimes I would try this knack out, like a professional tenor singing in the shower at home, for the sheer pleasure of exercising it. I would choose a young thug ("hoods" we then called them), or a shy girl, or someone whose background was utterly different from my own, and set out to win him or her over to my ever-enlarging stable of friends. Almost always I succeeded. It was pure art, really—friends for friends' sake. In those days, had I had a reasonable grasp of grammar and syntax, I could have written a book entitled *How to Win Friends Without Caring in the Least About Influencing People.*

I merely wished to be liked, and only by everybody I met. To be thought a Good Guy by all—this didn't seem too much to ask. Occasionally it would get back to me that someone or other didn't understand what lay behind my considerable popularity. I felt my appeal ought to have been self-evident to him; I was, self-evidently, a Good Guy. Then there was small band of people around whom I stepped gingerly. They were insensate to my blandishments, these people—most of them boys but also a few girls—whom I thought of, even in high school, as "in business for themselves." In a rough sense, each of us is in business for himself—each of us, that is, is pre-eminently concerned about his own preservation and rise in the world and has a necessary and probably sensible selfishness—but these people were rather more selfish than was either necessary or sensible. They were generally rather intense and (no rather about it) humorless. The very notion of the Good Guy, with all his airy friendliness, was alien to them, and so, consequently, was I. It only now occurs to me that I was also possibly in business for myself in those days. My business was being popular. It was a pleasant enough line of work, requiring no character whatsoever.

I can write all this now chiefly because I am—as a great
many people will tell you—no longer a Good Guy. I may not
even be, to shift at last to lowercase spelling, a nice fellow. I
have not yet arrived at the stage of Evelyn Waugh's character
Gilbert Pinfold, who of himself asks, "Why does everyone
except me find it so easy to be nice?" but I find I do not much
mind making enemies. Some enemies seem to me eminently
worth having. This is something that the old Good Guy in me
failed to understand. Chiefly through writing a good deal of
journalism and literary criticism, I have by now acquired, I feel
certain, an ample supply of enemies. If the people I have written critically about feel as I do about the people who have
written critically about me, my guess is that they have not
altogether forgotten me and that, should my name ever crop
up in their presence, it is cause for them to murmur a brief
Bulgarian curse or a stirring undeleted epithet.

Perhaps because, as a former Good Guy, it has taken me
so long to acquire enemies, I like to dwell upon them and on
occasion I have even dreamed of them. In one such dream the
people I have written harshly about are gathered together in
a large room in a Manhattan hotel to throw a party for me.
There they stand, as in a drawing out of *Esquire:* Joseph Heller,
John Updike, Norman Mailer, William F. Buckley, Jr., Gore
Vidal, Renata Adler, Philip Roth, Ann Beattie, Gabriel García
Márquez, and others too numerous to mention. In this dream
I sit alone, in white tie and tails, at a long dais. Everyone in the
room is standing, champagne glasses raised in my direction,
waiting for me to speak. "Sorry, gang," I announce at last, a
wide smile plastered across my face, "but no more Mr. Good
Guy."

If early life taught me how to gather a wide acquaintance-
ship, and later life how not to fear enemies, the great mystery
remains friendship. Aristotle, who devotes fully two books of

the *Nicomachean Ethics* to the subject of friendship, begins by remarking that "without friends no one would choose to live," which seems to me quite true. Yet the quality and variety of friendship are nearly inexhaustible, and, as Aristotle says, "not a few things about friendship are matters of debate." The first matter for debate, perhaps, is one's own interest in friendship —or, more precisely, one's own devotion to friendship. "The only way to have friends," writes Joubert, "is to throw everything out the window, to keep your door unlocked, and never to know where you will be sleeping at night. You will tell me there are few people mad enough to act like this. Well then, they shouldn't complain about not having any friends. They don't want any." I suspect Joubert is correct about this, even though it means that I, who value my friends, do not qualify as someone absolutely devoted to friendship. I want to have friends, but on my terms—and, as I grow older, these terms grow more and more strict.

Although not usually at its center, friendship plays a part in many of the greatest literary works. Straightaway there is the friendship of Achilles and Patroclus. Cervantes presents, in Don Quixote and Sancho Panza, a lovely instance of a friendship between unequals and opposites. Dickens provides many of his young heroes with charming, self-effacing friends— Tommy Traddles, Herbert Pocket, etc.—of a kind we could all use in our corner. The friendship that develops between Huck Finn and Jim is of course one of Mark Twain's great touches—perhaps his greatest touch. The delicacy and subtlety required in friendship—almost always referred to as "personal relations"—is nearly the entire subject of E. M. Forster. In Henry James it is not so much friendship as the betrayal of friendship that looms so large. But the novelist of friendlessness is Joseph Conrad, whose heroes are among the loneliest figures in literature and among the most moving in part because of their solitariness, which gives them their tragic dimension.

Possibly the greatest literary friendship on record, and the most literarily consequential, was that between Montaigne and the poet and magistrate Étienne de La Boétie. The two men met when Montaigne was thirty, La Boétie thirty-three. Their rapport was immediate and perfect; each was able, in letters and in person, to reveal his soul to the other. In 1563, four years after they met, La Boétie came down with an intestinal ailment from which he died, with Montaigne at his bedside. Montaigne was permanently bereft. Donald M. Frame, Montaigne's biographer and translator, believes that "there is much to show that the *Essays* themselves are—among other things—a compensation for the loss of La Boétie." With Étienne de La Boétie gone, Montaigne had no one to speak with and write for but himself—and the world. La Boétie is the friend, and theirs the single dominant friendship, referred to when, in his essay "Of friendship," Montaigne writes: "In the friendship I speak of, our souls mingle and blend with each other so completely that they efface the seam that joined them, and cannot find it again. If you press me to tell why I loved him, I feel that this cannot be expressed, except by answering: Because it was he, because it was I." The void left by the death of La Boétie was never to be filled by Montaigne; references to him in the *Essays* are frequent; eighteen years after his friend's death, Montaigne can still be troubled by thoughts about him. Which is greater, having known such a friendship or its loss, is a question that troubled Montaigne his life long.

Such a friend is rare at any time, in any life. I have never known such a friend in my own life, and I am not at all sure I should want one. (I exclude my wife, whom I consider to be in the realm above that of friendship.) As a boy, I recall how important it seemed to have a best friend; and I, as someone who had made friends rather easily, had, seriatim, several best friends. I might have a best friend for a summer, or a school term, but gradually we would drift not quite apart but to a friendship of lesser intensity. In a best friend I desired someone to pal around with, someone to rely on, someone occasionally to confide in. I required no full communion of souls, not being myself a very soulful character. The notion of the best friend carries over into adulthood with marriage, where, traditionally, the groom appoints a best man, who is presumably his best friend. I have been married twice—I believe I got it right the second time—but the combined total attendance at both my weddings was two; I had witnesses in place of best men. Even now I do not feel the want of a best friend, but I do have a number of good friends whom I cherish.

Was it Plutarch who said that one didn't need more than seven friends? Until this moment I have never counted mine, but—dead on, Plutarch—it turns out I can think of exactly seven friends, very good friends, whose death or disappearance from my life would devastate me. I can think of a second tier of ten or so friends who enrich my life but with whom the same degree of easy intimacy and depth of feeling does not quite exist. I can think of a third tier of twenty or so people whom I am always pleased to see or hear from, in whose company I feel perfectly comfortable, and with whom I believe I share a reciprocal regard. (Although they are more than acquaintances, are the people in this third tier truly friends? There ought to be a word to denote relationships that fall between that of acquaintance and friend, but there is not; the language —as Flaubert once remarked in attempting to express his love for his mistress—is inept.) After this third tier, in the stadium of my social life, we next move up to the grandstand of acquaintances and the bleachers of business associates. The first tier has not changed, and some members of it I have known for forty years. Some come down from the third tier to sit in the second; and a few from both the second and third tiers have departed, either through death or disagreement, before the game (my game) is done.

"How many intelligent people do you know in this city?" a famous writer once asked me. Ours is a city of roughly seven million people, of whom he said he had discovered three who were intelligent. High standards, these, and behind these standards was the clear implication that he valued intelligence above all else in friends. I hope I don't insult my friends when I say that it is not chiefly for their intelligence that I value them, even though all are intelligent. Some I value for their point of view; some for their loyalty and steadfastness; some for their seriousness and integrity; and two or three for their goodness, by which morally freighted word I mean to imply a combination of all these qualities.

When I think of the qualities that might unite the first tier of my friends, I am hard-pressed to come up with any persuasive pattern. I share interests with all of them, but they are not the same interests. Three of the seven are not bookish; four of them have politics different from mine. These same four are my exact contemporaries and indeed were high-school classmates; the other three are older than I, one of them more than twenty-five years older. Sexist swine that I am, all seven are men. (About women as friends, more presently.) None is orthodox in his religious views, and from two of them I have never heard any talk of religion at all; and although one would think one ought to know this about good friends, for all I know these two are atheists. (Must make a mental note to ask.) Two —not the same two—do not live in the same city as I do. Some among these seven good friends of mine have never even heard the names of the others. All seven are united in two things:

first, none is what I think of as a high-maintenance friend—
someone, that is, who requires regular ministering to in the
form of visits, daily telephone calls, or lengthy letters; and,
second, all have agreed to appreciate me.

Along with appreciation of me, we also, my close friends
and I, do not disagree strongly on any important subject. I am
not certain how much disagreement a close friendship can
bear. I don't think I could have a close friend who is a racist
or an anti-Semite. I am not sure I could have a close friend who
despised my politics; yet agreement on politics, though pleasing in a friend, is not for me, I like to think, decisive. I have
found myself among fairly large groups in which nearly everyone agreed with my political views, and a most comforting
feeling such an atmosphere can provide. But I have always
been impressed by Tocqueville's remark, made in his *Recollections,* that in politics "shared hatreds are almost always the
basis for friendship." Hatreds, even cozily shared ones, are not
a good basis for friendship; they too soon lead to one's having
to accept the enemy of one's enemy as one's friend. The enemy
of one's enemy, after all, can turn out to be himself a terrible
character. Politics may make strange bedfellows but finally not
very good friends, as witness John Reed, he of *Ten Days That
Shook the World,* writing to H. J. Whigham, his editor on the
Metropolitan Magazine: "You and I call ourselves friends, but
we are not really friends, because we don't believe in the same
things, and the time will come when we won't speak to each
other."

Perhaps the reason the number of people I currently call
friend seems so large has to do with my age, which is pretty
near smack-dab middle age. Being middle-aged, I am able to
have friends chronologically on either side of my own age:
friends ten or twenty or even thirty years older than I and
friends ten or now even twenty years younger. Meanwhile I

retain my contemporaries, upon whom death has thus far made no inroads. With older friends, my age sometimes seems to dissolve, and in some cases I have felt something akin to experiential seniority to people twenty or so years older. I have been lucky in having some of the most interesting older people I have met take me seriously.

I had a friend whom I much admired, a man in his middle-eighties, whom I never met but knew only through correspondence. He first wrote to me about something I had written in *The American Scholar*; I answered his letter; and each time I wrote anything in this or any other magazine he would write to comment upon it and to dilate upon the same subject, usually turning out something much more interesting than I had written. In his business life he had been in advertising, and as the editor of the leading trade publication for the advertising industry he told me he saw it as his job to try to make advertising less vulgar. "You have only to look about you to see how successful I have been," he added. He had delicious irony and, being of an advanced age, he felt no need to dawdle over clichés or empty pieties. He seemed to read all the intellectual magazines, loved Trollope, closed out each evening with a page or two of Burton's *Anatomy of Melancholy* "because I find a page or two of his magnificent prose gives me a fitting way to end the day," and he even took the icy plunge into contemporary philosophy. He described himself to me as a compulsive reader, and once, before a national election, noted:

Are you inflicted these days with fervid pleas to save the country? I get at least one in every mail. I will, for the sake of something to read, read an invitation to attend the opening of a new cleaning establishment but I will not punish myself by reading campaign letters. After all, even a compulsive reader has limits.

I soon found that part of the pleasing afterglow of publication was receiving a letter from him. Thinking to deepen our relationship, I once wrote to him when I was planning a visit to a large city near his own smaller one to invite him and his wife to lunch. He wrote back to say that his eyesight was no longer good enough for him to drive on freeways, his hearing was all but shot, and, since he went out less and less, he really didn't have any fit clothes for dining out. He thanked me for my invitation but would have to refuse. Besides, he said, nowadays he was much at his best in his letters. I never made another such invitation and we continued to exchange letters for a year or so more, when, one early summer's day, I received a letter from his daughter that began, "My father . . . died June 15th after a three-day illness. I know how much his correspondence with you meant to him. When he came home from the hospital last fall, the first thing he did was to have me sit down and type a letter to you on the horrors of modern baseball." A friend unmet but still missed.

Friendships with the young are very different. I have a number of such friendships, almost all of which have derived from my work as a teacher and a writer. I never set out to make them. But over a decade as a university teacher I have found eight or ten students to whom my heart has gone out. All of them wish to be writers or to do one or another kind of literary work, and they, I assume, have found my acquaintance useful. I am a touch flattered by these friendships, for they function in the way that Aristotle prescribed for friendships between the young and the older—that is, these young friends honor me and I in my turn try to be helpful to them. With one exception, I do not have what Aristotle termed "friendship of the complete type with them." This is in part because we do not share a common past; in part because they, being young, live largely in the future while I try to live in the present; but in greatest part because, for now, we are not equals. I hope I do not treat them with condescension, yet the fact is that thus far along I have achieved more in the line of work to which they aspire, and it is this, achievement, that makes us unequal. (As they grow older and achieve more, this inequality will narrow.) I have been on the other side of such relationships, the younger man who pays homage to the older who repays him in the coin of utility: by advice, by helping through his connections, by permitting conversational intimacies. Perhaps because I have benefited from such relationships, I feel gratified to enter into similar ones myself, now in the role of senior man. I feel as if I am passing on the baton that had earlier been passed on to me.

I have found the most delightful of such unequal friendships to be the most unequal of all—that between a parent and his children. Here, again, Aristotle is my guide; he notes that the inequality derives from the fact that a parent may disown a son or daughter for dishonorable behavior but, because his or her debt is too great, a son or daughter may not disown a parent. Is it possible, though, to declare one's child one's friend? Is blood thicker than friendship? I have felt something very akin to friendship with both my sons, and felt it fairly early in their lives. I remember an autumn afternoon on which I went with my eldest son, then fourteen, to Sears, Roebuck to get new tires for my car. I thought the job could be done in an hour; it turned out to take four. We had lunch in a Chinese restaurant. We walked the streets of the neighborhood. We babbled away to each other on all sorts of subjects. Because the car was still not ready, we sojourned to the appliance section of the Sears store to watch a bit of the U.S. Open tennis tournament while we sat on rolled-up rugs. "What a boon companion this kid is," I thought. "If he weren't my son, I can imagine him, when grown older, as my friend."

There have been times in my life when I felt I required no further friends; I said to myself, as one says when dealt a set

hand in draw poker, I'll play with these. But this hasn't been
so, and I am pleased that it hasn't. Even now, in middle life,
I continue to gain friendships while I watch other friendships
lapse or otherwise fall away. I am not quite up to the ratio of
Evelyn Waugh, who in this connection reported: "In the first
ten years of adult life I made a large number of friends. Now
[Waugh was forty-three when he wrote this] on the average I
make one new one a year and lose two." My own efficiency
is not so high. I say "efficiency" because there are times when
those of us who are promiscuous in our choice of friends feel
we could do with many fewer. These are the times when the
duties of friendship seem greatly to outweigh its pleasures.
Lunches to attend, phone calls to return, letters to answer,
obligations to repay—sometimes the duties of friendship (and
these are the lighter duties) seem all too much. And they are
often too much, unless, of course, one is friendless, in which
case one pines for lunches to attend, phone calls to return,
letters to answer, and obligations to repay. Friendship may
know no happy medium.

   Not everyone has the same appetite for friendship. P. G.
Wodehouse once claimed that he required few friends. But
then he was happily married and happy in his work, and this
combination of good fortune doubtless lessens the need for
friends. Friends are more important to the unmarried or the
less-than-happily married, I think. That very social being,
Henry James, who was a good friend to so many people and
who always took the obligations of friendship with the utmost
seriousness, nonetheless seemed, for much of his later life, a
friendless man; and toward the end he remarked, plaintively,
that he felt himself quite without contemporaries. Mencken
claimed not to care much for the company of writers, yet for
a long stretch he befriended, and championed, that otherwise
lonely figure, Theodore Dreiser. Max Brod was a supremely

good friend to Kafka. One senses that Melville did not get anywhere near the spiritual sustenance he had hoped for from his friendship with Hawthorne. The friendship award in American literature, however, ought to go to William Dean Howells, who proved so good a friend to Henry James and Mark Twain, two writers who had very little use for each other.

Howells never had to introduce James to Twain, luckily enough for him, for introducing two of one's friends to each other can produce a tense moment. How delightful when they turn out to appreciate each other! How dreadful when they don't! Then there is the tricky terrain when one of your friends attacks another of your friends to you. Obviously, one must stage a defense; just as obviously, it must be a careful one, so that in defending your attacked friend you do not seem to attack the attacker. I have a close friend many of whose own friends I heartily despise and at whom, in lulls in our conversation, I sometimes like to toss verbal darts. I sympathize with my friend—I have been placed in this position myself—but not enough to let up on him. Why does it bother me that a man I like so much has friends I so dislike? Do I see it as a judgment on me? How, after all, can I have so good a friend who has such miserable taste in choosing friends?

What kind of friend am I? I try to be good but know I am not great. Perhaps it is that I am able to live very comfortably within my family, that my work fills up larger and larger portions of my days, including weekends; but I think it is accurate to say that I do not so much depend upon as enjoy my friends. Certainly, I am less and less aggressive in friendship; increasingly, I hang back and wait for friends to get in touch with me. I allow long stretches to pass in which I do not see people I care a good deal about. More and more I feel at greater ease as a guest than as a host. Apart from a small circle of very dear friends, the effort required of friendship seems to me harder and harder to make. Not long ago I let a close friendship die because I had heard that this friend had said things behind my back that were painful to me; more recently, I informed a friend who had moved to another, distant country that I could not keep up my end of our correspondence; since then a business associate with whom I was on my way to forming a friendship accused me of sharp dealing in a publishing matter, and so I suggested to him that, if he really believed what he said, we cease to speak to each other for a period of five years (we still have two years to go). Fifteen or twenty years ago I would have acted differently in each case: confronted my friend with what he said, kept up my end of the correspondence, argued my innocence with meticulous care. No longer.

As one grows older, one realizes better the limits of friendship. In my case, I have begun to realize how far I wish to go with my friendships, which is to differing limits with different friends. At the lowest end of the scale, I have false friends: I deem them false not because of any hypocrisy on their part or mine but because our friendship is made up of pretense on both sides, and it is the taste for cordiality that makes this pretense possible. As a former Good Guy, I retain a special weakness for entering into this kind of friendship, which is, like a magician's trunk, hollow at bottom.

Next on the scale are casual friendships, such as the one I have with the salesman at the shop where over the years I have bought my suits. This man and I have never addressed each other by any but our last names. Since I sometimes go two or three years without buying a new suit or jacket, the time between our meetings is ample. Yet when we do meet a fine feeling prevails, and I believe that this feeling is not owing to salesmanship alone. We have a certain regard for each other;

we enjoy talking together about nothing in particular: my work, his travels, the city in which we both live. The last time I was in the shop I learned that, within the same month, his wife had died of cancer and he had had a stroke. People I have known better than he have died or suffered affliction, and yet their troubles have affected me less—or at least I have thought less about them. In friendship "casual" can be a tricky term.

I have other friends whom I don't think of as casual at all, whom I genuinely like, yet whom I am perfectly content to see on the most limited basis. I have a friend from college days with whom I go to one, sometimes two baseball games a year; we do not meet in winter. I have some friends I see only for lunch (and one or two with whom I am always planning to meet but never do meet for lunch). I have friends whom I see only when their wives are along; I have other friends whose husands or wives I have never met. I have a friend who lives a mere two miles from where I do and whom I generally meet but once a year and sometimes less frequently than that. I have a category of friends whom I am pleased to run into but do not wish necessarily to see again soon; there is always a slightly embarrassed silence when we part without either of us saying, "We must get together again soon."

At a high-school reunion I attended—this was for the school at which I was not voted Most Popular, Best Liked, Most Friendly, etc.—I felt an odd mixture of elation and sadness, for such events, I realized, are really graveyards of dead friendships. It was lovely to see all these friends from my past. As Logan Pearsall Smith once put it, "The mere process of growing old together will make the slightest acquaintance seem a bosom friend." Hence the elation. The sadness came from the knowledge that there was no real hope of renewing any of these relationships, that at such meetings we jump back to our youth for this one night, but that by morning we shall recall why we haven't stayed friends through the years—because, that is, life has dragged us elsewhere and there is no point in pretending that we can drag ourselves back.

I number more than a few women in the second and third tiers of my friends, and yet I must add that I think of women as belonging in a different category of friends. Montaigne thought women incapable of friendship: "Besides, to tell the truth, the ordinary capacity of women is inadequate for that communion and fellowship which is the nurse of this sacred bond; nor does their soul seem firm enough to endure the strain of so tight and durable a knot." From such remarks are movements such as Women's Liberation made. One of the nicest consequences of the current Women's Liberation movement, I should say, is that it has brought out the fellowship (Flaubert is correct; the language is frequently inept) between women, making friendships between women seem, to pick up Montaigne's phrase, "tight and durable" indeed. But friendships between men and women are something else again. La Bruyère speaks interestingly to this point:

Friendship may exist between a man and a woman, quite apart from any influence of sex. Yet a woman always looks upon man as a man, and so a man regards a woman. This intimacy is neither pure friendship nor pure love. It is a sentiment which stands alone.

I once asked Lillian Hellman about Edmund Wilson, a writer I much admired but never met and who, from his letters and diaries, seemed damned unpleasant. "You have to realize," she said, "that there were really two Edmund Wilsons: the man's and the woman's Edmund Wilson. If you were a man, Edmund had to prove his superiority to you by demonstrating that he was smarter than you. He was the intellectual equivalent of the playground bully. But if you were a woman, he could be very gentle, sweet, *galant*, even when he had no sexual interest in you. I of course knew him as a woman, and so have nothing but nice thoughts about him."

This seems to me very penetrating, and not alone about Edmund Wilson. I suspect we are all a bit two-faced in this regard, depending upon which sex we are facing. In discussing friendship, the moralists almost invariably contrast it with erotic love, holding friendship to be on a different level because of its disinterestedness, a quality to which erotic love can never lay claim. Too often when even the most decorous men and women are together the sound of flutes can be heard off in the forest, albeit neither party is prepared to gambol to them. Still, the gentlest wind of Eros can give an odd twist to a friendship between a man and a woman. Is it correct to say that when men and women are together they find it difficult to be themselves? Or is it more correct to say instead that they are most like themselves?

Let the flutes resound, let the winds of Eros blow the roof down, I know I am not ready to give up any of my female friends. I am not, in fact, ready to give up any of my friends. Aristotle says that a happy man has need of friends; I am not sure I qualify as his happy man, but I know I have need of mine: for the delight and support and affection they give. He also says that "it would seem actually impossible to be a great friend to many people," adding later, when considering the question of whether we need friends more in good fortune or in bad, that "the presence of friends . . . seems desirable in all circumstances." I agree on both points, while recognizing that I for one may have more friends than the philosophical limit allows. Still, this comes under a category that Aristotle, for all his marvelous comprehensibility, does not consider—that which I think of as the Happy Problem. For now I am fully prepared to live with mine.

A Fat Man Struggles to Get Out

H OW DO THINGS STAND with you and the seven deadly sins? Here is my scorecard: Sloth I fight —to a draw. I surrendered to Pride long ago. Anger I tend to give in to so often that it makes me angry. Lust I'd rather not discuss. I haven't thus far done well enough in the world to claim Avarice as anything more than a theoretical sin. I appear to be making some headway against Envy, though I realize that it's touch and go. Of the seven deadly sins, the only one that has a continuing interest for me is Gluttony. But "continuing interest" is a euphemism; by it I mean that Gluttony is the last deadly sin that excites me in a big way—so much so that, though I am prepared to admit that Gluttony can be deadly, I am not all that prepared to say it is a sin. As soon as I pop this chocolate-chip cookie in my mouth, I shall attempt to explain what I mean.

I am not beautiful and I am probably not very fit, but I am, at least in a rough geometrical sense, in shape. I weigh what the charts say I ought to weigh. To some people I may seem slender. For the most part, I am not displeased with my physique. Certainly I have no wish to be fat; flabby I should

heartily dislike; portly is a touch more than I should prefer—
but, let me confess it, stout, solid dignified stout, doesn't sound
that bad to me. Was it Cyril Connolly who said that within
every fat man a thin man struggles to get out? With me the
reverse condition obtains: I am a relatively thin man in whom
a fat man struggles, sometimes quite desperately, to get out.

That fat man is no gourmet. He cannot claim to be a
gourmand, which A. J. Liebling, a fat man who did get out,
once defined as someone who loves delicacies and plenty of
'em. My fat man is less discriminating. He longs for quantities
of sandwiches and great mounds of rather greasy french fried
potatoes followed by great hunks of cake, a little snack washed
down with tankards of soda pop (with Pepsi-Cola, to be specific, and not the no-calorie, caffeine-free, unleaded kind, either). Ribs, pizza, raw oysters, servings of ice cream that cover
the entire surface of dinner plates—these are the names of some
of my fat man's desires. He is always on the lookout for inexpensive restaurants that serve in impressive tonnage—restaurants out of which he dreams of walking, a toothpick clamped
in his mouth, remarking to himself, "Yes, indeed, a slap-up
meal; they did me very well in there."

You can see why this fat man cannot be turned loose. I do
on occasion let him out for a weekend or a holiday, in what
I suppose is the gastronomical equivalent of a work-release
program. But set scot-free, left to forage full-time for himself,
this man would kill me with his teeth and bury me with a fork.
Clearly a dangerous character, he must be held under lock and
key and, when let out, kept under the strictest surveillance.
Moderation is a principle he does not recognize, deferred gra-
tification is a phrase of whose meaning he remains ignorant,
compromise he won't even consider. All this being the case, I
can only say to him, as I frequently do, "Sorry, Tons-of-Fun,
it's the slammer for you."

Perhaps I would be better off in the condition of a friend who one day told me that, as the result of a boyhood fistfight in which his nose was so badly smashed it had to be remade, he had lost roughly eighty percent of his sense of taste. To him food was now almost sheerly a matter of fuel. I greeted this announcement with a mixture of envy for his release from a troubling passion and sadness at his deprivation. I have known others who could eat until the cows come home, and then slaughter the cows for a steak sandwich—all without the least effect on girth or chin or limb. These, in my view, are among the favorites of the gods. To me the gods have dealt differently, bestowing upon me an appetite that is matched only by my vanity. I wish to live fat but be thin.

I was not bred for the kind of careful abstinence that is the admired eating standard of our day. A finicky child, I was catered to in my extreme fussiness. (Freud says that a man who as a child feels assured of his mother's love is likely to think himself a conqueror; I say this same conqueror is likely to have a weight problem.) Whatever Joseph wanted, Joseph got—in my mother's kitchen, Lola had nothing on me. In adolescence, my tastes in food broadened and my appetite deepened. Ours was always an impressive larder. I can recall many a night, before settling in to sleep, fixing myself a little snack that might consist of, say, a dozen or so cookies, a pint of butter-pecan ice cream, a gross or so of grapes, and four fingers of salmi. Nor was sleep after such a repast in any way a problem. Today, of course, this kind of snack, attempted at my age, could only be construed as a suicide attempt.

My mother knew I ate huge portions at home, but she could not know that the ample meals she served me were perhaps half my daily ration. She could not know because I did not tell her. As a serious eater I hadn't, you might say, come out of the pantry. But out of the pantry I surely emerged. After a breakfast at home of orange juice, eggs, and toast, I would, upon arrival at high school, generally plunge into a smoke-filled school store called Harry's, where, to fortify myself for the strenuous mental effort that lay ahead, I engorged something known as a chocolate square (approximate weight: one-third pound), a small stein of root beer, and the smoke of two Lucky Strike cigarettes. Often with friends I would take tiffin at a nearby Jewish delicatessen called Ashkenaz; the meal usually consisted of soup, corned-beef sandwiches, and other of those Jewish foods that, as one sour-stomached Jewish gentleman I know has put it, have caused more difficulties for the Jews than Pharaoh himself. After lunch it was back to the classroom, where, on a full stomach, I was easily able to ignore what should have been the rudiments of my education. After school, a *flâneur du gastronomique,* I might knock back a small bag of french fries liberally slathered with ketchup, which, most afternoons, along with perhaps a banana and six or seven cookies, would see me through to dinner.

Proust famously used food—his little fluted madeleine cake—to beckon memory; working at things the other way round, I beckon memory to recall food. I remember a Rumanian Jewish restaurant to which my parents used to take us where the waiters seemed to have stepped out of Jewish jokes. Once, as a small boy, when I asked one of them if the restaurant had any soda pop, he, towel over his shoulder, pencil poised over his order pad, sourly replied, "Yeh, ve gots two kinds. Ve gots red and ve gots brown." I remember when a small chain of rather deluxe hamburger restaurants named Peter Pan was caught serving its customers horse meat and, in a gesture to return to the public's good graces, gave away free hamburgers for a day, thus creating a living fantasy in which every boy could be his own Wimpy. In the autumn of 1952, Dwight David Eisenhower was elected president, elaborate peace negotiations were under way in Korea, François Mauriac won the Nobel Prize for literature, and I, a freshman in high school, tasted pizza for the first time and thought I had died and gone to heaven.

That same year, in an episode of shame, I recall walking along the avenue with my faithful companion Robert Ginsburg, who, always the tempter, suggested we buy and share and dispatch a cake. Dispatch it we did, but I cannot say neatly. As in so many of our combined enterprises, an element of planning was missing. In this instance, the cake now purchased, we noted the absence of utensils for cutting it—a large chocolate affair with a combined chocolate and pistachio frosting—and, once cut, for conveying it to our mouths. We could have brought the cake home, there to have an ample slice in his or my mother's kitchen. But we did not want a slice of cake, however ample—we wanted an entire cake. So we ate it, walking along side streets, prying great fistfuls away from the cake and stuffing them into our mouths in the style we designated "one billion B.C." We are talking about two reasonably well brought up middle-class boys here, you understand, but true hunger, to the truly craving, will turn even a middle-class lad into a savage.

Middle-class and middle western, I should have added, for when I think of the ideal middle-class meal of my youth, eaten in a restaurant, it comprises the following plain but to me, then as now, quite pleasing Middle Western menu: it begins with a shrimp cocktail; followed by a wedge of iceberg lettuce with thousand island dressing; followed by a rather thick slab of medium-rare prime rib of beef, with a baked potato (not cooked in aluminum foil) lavished with butter and sour cream with chives; and concluded with strawberry shortcake and coffee. This is, you will recognize, almost an entirely prelapsarian meal; it could only have been eaten in good conscience before the vile knowledge that certain foods can clog arteries, set tumors growing, send up blood pressure. If you are someone who would like to get to ninety-six or ninety-seven, and hence someone attentive to death by cancer, heart attack, or stroke, what you are permitted from that meal I have described, once the calories, the cholesterol, and the caffeine are removed, is a plain baked potato on a bed of undressed lettuce with a few strawberries atop it nicely garnished with chives. Dig in.

I mock such curtailment of pleasure—I hate it, truth to tell —yet I am myself victim to it. Far from always but still all too often, I look down at the plate set before me to find potential death through possible heart disease or cancer lurking there— and if not death, social disgrace through overweight. Until roughly twenty-five years ago, those of us born into industrially developed countries, though we may not have known it, were all living in the kitchen of Eden. The snake responsible for casting us out is named Diet: today few are the people who are not dieting for health, for beauty, for longevity. *Eat to Win* is the title of a recent best-seller that supplies diets and menus for people who wish to stay young and athletically competitive. The well-named *Self* magazine calls it "the eating wave of the future." *Eat to Win?* Whatever happened to, eat to eat?

Not that I am above diet. I spend a serious portion of my life attempting to lose the extra four or five pounds that clearly wishes to adhere to me. I gain it, I drop it off, I gain it, I drop it off—we are, those four or five pounds and I, like a couple who cannot agree to live peaceably together but who refuse to separate permanently. I need no reminder when they have returned: when the press of my flesh rubs the waist of my trousers, it is time to miss a meal, hold the fries, play strong defense generally. Aggravation makes the best diet, in my view, and once, in a troubled time in my life, I dropped off fifteen pounds without consciously attempting to do so. Another time I set out to lose twenty pounds; I did it, and I wish to report that the feeling upon having succeeded in doing so is one I describe as "fatness of soul." One is so splendidly well pleased with oneself. An element of fanaticism slides in. One has lost twenty-pounds—why not twenty-five? A friend described my play on the racquetball court as quicker than a sperm. I thought I looked wonderfully well when I had lost all that weight: so lithe, so elegant, so youthful. Apparently this was not the effect I everywhere conveyed, for more than one person, during this period, asked my wife straight-out if I were suffering from a wasting disease.

Because of this little experience I believe I can understand something of what goes on in the mind of the anorexic. The anorexic is the reverse of the glutton, but it is well to remember that the anorexic is the other side of the same coin. (The currently accepted definition of anorexia nervosa is "a serious illness of deliberate self-starvation with profound psychiatric and physical components.") As food excites the glutton, so does it repel the anorexic (most of whom are adolescent girls or youngish women). The glutton's idea of a jolly fine time is precisely the anorexic's idea of hell. As the glutton in extreme cases will have to have his jaw wired to prevent him from eating, the anorexic will in equally extreme cases have to be hospitalized and force-fed through tubes.

For the true glutton, as for the true anorexic, food may well not be the real problem; the love and hatred of food, when they take on such obsessive energy, doubtless mask deeper problems, distinctive in individual cases. But it is interesting that reactions to food can be a significant symptom in serious psychological disorders. Freud, that suspicious Viennese, thought that a great deal more was going on at the table than met the fork. Unquestionably there sometimes is. But I prefer to stand on this question with Cyril Connolly, who put into the mouth of a character in his story "Shade Those Laurels" the lines: "They say that food is a substitute for love. Well, it's certainly a bloody good one."

I like my gluttons mildly obsessive but not compulsive. I prefer to think that in their pursuit of food they are not crying out for attention never given them by a thoughtless mother but instead are trying to duplicate the lovely meals given to them by a thoughtful mother; or, if not that, then I prefer to think they are simply hungry—most of the time. Consider Falstaff, about whose childhood and parentage Shakespeare supplies us with no helpful information. He is perhaps a bit more of a soak than a pure glutton ought to be, but he is otherwise an ideal type, and one who oughtn't to be made to lie still for psychoanalysis. Friar Tuck, Robin Hood's man, is another in the line of delightful fat boys. Let us not neglect, in toting up our serious trenchermen, the monks in Rabelais, whose merest snack could render any forest full of endangered species. The great gluttons of the movies of my boyhood were an Austro-Hapsburgian character actor named S. Z. ("Cuddles") Sakall and Sydney Greenstreet; Sakall played his fat man sweet, as if he were a walking piece of very creamy pastry, while Greenstreet played his menacing, as if he were a hard dumpling that, should it roll over you, could cause serious damage.

The literary hall of avoirdupois has no shortage of tenants. Those two butterballs, G. K. Chesterton and Hilaire Belloc, gain admittance without question. Balzac, who was a bit of a pudge, deserves a place. So, too, does Henry James, who fought weight all his life and, as photographs from his later years reveal, was finally defeated. Mustn't forget Edward Gibbon, that chubby, inelegantly formed little man who wrote only streamlined, elegantly formed sentences. The nineteenth-century French writers Sainte-Beuve, Gautier, Flaubert, and

Edmond Goncourt, while not quite Keystone Kops, were nonetheless all nice-sized boys, the result no doubt of those elaborate meals at Magny and other Parisian restaurants. E. R. Curtius has commented on the corpulence of Friedrich Schlegel. Among American writers William Dean Howells and Wallace Stevens were, to put it softly, heavyset. Poor Oscar Wilde emitted such pointed wit from a rather pasty, lumpy body. Evelyn Waugh ended his days with his trousers let all the way out. Edmund Wilson was no flyweight. No shortage of embonpoint among the literati.

But then there are those anorexics of culture who seemed to exist on aperçus and orchids: Ronald Firbank, Aubrey Beardsley, Lytton Strachey, and Proust. As anyone who has read Céleste Albaret's memoir of her employer, dear M. Proust, can tell you, that Marcel could be a very picky eater. Still, I believe I should rather have Proust over for dinner than Kafka, who doesn't seem a man easily fed. Yet it may well be that it would be more pleasant to have Kafka for dinner than to go out oneself for dinner at the home of Leonard and Virginia Woolf, whose gaunt looks scarcely suggest that they set a very handsome table. Judging now from their girths and from what is known of their appetites, I shouldn't mind dining, at a table for five, with Samuel Johnson, H. L. Mencken, A. J. Liebling, and Jean Anthelme Brillat-Savarin. How fine the talk would be! Separate checks, of course.

When an adolescent I used to lunch from time to time with a man who, I estimate, weighed in at roughly 350 pounds. He worked for the father of my friend Robert Ginsburg. He had all one would expect in the way of jollity from a large and gluttonous man. He called himself the Fat Man. How fat was he? A single detail will suffice for description. In his car he kept an old towel—his *shmatte*, he called it—which, when driving, he laid across his belly to prevent the steering wheel from wearing away his trousers.

The Fat Man was Robert's and my Falstaff, though it is fairly certain that neither of us will go on to become king of England. Like Falstaff, he commanded a highly colorful vocabulary. When a driver in a car behind him honked, his standard riposte was, "Blow it out your duffel bag, knucklehead." He introduced us to various of the gaieties of the flesh, overeating not least among them. He knew the best inexpensive restaurants in every neighborhood in Chicago. He enjoyed his vittles and piled them high upon his plate. He was once described as eating corned-beef sandwiches as if they were cornflakes. He seemed to take minor offense if his luncheon companions failed to eat heartily. Robert and I did our best never to give offense. "Have another piece of cheesecake, boys," the Fat Man would say, "you owe it to yourself." *You owe it to yourself*—a finer glutton's motto cannot be devised. A philosophy of life is contained in those five short words.

The Fat Man died before the advent of nouvelle cuisine, but I feel confident in my belief that he would have found it, as a serious feeder, laughable. I have eaten perhaps a dozen such meals, all very expensive, and the majority of them, I am pleased to report as a partial excuse, on other people's expense accounts. The dishes to be had in such restaurants, as the carefully coiffed waiters who tell you about them like to say, "make a very nice presentation." I suppose a lot depends upon how hungry one is for a very nice presentation. I have eaten dishes in such restaurants wherein, at moments, I thought I was devouring a Kandinsky or a Frank Stella painting. Then there are those bloodless specials to deal with. "May I tell you about our specials?" the waiter will ask. ("Of course not," an acquaintance with more social courage than I has taken to retorting.) "Chef Yoshie has prepared tonight a delicate terrine made up of twenty-six pâtés and a sausage composed of the spare parts of a 1973 Ford Pinto. We also have medallions of pigeons' heels in a savory hot fudge sauce, with just a hint of tarragon." Something there is about the announcement of those specials that makes a genuinely crapulous man yearn for a bowl of chili and large side order of mashed potatoes.

Worse news: it's spreading. An informed source, as they call them at the *New York Times,* informs me that there is now a nouvelle Mexican restaurant in Dallas. One morning a few years back I was hit by specials at breakfast in San Diego. In my own city, Chicago, theme restaurants have had a long run, and so we have beaneries with such names as Jonathan Livingston Seafood and Lawrence of Oregano. We also have nostalgia dining, with one popular joint got up as a 1950s diner, with waitresses who chew gum, fifties tunes on the jukebox, the whole bit. I am told that the food isn't bad, though I haven't visited it because I fear the place must be chiefly frequented by what I think of as "fun couples."

I prefer my restaurants shorn of fun couples. I don't like restaurants where status is the true entrée. Nor do I want too many vegetarians on the premises. "Vegetarianism is harmless enough," said Sir Robert Hutchison, a former president of the Royal College of Physicians, "though it is apt to fill a man with wind and self-righteousness." I like some burly guys around— eight or ten size 48 suits in the place. I like a restaurant where you can get a virile BLT club sandwich ("one of those complicated American sandwiches, with lots of layers," as an English friend once described it), where they know the meaning of creamy coleslaw, where they serve a significant hamburger. I don't wish to seem more Philistine than I am, but I'm talking about that disappearing commodity—plain but serious grub.

I prefer women, too, to be of hearty appetite, though a

gluttonous woman seems to me less than appealing. Samuel Johnson took this thought a step further: "If you once find a woman gluttonous, expect from her very little virtue." The strumpets in *Tom Jones,* in corroboration of Johnson's point, were powerful trencherwomen. Although slender herself, Edith Wharton was a woman with an eye always out for the main course. Certainly in her novels she was attentive to the food her hostesses served, and described food very well. In *The Age of Innocence,* in the character of Mrs. Manson Mingott (oddly enough, herself a stingy hostess), Edith Wharton provided the one hugely fat female character I can think of in American literature:

> The immense accretion of flesh which had descended on her in middle life like a flood of lava on a doomed city had changed her from a plump active little woman with a neatly-turned foot and ankle into something as vast and august as a natural phenomenon. She had accepted this submergence as philosophically as all her other trials, and now, in extreme old age, was rewarded by presenting to her mirror an almost unwrinkled expanse of firm pink and white flesh, in the center of which the traces of a small face survived as if awaiting excavation. A flight of smooth double chins led down to the dizzy depths of a still-snowy bosom veiled in snowy muslins that were held in place by a miniature portrait of the late Mr. Mingott; and around and below, wave after wave of black silk surged away over the edges of a capacious armchair, with two tiny white hands poised like gulls on the surface of the billows.

The really fat woman has never been an ideal in Western history, though the zaftig or appealingly buxom woman à la Rubens or Renoir of course has. The past fifteen or twenty years have been hard on women in this regard, for they have been years that, despite all the new freedoms attained, have left women hostage to the look that Tom Wolfe has called "starved to perfection." I have known more than one woman who has sacrificed her good looks through the kind of carrot-and-cel-ery-stick dieting that is required to achieve this look of upper-middle-class emaciation. It was Proust, I believe, who said that, beyond a certain age, most women can retain either the beauty of their figure or the beauty of their face—but they cannot retain both.

This was no very great problem for the wives and mis-tresses of Louis XIV, who, portraiture makes plain, liked his women zaftig. Dining with Louis, they could scarcely have been otherwise. Although not a fat man himself—he was fortu-nate in being tall—he was one of history's profound feeders. "His appetite," writes Nancy Mitford in *The Sun King*, "as-tounded the onlookers and frightened the doctors." Dinners at Versailles, one must allow, were impressive. The king ate, again according to Miss Mitford, "a meal composed of four plates of different soups, a whole pheasant and a whole par-tridge or chicken or duck (according to what game or poultry was in season) stuffed with truffles, a huge quantity of salad, some mutton, two good slices of ham, a dish of pastry, raw fruit, compotes and preserves." In Louis XIV divine right was reinforced by divine gastronomical might, for he was beauti-fully equipped for adventures of the table: at his autopsy he was discovered to have a much larger than average stomach and bowels double the normal length.

The Romans were not famous for being dainty feeders; no people who had thought to devise the institution of the vomitorium could have been. The towering glutton among the Roman emperors was Vitellius, who, even on campaign, Suetonius tells us, "always kept a lavish supply of delicacies within reach of his hand." At home he did not dine but ban-quetted—three and often four times a day. If Vitellius invited himself out, such were his expectations that it rarely cost his hosts fewer than 4,000 gold pieces to set out a table for him.

Suetonius notes: "Vitellius paid no attention to place or time in satisfying his remarkable appetite. While a sacrifice was in progress, he thought nothing of snatching lumps of meat or cake off the altar, almost out of the sacred fire, and bolting them down; and on his travels would devour cuts of meat fetched smoking hot from wayside cookshops, and even yesterday's half-eaten scraps." Talk about fast food.

Suetonius cites gluttony and cruelty as Vitellius's two reigning vices. Is there a connection between the two? Many a cruel ruler has been a fat boy—Nero and Henry VIII leap to mind. Unfortunately, the data are missing for even a wild generalization. Yet this much can be risked: the possession of power appears not in the least to slake other appetites, food among them. King Farouk of Egypt was a complete tub. Mao Tse-tung was clearly a man who could make his chopsticks fly. The grandfather of the current Aga Khan carried pro football weight without pro football muscle. William Howard Taft, our twenty-seventh president, was built like two walruses with a single head. After Lenin and until Gorbachev, the Soviet Union has not known a leader of normal girth, which has doubtless contributed to the just fame of Soviet tailoring in the fashion capitals of the world. Attaining power, then, seems to be no satisfactory substitute for the passionate craving for food; it merely gives one a chance to sit down to some real meals.

But I see that I have progressed thus far into this essay without rolling out the sweets trolley. The time has arrived. The sweet tooth is an affliction that leaves some people quite untouched. I am not among these people; neither was Evelyn Waugh, who once called gluttony "the master-passion of boy-hood" and who knew that many a glutton sets out on his unappeasable path through a childhood craving for sweets. Writing of his fifth-form visits to The Grub Shop near his public school, Waugh wrote: "No subsequent experience of the haute-cuisine or the vintage can rival the gross, innocent delight in the commonplace confections that now began to reappear." The shop offered cakes and buns and ices and chocolates and various whipped-cream contrivances. This sounds quite superior to the sweet fare of my boyhood—about which more directly—but then the English is so much more a tea and tiffin culture than the American. In *A Passage to India* E. M. Forster writes that Aziz "had been warned that English people never stop eating, and that he had better nourish them every two hours until a solid meal was ready." Aziz was well advised, I think, for the English remain, even after the sun has long set on their empire, the world's greatest nation of noshers. What else is an English tea but the nosh regularized and turned into an institution?

The shop across from our grammar school was called Miller's, after its owner, a Jewish immigrant who lived upstairs from it with his wife and daughter. The shop sold a few groceries, some sandwich makings, detergents, school supplies. But its main attraction and, my guess is, its main source of revenue was a glass cabinet three feet high and perhaps ten feet across that sold the most delightful small poisons and tooth destroyers, which went by the name of penny candy. Gums, waxes, licorices, gelatinous and sticky substances in every color and shape were available in that glass cabinet. Before school, at recess, during lunchtime, after school, children pressed up against it, calling out, "Gimme a wax lips, two machine-gun belts, a jujubes, and three Fleers bubble gum." But before Mr. Miller, bending to the cabinet with noticeable effort, could get these things, another kid would demand, "A pack of Bazooka, three jawbreakers, a mustache, and four cents' worth of red licorice whips." Running that shop required the patience of a saint. Mr. Miller, I regret to have to report, didn't have such patience, and so would regularly break down, crying out to the heavens, yelling at a child, occasionally chasing an older boy out into the street. Those sessions could not have lengthened Mr. Miller's life, but I do know that my regular visits to his shop as a boy have continued to enrich an impressive line of my own dental specialists.

An habitué of Miller's I shall not soon forget was a boy of my own age whom I shall call Mick Stone—a name that rhymes with his own true name and that speaks to his considerable bulk, for at the age of thirteen he already weighed in at roughly 190 pounds, or some fourteen stone. He was the first true glutton I had met. A slow-moving and somewhat morose lad, as free from malice as he was from wit, he must have concentrated all his mental energies on thoughts of food. He was no mere theoretician. At recess, over at Miller's, he sprang into action. A cash outlay of a quarter at Miller's in those years —a time when a bottle of soda pop cost a nickel—identified one as a high roller. Mick Stone must have spent nearly a dollar daily. He was a boy who unfailingly put his mouth where his money was. There on the playground he would wolf down a box of twelve doughnuts, or five or six packages of Twinkies and as many Mounds bars, or four Dreamsicles, a full jelly roll, and a simple Butterfinger. Recess, it is important to understand, was only fifteen minutes. Thus fortified, he would return to class, refreshed and free to turn his full attention to thoughts of lunch.

My reaction to the gluttonous Mick Stone was one that combined amazement with vague envy. I knew that as a feeder he was way out of my class; I knew that I didn't want the encumbrance of vast flesh that was only the most evident wage of his particular sin. Still, I envied the fact that he was someone who would have no traffic with moderation. Food is not a thing that easily allows for moderation. Consider ice cream. I know of only two conditions in which I have ever existed with regard to ice cream: I leave the table either not having had enough, or I leave having had too much. Sometimes a single spoonful can make the difference between not enough and too much. Enoughness, in relation to ice cream, is not a state I have known; I am inclined to think it may not exist.

It may be a mistake to attempt moderation in eating. Instead one must make a choice: either to eat away, let 'er rip, and suffer the consequences; or hold back, bail out well before fullness, and also suffer the consequences. I have decided on the latter course, with occasional forays into gluttonous feeding. It seems to me the wiser way, allowing for a longer life, provided I do not go down in an airplane crash, or under the wheels of a truck, or through an arbitrary disease. Meanwhile, the consequences are a persistent hunger nibbling away at the edge of my consciousness. I suffer from a condition that not Freud but I have named Entrée Envy: a certain sign of the potential glutton, Entrée Envy involves a quick check at restaurants to make sure that no one at my table has ordered better than I and a feeling of sadness upon discovering that someone else has a fuller and more interesting plate. I also tend to hear the following lines from an old Negro blues tune, which I have rewritten slightly to read:

> I may be beautiful but I'm goin' to die some day,
> I may be beautiful but I'm goin' to die some day,
> So how's about a little feeding before I pass away.

Somerset Maugham, at the beginning of a story entitled "Virtue," tells that, when he was young and poor, he resolved that, if he were to become rich, he would smoke a good cigar every day of his life after lunch and dinner. It is, he claims, the only resolution of his youth that he ever kept. It was also "the only ambition I have achieved that has never been embittered by disillusion." (Freud, that connoisseur of disillusion, was another regular cigar smoker.) Does food bring disillusion? In the same paragraph Maugham talks about oysters and lamb cutlets; and the thought of evolution and the "millions upon millions of years [these] creatures [have taken to] come into existence to end upon a plate of crushed ice or a silver grill," he says, leaves him sad. I must say that the fat man inside me has never had such solemn thoughts. For him life is strictly man eat cutlet and, so to say, no bones about it. And yet ... and but ... and still ... and however ... disillusion remains after the dessert dishes are cleared. There was all that happiness upon the plate and now it is gone.

I had planned to end this essay with a chronicle of a day in which I let my fat man loose upon the countryside. It was to be a story whose cast included German pancakes and French pastry, pizza and ribs, corn and potato salad, steaks and rich fowl, a small tub or two of sweet butter. I thought I might order two entrées, a thing I have never done. But I find I cannot bring myself to do any of it. The flesh is willing but the spirit is weak. I have been living carefully too long. After such a day, I fear belly vengeance; I see a picture of my wife driving up to an emergency room with me stretched across the back-seat, a cool compress across my brow, groaning and pledging repentance.

There is, then, a deep fraudulence at the heart of this essay. While writing it I ate a fruit salad, munched on salt-free crackers, drank the abysmal brew known as diet soda, kept a post-card-size picture of the obese Orson Welles taped to my refrigerator. More shocking to report yet, while writing this essay I actually lost two pounds. Oh civilization! Oh bloody discontents!

Everybody's Talking at Me

I N THE REALM of boredom, as in so many others, it is
better to give than to receive, and I would have it
known that, as a university teacher, I give—and give plenty—
at the office. With the aid of my scintillating talk, I have in my
day put a student or two to sleep. When first I noted this
strange power, I was a touch alarmed and more than a touch
resentful. In the fullness of time I have gotten over both the
alarm and the resentment. Except in seminar rooms, where
there is the danger of injury through their striking their heads
against a table top, I allow such students to snooze away,
drawing the line only at passionate snoring. I suppose I could
wake them, but I don't like a scene. Besides, my reasoning is,
if my students cannot arise from my classes inspired, at least
they will awake refreshed.

To treat a brawny lad or an indelicate lass, after a night of
who knows what wild roistering, to a brief nap through the aid
of my sometimes intricate commentary on the novels of Joseph
Conrad or Henry James seems to me no grave disgrace. It
happens to others and, I prefer to think, perhaps even to the
best of teachers. For all one knows, Aristotle may well have
sent his lot of Athenian youths into the arms of Morpheus with
his lectures on Prior Analytics; doubtless at times even his best

student's attention must have strayed. To be a bit boring is part of the job of the teacher; it is, you might say, ed. biz, not everything about which is appealing.

But it is given only to a few to bore a throng. I am one of those few. The throng in question numbered on one occasion somewhere between six and seven hundred; the setting was a middle-western university, to which I had been invited as a guest lecturer. The school had decided to use one of my books for its freshman composition course—provided, that is, that I agreed to visit the campus, meet with the students, and deliver a lecture. In teaching the book and bringing its author to the school, officials there apparently wished to demonstrate to the students the imperfection of the work and the life both. Financially it seemed a good deal. Driven by lucre, flown by United, I arrived on campus with a typed, double-spaced, twenty-one-page lecture entitled "Is There a Literary Life Before Death?" clutched in my warm fist.

A hectic visit was planned. Dollar value was to be exacted. Mine was one of those schedules that read "11:00–11:10—author free"; otherwise the author was fully occupied. The two hours before the lecture were given over to a dinner with students and a fireside chat with the author. At roughly a quarter to eight the author was marched over, without aid of tumbril, to the large church in which his lecture was to be given. A church, according to Mark Twain, a practiced lecturer, is a fatal setting for a secular talk; people are unaccustomed, and hence unwilling, to give way to laughter in a church. About many things Mark Twain did not know diddly, but about lectures in churches he was brilliant. At five of eight the students and a few faculty members filed in; the author later learned that attendance at this lecture was compulsory. A compulsory lecture delivered in a church—this, then, was my assignment.

But I had a secret weapon. In my hand was not a list of fifty-seven Communists currently working in the State Department but an hour-long talk completely over the heads of my audience. I did not know this when I began, but it soon became evident. I started with a little joke. "The title of my lecture," I announced, "is, 'Is There a Literary Life Before Death?' Please note that I do not intend to discuss the other side of this question: Is there a literary life after death? That is the more interesting question, but on it the data just now is rather thin." This was greeted by puzzled silence. My lecture proper began with what I thought was an amusing anecdote. Apparently I was alone in thinking it so. Before I arrived at page 2 I had to allow to myself, No doubt about it, this is not going smoothly.

I thought I had interlarded my lecture with witticisms, aperçus, interesting formulations. My audience, again, evidently, thought otherwise. Occasionally, the sound of a raucous masculine laugh rang out, echoing in the vasty deep of the church. Where are you, brother? I wondered, as I droned away at my lecture. I scanned the church to find the eyes of this solitary appreciative auditor, but all I could discover were the eyes of youthful students that wore the ophthalmological equivalent of Gone Fishing signs. As I finished each page of this lecture, I felt I would have done well to fold it into a paper airplane and sail it over the heads of my audience, there to follow the words printed upon it, which had also sailed over their heads. I felt I was standing at that lectern in that church for something like a fiscal quarter—and a very poor fiscal quarter at that. Will time, I asked myself, drag so in hell?

And then something rather odd happened. I began to be amused by the comedy of my own situation. Here I was, babbling away, boring the pants off some six hundred or so students, causing them to long for their beds and to be at last rid of me, the man who was keeping them from beer and sex and who knows what other diversions. I thought of Henry James who, when relieved of his job as correspondent for the New York *Tribune* after being told that his articles had been above the heads of that paper's readers—"too good" for them is the way the editor put it—of Henry James who replied that "If my letters have been 'too good' I am honestly afraid that they are the poorest I can do, especially for the money."

Certain phrases in my own lecture now nearly caused me to laugh aloud. One in particular that really got to me was the front portion of a sentence that read: "The best guide to this life are the Brothers Goncourt, Edmond and Jules, who in the journals that they wrote in collaboration—and which Edmond continued after the death of Jules in 1870. . . ." Reading this sentence I thought, No doubt these kids cannot have heard of the Goncourt brothers—neither after all had I at their age—but I am fairly certain that they never even heard of 1870. I proceeded, slowing my pace now, quite enjoying myself, and finally rather sorry to end, which I did to applause of a strength that did not quite merit the word *wan*. Somehow I was able to restrain myself from blowing kisses and bowing deeply from the waist.

Not all my public performances have been so uniformly dismal. One of the nicest days of my adult life was the day I gave the H. L. Mencken Memorial Lecture at the Enoch Pratt Free Library in Baltimore. It was a sunny Saturday afternoon, and, standing out in front of the library, I recall wondering whoever would wish to waste such an afternoon on listening to a lecture. As I entered the hall in which the lecture was to be given, I encountered a friend. "Kenneth," I said, "what are you doing here?" "I don't know," he answered. "Frankly I'd rather be in Fenway Park." So, truth to tell, would I. But more than four hundred people showed up—an overflow crowd.

And a fine crowd it was, composed not principally of professors or students but of a lovely diversity of people, of all ages
and social classes, who were there less to hear me than to honor
the memory of H. L. Mencken, their city's great writer. Afterward Mencken's bartender at the Rennert Hotel came up to
show me a letter from Mencken, which he had had framed, that
congratulated him, the bartender, on his craft.

I could be mistaken—the distorting egotism of the performer is never to be trusted in these matters—but I thought
the lecture went very well. The audience laughed where I
hoped it would and seemed thoughtful where I had hoped to
provoke thought. The applause at the close felt neither per-
functory nor phony. A coffee was served after the lecture, to
which the public was invited, and a dinner of the Mencken
Society was held later in the evening in a magnificent room of
the Peabody Conservatory Library. An official of the Pratt
Library handed me my check in an envelope, and it turned out
to be for more than had been promised. At the coffee a stream
of people came up to tell me how much pleasure my lecture
had given them—and I determined to believe them. At the
dinner I asked the man who was the outgoing president of the
Mencken Society, an insurance man in his sixties, what it was
he liked about Mencken. "Reading him," he said, "makes me
happy." So, I thought, has this day in his honor in his native
city made me happy.

Yet lecturing, it has not taken me long to appreciate, is not
my métier. I like the money when it is more than I deserve;
I like the sociability between lecturer and audience when it
exists; I like the applause and praise when it seems genuine. It
is, really, only delivering the lecture that I don't much care for.
Part of it is the nervousness I feel about being able to please
a crowd. A recent survey revealed that Americans fear only
cancer more than public speaking. Although never surveyed,

I am one of those Americans. I scarcely ever speak before more than ten people without an initial flutter of nerves. The word *flutter* suggests butterflies, the reigning metaphor for such nervousness. I feel too old for butterflies; perhaps what I get are moths. In any case, something is fluttering when the prospect of speaking to an audience of any substantial size is before me.

But for me there is a deeper problem than nerves, and this is that I do not think all that much of the lecture either as a form of entertainment or as a medium of education. Today I give lectures, but, with rare exceptions, I do not go to them. As a college student, of course, I was bound to attend my share of lectures, but I remember chiefly two things about my attendance at such lectures: a frantic mental scampering to take notes on material that I judged might be on examinations (six characteristics of the late Renaissance—that sort of thing) and a heavy boredom that all too often elided nicely into slumber. Occasionally, during my student days, I would note items of intellectual style in a lecturer—the dramatizing quality of German lecturers, the casualness of English ones—or acquire such little intellectual tips as the proper pronunciation of *banal*. Sometimes I would go to a lecture or a reading to see an artistic celebrity; for precisely this reason—to *see* quite as much as to hear—I went, as a young man, to poetry readings given by Marianne Moore, e. e. cummings, and Carl Sandburg. I went to these readings, in effect, as an intellectual and artistic groupie. On occasion I even now go to a lecture by a scholar I revere: Arnaldo Momigliano or Hugh Trevor-Roper or E. H. Gombrich. In middle age, I remain an intellectual groupie.

Far and away the most effective lectures I have ever attended were those I went to as a private during basic training in the peacetime army. What they effected was deep and contented sleep. The army could do with subject matter what it did with food: make it all seem alike and all supremely boring.

Be the subject Communism or chemical warfare or nuclear attack, lectures in the army, listened to on cold mornings in Fort Leonard Wood, Missouri, while I was wearing fatigues, boots, and a field jacket, could unfailingly put me out in somewhere under three minutes. In this they surpassed even a session of papers on literary theory at a meeting of the Modern Language Association. How I wish I had tapes of those army lectures in my possession now to replay on the infrequent nights when I suffer insomnia!

The world has never known a shortage of brilliant lecturers. Charles Dickens was famously successful as a lecturer, though his lectures were chiefly composed of dramatic readings of his own work. Mark Twain's lecturing consisted of comic turns, which he did consummately; and throughout his life he was able to call on his ability as a lecturer as a means of refilling the coffers he repeatedly emptied through his many bad business investments. Oscar Wilde's lectures in America were a very great hit, and Wilde was fond of comparing his own success in this line with Dickens's. As a lecturer, Wilde came on as an exotic; from St. Louis he instructed his agent to acquire for him "a sort of Francis I dress: only knee-breeches instead of long hose. Also get me two pair of grey silk stockings to suit grey mouse-coloured velvet. The sleeves are to be flowered—if not velvet then plush—stamped with large pattern. They will excite a great sensation. . . . They were dreadfully disappointed at Cincinnati at my not wearing knee-breeches." Emerson, as his biographer Gay Wilson Allen remarks, looked to lecturing "to be his own salvation, both for sanity and solvency"—and so it proved.

Dickens, Twain, Wilde, Emerson, all were, quite apart from their distinctly different geniuses, considerable showmen. Without this element of showmanship there can be no exciting lecturing, for entertainment is intrinsic to the successful lec-

ture. Writers without a showman's flair have fared poorly as
lecturers. Melville, though he needed the money desperately,
was unable to make a go of it as a lecturer. Walter Pater's
lectures were said to be inaudible; "a form of self-communion,"
Max Beerbohm called them, adding: "He *whispered* them." E.
M. Forster did a certain amount of lecturing over the course
of his life, but not, apparently, altogether successfully. Kather-
ine Anne Porter recalled hearing him lecture to a political
conference in Paris in 1935: "He paid no attention to the micro-
phone, but wove back and forth, and from side to side, gently,
and every time his face passed the mouthpiece I caught a
high-voiced syllable or two, never a whole word, only a thin
recurring sound like the wind down a chimney as Mr. Forster's
pleasant good countenance advanced and retreated and returned." At Harvard, Lee Simonson remembered Santayana
lecturing his students while "gazing over our heads as if looking for the sail that was to bear him home," to Europe presumably.

Henry James did a good bit of lecturing on his final trip
to the United States in 1906, but his lectures, one gathers,
received less than a triumphant greeting. During a lecture
James gave in Chicago he noted that only three men were in
the audience—thus fortifying James in his belief that in America culture was almost exclusively the possession of women—
and two of the three were sound asleep before he had unwound
his intricate first paragraph. Wallace Stevens preferred neither
to lecture nor to give readings of his poetry. It was reported
that three members of the audience fell asleep and many others
fought drowsiness when Albert Einstein, in 1934, set out his
theory of relativity in English in a lecture hall at Carnegie
Tech.

When Max Beerbohm was asked to lecture in America, he
said he would be pleased to do so only if he could deliver his

lectures out of doors at the Castle Garden and if the audience
was limited to twelve people. The offer was withdrawn. Beerbohm later made a great success giving radio talks over the
BBC during World War II, but he later refused to appear on
television, arguing that a radio talk was a work of verbal art
while an appearance on television, in the words of his biographer David Cecil, was "the naked unedited exhibition of a
personality"—a case, to reverse the old maxim about children,
of its being better to be heard than seen. A number of other
cultural figures have preferred to be neither seen nor heard. In
Edmund Wilson's infamous postcard bearing the rubric "Edmund Wilson Regrets That It Is Impossible For Him To," two
of the items appearing under that rubric are "Deliver Lectures"
and "Give Talks And Make Speeches." Maxwell Perkins es-
chewed lecturing and so, too, did S. J. Perelman. E. B. White
chose not to lecture and must have disappointed many a college president who thought him the perfect commencement
speaker, which when younger he probably would have been.

Then there is the category—into which I fall—of those
who wish they were superior speakers but know that they are
not. Tocqueville is perhaps the most distinguished man among
our number. As a member of the French Assembly during the
fateful year of 1848, Tocqueville hoped to lead his party but
soon discovered that his considerable talent as a writer did not
translate into talent as a speaker. "But skill as a writer is more
hindrance than help to a speaker, and vice versa," he noted in
Recollections. "For a well-written chapter is about as different
as possible from a good speech. I soon noticed that and saw that
I was classed among those speakers who are correct, straight-
forward and sometimes profound, but always cold and consequently powerless. Certainly my trouble is not any lack of
passionate feelings, but on the rostrum a passion for expressing
myself well has always momentarily driven out all other pas-

sions." Tocqueville's is, of course, exactly the correct, indeed the crucial, distinction—that between writing and speaking. The first is an intellectual act, the second, though not devoid of intellect, is finally a performance art.

This always comes as news, and as rather bad news at that, to those of us who write fairly well. (Between the pen and the lip is many a slip—too many, I regret from experience to report, for I believe I have made them all.) When I began teaching I thought to lecture my students about the authors whose books we were reading. I filled these lectures with facts, anecdotes, curiosities, things that I myself found interesting or sometimes merely amusing. My students scribbled away, furiously taking notes. I told them they need not bother, for they would not be examined on any of this material. Industry was instantly replaced by torpor. As I prattled away, I felt I had the attention of perhaps five or six students in a class of thirty; the remainder of the class was simply not returning service. To be fair to them, these little lectures were respectable enough as compositions but not very successful as lectures. They were over-freighted with fact, for one thing; for another, though they read well enough on the page, they did not always read smoothly from the lectern. I could feel my subtleties miss the target, my ironies fizzle, my parentheses evaporate. I looked up from my text to catch the pretty Miss Goldstein's eyelids at half-mast; the red-haired Mr. Pipal, eyes completely shut, was well out of the intellectual struggle. I droned on, slowly coming to an awareness that, pedagogically, what one thinks is not necessarily what, from the lectern, one can say. Or, to put it another way, I agreed with everything I said; it was the way I said it—which was the way I would have written it—that was wrong. To underscore my point, I invite you to read this paragraph aloud, as if it were part of a lecture. As such, I believe, it is a dud.

In his essay "On the Difference Between Writing and Speaking," William Hazlitt notes: "It is a common observation that few persons can be found who speak and write equally well." The chief distinction, according to Hazlitt, has to do with time; more time is allowed for writing and reading than for speaking and listening. "In reading," Hazlitt writes, "we may go over the page again, whenever anything new or questionable 'gives us pause'; besides we are by ourselves, and it is *a word to the wise.*" Listening to a lecturer, or an orator of any sort, words whiz by; one may be swept up by them, or entertained by them, or infuriated by them. But they are not around long enough to be argued with, as they can be in rereading a questionable passage in a book, for the lecturer is on to other words, while books, centuries before television was invented, have always permitted the mental equivalent of instant replay.

Along with its intellectual component, a lecture or speech is also sound and gesture, accent and emphasis, face and, yes, even garb (recall Oscar Wilde's knee-breeches). These supposedly extraneous elements can loom larger than one might prefer to think. "The most dashing orator I ever heard," writes Hazlitt, "is the flattest writer I ever read." Reading that sentence, I remember some twenty years ago working for a large educational corporation whose president used to speak fairly regularly on something he called "the knowledge explosion." He was an elegant man; he had interesting hands, which he used to fine effect. He had earlier been a colleague of Edward R. Murrow, which lent him a certain authority. He wore very good clothes. He was perpetually tanned and his face was intricately lined; his hair was gun-metal grey admixed with white. When he spoke about the knowledge explosion, one couldn't take one's eyes off him; one could almost hear a bomb go off, see a cloud go up.

A friend who worked for the same corporation, a young

man no less intellectually skeptical than I, determined to get the president to write up his thoughts on the knowledge explosion for *Harper's* or the *Atlantic* or the *New York Times Magazine*. As the president of a large corporation, he said he hadn't time. My friend persuaded him merely to talk further with him about the subject, saying that he would ghostwrite the article for him. They spent a few sessions together, my friend pressing, probing, prying ideas about the great knowledge explosion out of him, or at least trying to do so. None, apparently, were there. After a week, my friend, defeated, announced that the explosion didn't seem to exist, that all the president had in mind were the rather dull notions that more people than ever were attending colleges and that computers figured to become more and more important in education. It was a wonderful speech; there just happened to be nothing behind it.

This is not, I suspect, an altogether uncommon experience. I recall not long afterward reading the speeches of Adlai Stevenson and being hugely disappointed by them. They seemed so witty, so winning, so wise when Stevenson delivered them; they were so inert, so cliché-ridden, so commonplace on the cold page. I thought Mario Cuomo's keynote speech at the 1984 Democratic Convention easily the most powerful piece of political oratory I had ever heard; reading it the next day in the *New York Times* I thought it seemed thin stuff. But the difference between speaking and writing doesn't apply to politicians alone. One of the great publishing disappointments of recent years for me has been the three volumes of Vladimir Nabokov's lectures. I know extremely intelligent people who heard Nabokov deliver many of these lectures and were tremendously moved by them. Bound in books these lectures seem scarcely more than highly interesting summaries of works with occasional side comments. My guess is that the students who were moved by Nabokov's lectures were moved by Nabokov himself, the last aristocratic Russian writer, a living link to Tolstoy and Turgenev. I don't for a moment think these people were callow or even in any way wrong to be greatly moved by these lectures. I believe instead that, as one says after recounting a story that does not quite come off, you had to be there.

There are lectures and there are lectures, and then there are lectures. There are the lectures that one gives to students, and there are the lectures one gives to something called "the general public," and then there are the lectures that, while not necessarily excluding these two former groups, scholars give to their peers. Lectures can be turned into books, and lecture series—the T. S. Eliot Lectures or the Christian Gauss Seminars—have been the occasion for books. Lectures can be to books what out-of-town openings used to be to Broadway plays—trial runs in which one works out the kinks and papers over the chinks before the final production. Different lecture audiences require different lecturing etiquette. Lectures to serious scholars seem to require a prepared text, from which one reads; lectures to the general public seem most impressive if delivered without a text or with a text that one only infrequently glances down at; lectures to students seem to call for rather elaborate notes, preferably neither turning yellow nor beginning to shred at the ends and dropping from the lectern, in the manner of heavy dandruff.

The appetite for lecturing varies vastly among people who are called upon to do it. Some adore doing it, some do it out of necessity, and some loathe it. I am someone who satisfies all three conditions: I adore doing it, I must do it, I loathe doing it. I have never given a lecture without traces of the nervousness associated with stage fright (those damn moths); yet, in the very midst of a lecture, the ham absolutely triumphant in me, I have said to myself, "God, I am enjoying this." But I cannot say that I have ever felt like the narrator of Chekhov's

"A Dreary Story," emeritus Professor Nikolay Stepanovitch, who says: "No kind of sport, no kind of game or diversion has ever given me such enjoyment as lecturing." In his story Chekhov compares the good lecturer to a good symphonic conductor, someone who has to be aware of twenty things at once. He has his professor remark:

Before me a hundred and fifty faces, all unlike one another; three hundred eyes all looking straight into my face. My object is to dominate this many-headed monster. If every moment as I lecture I have a clear vision of the degree of its attention and its power of comprehension, it is in my power. . . . At one and the same minute one has to play the part of savant and teacher and orator, and it's a bad thing if the orator gets the upper hand of the savant or of the teacher in one, or *vice versa*.

You lecture for a quarter of an hour, for half an hour, when you notice that the students are beginning to look at the ceiling, at Pyotor Ignatyevitch; one is feeling for his handkerchief, another shifts in his seat, another smiles at his thoughts. . . . That means that their attention is flagging. Something must be done. Taking advantage of the first opportunity, I make some pun. A broad grin comes on to a hundred and fifty faces, the eyes shine brightly, the sound of the sea is audible for a brief moment. . . . I laugh too. Their attention is refreshed, and I can go on.

Chekhov's Professor Nikolay Stepanovitch feels that "only at lectures have I been able to abandon myself entirely to passion," but for others who lecture the passion dies fairly quickly. A young and very popular professor at the university at which I teach has told me that, after giving the same course of lectures for the past several years, he now slips his lecture for the day out of his desk drawer and goes forth to deliver it to some four hundred students with no more excitement than he might feel at going out to buy the morning newspaper. It is because it has become so easy for him that he is thinking of abandoning this course to teach another. Others feel such extreme tension at the prospect of lecturing that there is no room left over in their psychic economies for passion. Many is the story of university lecturers who, in their violent nervousness, quietly go off to vomit before lecturing. William Hazlitt had to be pushed onto the stage when he began lecturing, and his first public lecture, on the subject of Hobbes, according to his biographer Herschel Baker, "was read so fast, and in such a low, monotonous voice, that it was hardly understood." It is good to be able to report that Hazlitt, who desperately needed the money from lecturing, became in time better and better at it.

Was it in A. J. P. Taylor's autobiography that I read about the English don who so loathed lecturing that he always chose the most obscure and unpromising subjects for his lectures, in the hope of attracting fewer than three students to them, which would allow him to cancel the lectures? His colleagues, good chaps, tumbling to his trick, regularly paid three students to show up at each of these lectures, thus forcing him to go through the full torture. A. J. P. Taylor's exploits as a lecturer run throughout his autobiography, and in his recent book, *An Old Man's Diary*, Taylor writes: "The achievements I am most proud of apart from my books are two lectures: The Ford Lectures given as long ago as 1957, and the Romanes Lecture given in 1982—both, I need hardly say, without a script or notes." Taylor not only lectured without a script or notes (though he would when required carry cards with long quotations on them), but even refused to use a lectern. As a nervous lecturer, I must say I find this impressive. As he was standing there unprotected by a lectern, what did he do with his hands? How did he keep his feet still? If I had my druthers, I would lecture wearing a life jacket, a parachute, a crash helmet, and a bowie knife strapped to my calf.

The lecture as an educational form came to the United

States fairly late in the nineteenth century. It was an import from the Continent, chiefly from Germany, where professors were great figures. German professors were scarcely considered teachers; they were scientists and thinkers who, in their lectures, shared their researches and thoughts with their students. Soon, in the United States, much more prestige attached to lecturing from a raised platform, from on high, than from working down in the trenches putting students through recitations. From the professor's standpoint, then, lecturing was greatly to be preferred. Was it—is it—preferable from the standpoint of education?

The late Alexander Gerschenkron, who was an economic historian at Harvard and himself educated on the Continent, has written about what he deemed the inefficiency of the lecture system in education. Gerschenkron was well aware of the psychic pleasures of lecturing—"Where else could a man get these regular opportunities for hearing himself talk undisturbed for an hour or so?"—but also well aware of its corruptions. (H. G. Wells thought George Bernard Shaw's mind had been "early corrupted by public speaking.") He believed that students like lectures, for it was, in his view, "a very commodious, passive way of learning or rather of satisfying the requirements." He also believed that students were "bored and like to be entertained, and a lecturer who knows how to display a sense of humor in relevant and irrelevant asides can be certain of approval." He knew that lectures given over and over again tend to harden into formulas and were the academic equivalent of long-running Broadway plays. Gerschenkron believed, too, that "a lecturer who thinks creatively on his feet and to whom many a new thought occurs under the stimulus of expressing himself aloud, and who, therefore, is likely to go off on all sorts of tangents, such a brilliant man is unlikely to find much favor with his listeners."

With certain rather lengthy and boring qualifications, I am inclined to agree with Alexander Gerschenkron. With the exception of certain scientific and highly scholarly papers delivered before an audience, lectures generally tend to be closer to intellectual entertainments than exercises in ratiocination. If proof of the assertion that lectures are chiefly entertainments is wanted, I would point to their increased popularity in our day. Although going to a lecture is not everyone's notion of a real night on the town, lecturers with fame or a reputation for brilliant talk are in great demand and are often paid fees not much below those earned by show-business personalities and concert performers.

When I was a student at the University of Chicago, I once went to hear Nelson Algren deliver a lecture, the proceeds from which were to go to the *Chicago Review,* the university's little magazine on which I was a sub-editor. I remember not a word of Algren's lecture—it was more in the nature of a talk —but I do recall clearly his introductory remarks. "For a thousand dollars," he said, "I will give a talk in a tuxedo. For five hundred I will wear a business suit. For two-fifty, I appear in a sport jacket, slacks, and necktie. One hundred dollars gets you a jacket and slacks but no tie. I'll let you guess what I am being paid tonight." Algren was wearing a pair of baggy washpants, none too clean, and a shiny shirt, which must even then have been fifteen years old, with a zipper running diagonally across it. This was Algren's characteristically delicate way of saying he was speaking for nothing.

Were he alive today, Nelson Algren might have to pep up his wardrobe; he might even have to buy a set of tails. Big bucks are to be had by those people whom the English describe as "namey." On the current chat market it is said that the highest fees are made by Alexander Haig and Henry Kissinger, who can get between $15,000 and $20,000 for a lecture. The Jefferson Lecture, sponsored by the National Endowment for the Humanities, pays $10,000. I imagine William F. Buckley, Jr., and John Kenneth Galbraith to be in the $5,000 to $7,500 class. The columnist George Will is said to charge $5,000 for a lecture in Washington, D.C., and $10,000 for a lecture outside Washington—a man, Mr. Will, clearly, who prefers not to pack his jammies. The economist Arthur Laffer, he of the Laffer Curve, asks $8,000. Imagine what he could do if he had a slider!

As for the chit for my own chat, it varies wildly, depending on the location (California in the winter is always tempting), the state of my own finances, the cause (if any). I find it is lovely to be invited to give a lecture, and hell to accept. I get especially edgy when, in connection with an invitation, the word *honorarium* is mentioned; I have come to read the word *honorarium* as a synonym for "small fee"; when someone mentions "a modest honorarium," I know the fee is likely to be in the category known as "negligible." I was not long ago invited to give a lecture at Princeton for a fee of $800. I wrote back to say thank you, but since I am a nervous lecturer I generally try to get two or three times what I am worth, and, because you are offering me only roughly what I am worth, I must refuse. I not long ago received a call to give a commencement address; the terms were expenses, a modest honorarium, and, of course, they would "toss in an honorary degree." I had not thought of the phrases "toss in" and "honorary degree" in conjunction before. "Toss in the rear-window defogger," yes, "toss in the whitewall tires," no problem, but to have an honorary degree "tossed in" seemed to me to mark an advance of some sort.

I wouldn't say that it is the main attraction, but one always goes to a lecture anticipating little foul-ups, gaucheries, comic faux pas. As a form of "live" entertainment, lectures in the natural course of events often provide these. In this line once, when giving a classroom lecture on F. Scott Fitzgerald, I described the young Zelda Sayre, not yet Fitzgerald's wife, as the "ball" of Montgomery when of course I meant the "belle." Somerset Maugham, whose stammer made each of his lectures and speeches an act of bravery, in a speech at Yale during World War II referred to "the price of liberty" and then could not for the life of him remember what the price of liberty was. John Berryman, a drinking man, used fairly frequently to give lectures and poetry readings at which he thought he was perfectly charming when it was clear to everyone in the audience that he was perfectly drunk. Stories are not uncommon of older professors simply delivering a lecture to the wrong class, or the wrong lecture to the right class. In the long lore of lecturing, has any lecturer, I wonder, ever put himself to sleep with his own lecture and had to be gently awakened at the lectern?

My own favorite lecture story is about an Englishman who was delivering a public lecture about George Eliot, when in the middle of the audience he noticed a beautiful young woman raptly attending to his every word. He began to direct his lecture to her alone; as he went on he felt rather like a Spanish caballero serenading his lovely senorita. On and on he talked about George Eliot, and her eyes, shining with what seemed like great intelligence, never for a moment left his. At the end of the lecture there was applause, followed by the announcement that the lecturer would be pleased to answer any questions from the audience. The beautiful young woman raised her hand. The lecturer, anticipating a question of brilliant perception, called on her straightaway. In a husky voice, with a German accent, she said, "Zis Middlemarch, may I esk you, vat elze he write?" The lecturer's answer, quite properly, is not recorded.

A Mere Journalist

I BEGAN KEEPING A JOURNAL not long after it became clear to me that I wished to be famous. Perhaps that is not quite accurate, for, as I think back on it now, it occurs to me that I always wished to be famous. As other people have an imagination for disaster, I have had an imagination for fame. I can remember as a boy of nine or ten returning home alone from the playground in the early evening after dinner, dodging, cutting, stiff-arming imaginary tacklers on my way to scoring imaginary touchdowns before enormous imaginary throngs who chanted my name. Practicing free throws alone in my backyard I would pretend that I was shooting them at a crucial moment in a big game at Madison Square Garden. Later, as a boy tennis player, before falling off to sleep, I imagined the Duchess of Kent presenting me with the winner's trophy on the center court at Wimbledon. I wrote none of this down, because I had not yet become a scribbling man. Fame was still a general, not a particular, desire. Once I determined to become a writer the desire became quite particular. As for the extent of my fame today, it is best measured by way of analogy through an anecdote a friend told me about having once asked a historian of medicine at what point in history physicians began saving more patients than they killed. "I regret to report," the historian replied, "that we haven't achieved it yet." I can say roughly the same thing about my fame.

But should fame ever arrive, I shall be prepared for it. Off and on for more than twenty years I have been keeping a journal. One expects a famous writer to keep a journal. In my case, jumping the gun somewhat, I began keeping a journal well before I had done much writing. Yet one has to start somewhere, and why not with a journal or diary or notebooks? "I have never understood why people write diaries," Max Beerbohm said. "I never had the slightest desire to do so—one has to be so very self-conscious." No argument about the need for the journalist to be self-conscious, since the journal is the personal house organ for self-consciousness. But it is hard to believe that so subtle a writer as Max Beerbohm hadn't the requisite self-consciousness. My own guess is that Beerbohm didn't keep a journal or diary because he didn't need one; fame came to him early—while he was still at Oxford, in fact—and thus he was quite without need of what is the first function of a young writer's journal: a place to grouse, a place to dramatize one's condition in prose, and a place to bemoan the fact that, once again, this time in the instance of oneself, the world in its ignorance is failing to recognize another genius.

It may be, too, that, along with so many other arts and games, keeping a journal is an activity that one must begin while still fairly young. By thirty it may be too late to begin. For the journalist, habit is nearly everything. Mordecai Richler once remarked that, for a writer, all experience is divided between the time before he decides to write and the time after. After the decision has been made, life becomes in large part copy, all experience grist for a mill that closes down only at death. For the keeper of a journal, experience is turned into words before the sun sets twice; sometimes, like dry cleaners, he gives same-day service. When something of interest occurs in the life of a journal keeper, he not only notes it mentally but also notes that he must note it in his journal. A short while ago, for example, I was at dinner with a number of academic historians. The group among contemporary historians known as the cliometricians came up for discussion. "Whatever happened to the cliometricians?" someone asked. I thought immediately of the radical feminist historians, and I leaned toward a historian seated on my right, a woman of a certain age and the sophistication to go with it, and whispered, "They were replaced in academic fashion, I believe, by the clitoromeretricians." Not bad, I thought to myself; must note it down. You will find the remark in my journal under October 2, 1985.

You will find a great deal else besides such mots in my journals, but one thing you will not find is anything approximating a record of contemporary history of the kind available in the diaries of Harold Nicolson or Chips Channon or Richard Crossman. This for the simple reason that I have had no serious or intimate connection with contemporary history, and perhaps an insufficient interest in it. The only large public event noted in my journals is the assassination of John F. Kennedy and the dreary events surrounding his funeral. Even here, though, I noted his death, in the wholly egotistical manner of the journalist, less for its effect on the country than for its effect on the hero of my journals, me. What I thought of John F. Kennedy—which, at the time, wasn't very much—cannot be of any great interest to the world; nor, I have reasoned since, can what I think of other public events and political tendencies of our time be of any staggering significance. Who really cares what I think of, say, the Sino-Soviet dispute? (For the record, I happen to be rather partial to this particular dispute, which I hope will continue all of my days.)

Along with an absence of political content, neither will you find much in the way of spirituality in my journals. Unlike *The Intimate Journal of Henri Fréderic Amiel*, from whose pen flowed an abundance of such sentences as "Love that is sublime, single, invincible leads straight to the brink of the great abyss, for it speaks at once of infinity and eternity," my journal seldom strikes the religious note. In it my arguments with God go unrecorded. The closest I get to spirituality is self-pity, which, I recognize, is not quite the same thing. Especially when young, I could be very strong in the line of self-pity; I whined exceedingly well. Here, for example, is our hero on December 29, 1962, at the age of twenty-five, living in New York and working as an editor on a political magazine in a job he rightly realized was a dead end:

Well, I have worked one year at this job. What have I learned? What have I lost? What have I missed?

Learned: (1) A few writing tricks, though mostly tricks with other people's writing; (2) a trade, or—perhaps more accurately—a wide but not altogether firm knowledge of how to go about a trade; (3) a few pieces of extraneous information; (4) how to talk about politics—quite different from learning how politics truly work; and (5) how to read and judge a composition somewhat more surely than before.

Lost: (1) A good deal of, sadly, enthusiasm; (2) youthful intransigence on many subjects and issues where intransigence is the only proper attitude; (3) sympathy; and (4) some hair.

Missed: (1) Sitting down to do some writing that I might take pride in; (2) friendship.

As I grew older, this self-pity swelled and expanded nicely into a fine case of melancholia, so that, on October 28, 1970, after a falling-out with a dear friend, I discover our boy, now thirty-three, noting that "at such moments you know how tenuous are the strongest of human bonds—and you rediscover what you at this instant feel yourself a fool for ever forgetting:

that you are absolutely alone in the world." Returning to the subject some seven months later, he says of human loneliness and vulnerability, "Perhaps for the best, most of us are unable to keep this devastating fact in mind for much of the time. I am currently reading Conrad *(Victory)*, who never for a moment forgot it." Our jolly melancholic's notion of a good time is insomnia, that is if you believe an entry of February 16, 1971, which in part reads: "It is now nearly two in the morning, and unless I get extremely tired, I think I shall try to stay up to see the dawn in. I have ample provisions: cigarettes, tea, an all-night classical music station, the *Letters of Thomas Mann*, a new (to me) book of Wm. Hazlitt essays, some writing to do, and (for now) this notebook." Our hero had just gone through a divorce, of which, mercifully, his journal says little directly; but, not to worry, there is sufficient dolorosity to go round. Thus on July 20, 1971, we find him inditing, "Five years ago I found much about life absurd; nowadays I find many of the same things merely sad. It would be good to be able to regress a little in this sphere." As a Borscht Belt comedian might say, "Hey, c'mon folks, these are the jokes—yuk it up!" The comedian's name in this case might be young Jackie Werther.

Self-pity, melancholia, depression—best of course to do without all these; but if suffer from them one must, next best is not to impose them on others, or so I was brought up to believe. A journal, though, is not a bad place to deposit them. For people who do not slide easily into the public therapeutic mode, a journal can function as a book of consolation. For many among us, writing things out appears to be therapy enough; it is also a solution that cuts out the middleman, the therapist, thereby in one stroke eluding both the problem of transference and the transference of funds. There is, though, a middleman named Dr. Ira Progoff who wishes to cut himself back in. Dr. Progoff runs something called a "journal workshop," in which he holds out the promise, through the use of journals in something he calls the "Intensive Journal" process, of "a potential for growth in a human being . . . as infinite as the universe." (Beware doctors bearing botanical metaphors, and especially doctors bearing them into workshops.) But in any case Doc Progoff has come too late for me. In my journal, and as much as possible in my life, I have done my best to cease complaining and have taken as my motto the line from the beer commercial that runs, "I guess it doesn't get much better than this."

Not that I am committed to the cheerful view, or that I decided that complaint is always a mistake. But I do note, in my journal for April 17, 1975, the following shift in emphasis openly declared: "The time has come to turn this journal away from being a chronicle of complaint—an Iliad of woe—and into a name-dropping affair. Through my ersatz eminence as editor of a respected, if still less than dazzling, magazine, I find myself more frequently in touch with writers and intellectuals of some—how to say it?—standing. Might as well note down these meetings, for the practice they provide in portraiture and for a 20-watt light bulb on the age."

Here I have to report, with regret, that my journals are not, as the English say, as "namey" as a lively literary journal ought to be. Saul Bellow appears from time to time, Lillian Hellman is there, and so are John Sparrow and Martha Graham. I. F. Stone shows up when I am in Greece, and Henry Kissinger puts in a cameo appearance. But my journals contain no Mitford sisters, no Cyril Connolly, no Evelyn Waugh (insulting me as a boorish American, doubtless), no Diaghilev, no Virginia and Leonard Woolf, no André, Willie, or Morgan, no Prince of Wales and Mrs. Simpson, no royalty whatsoever, I regret to say. In his diary the snobbish Chips Channon reports once having two queens dine at his home on the same evening, but, in his utter elation, he became too drunk to recall anything about the evening. Unlike Chips Channon, or Harold Nicolson, or other keepers of namey journals and diaries, I do not leave my apartment often enough to compile a really interesting index—one of the kind that, under the letter *R*, for example, lists Walther Rathenau, Maurice Ravel, Max Reinhardt, Sir John Reith, Rilke, Rodin, and Ida Rubinstein.

"This afternoon Cocteau and Picasso suddenly entered my room and were just as suddenly gone again." That sentence, written by Count Harry Kessler, strikes me as precisely a sentence of the kind the keeper of a namey journal requires. In a single stroke it shows its author to be a man of the great world, as the German-born Harry Kessler, a cosmopolitan at home in art and politics and publishing, indubitably was. Kessler provides many such sentences: "In the afternoon visited Baby Goldschmidt-Rothschild. She received me in bed, between pink damask sheets and in blue pyjamas, the Chinese bed upholstered in yellow satin." "Maillol and Mlle Passavant lunch with me." "Luncheon at the Princess Bassiano's in Versailles with André Gide and others." "Sammy Fischer and his wife invited me to lunch with Gerhart Hauptmann." "Lunch with Albert Einstein, Nicolai, Rubakin, Sytin (the Russian publisher), and Hugo Simon to discuss Rubakin's people's library project." "Dinner at Martin du Gard's, with Helen, Paul Valéry, and Edmund Jaloux." One might think one could not hope to run so namey a journal on a low-calorie diet, yet Count Kessler was stiletto thin, thus rendering his diary, along with its being a splendid literary work, a simultaneous tribute to his energy and powers of abstinence.

If one cannot run a journal on meetings with famous people, for simple want of such meetings, then another possibility is to feature introspection and self-analysis. Introspection, even in a journal, has its limits. The diaries of Anaïs Nin, in which

I have never been able to make much headway, seem to me subject to this criticism. She is too intent on "the quest for the self," as she more than once puts it, but after a page or two I invariably find myself giving her quest a rest. Even the higher introspection of Amiel soon loses it edge. Better, perhaps, to keep introspection where it belongs—to oneself.

In my own journal I tend to serve up introspection with a La Rochefouauldian twist. "Vanity without foundation in either physical beauty or true talent is one of the most pathetic of human spectacles," I wrote on July 22, 1971, quite obviously referring to myself. "New bookcases," I wrote years later, "give one the splendid illusion that one can bring order to one's life." A week or so afterward I wrote: "I suppose I believe that art, like sex, is better for being made a bit difficult." And yet again, "Writing well is the best revenge," though what I had to revenge myself against is far from clear. This is La Rochefoucauld all right, but La Rochefoucauld, as I read it now, living well below what the old Department of Health, Education, and Welfare used to call the poverty level.

Sometimes my journal entries are little more than doodling in prose. In one such entry I describe what I call "a purist's dream," which is to write an entire essay in which no sentence begins with *it* or *there* and in which the words *but, yet, still,* and *however* never appear. Sometimes a single phrase will prompt me to repair to my journal, as when I describe a restaurant I had dined in the day before as the haunt "not merely of the old but of the militantly old," or when I refer to a greatly neurotic novelist of small talents I know as yet another case of "big wound, small bow." Like a precocious and rather spoiled child who runs off to his mother to report his smallest achievement, I run off to my journal to report my most fugitive thoughts. Five years into my career as a teacher, for example, I remark: "How, in its way, like courtship teaching can be, with the teacher as the male, the class a dumb but nonetheless desirable female who needs to be won each time afresh." Scraps of literary criticism go into my journal as well, so that, after finding myself disappointed with the closing chapters of *The Confessions of Saint Augustine,* I wrote, "As secular autobiography tends to grow dull once success has been achieved, so in religious autobiography dullness sets in once the autobiographer has found God." I also mark my own birthdays: "I am 41 today. Apart from this flu, I have no strenuous complaints. I am required to do nothing ignominious to earn my living; everything ignominious I do, I do of my own volition."

I have by now filled nearly nine hundred pages with such matter. "Who," Igor Stravinsky used to remark when presented with a new work, "needs this?" I suppose I alone do. Something in me impels me to record what I have thought, or experienced, or read, or heard. "Most of life is so dull that there is nothing to be said about it," E. M. Forster wrote in *A Passage to India.* I could not disagree more. I find keeping a journal quickens life; it provides the double pleasure of first living life and then savoring it through the formation of sentences about it. Here I recall the cliché philosophical problem about whether a tree makes any noise falling in the forest if no one is there to hear it. As someone who keeps a journal, I prefer to keep a record of all the trees I hear fall, and by now I seem to have piled up, in my various notebooks, a great deal of lumber.

A journal can also function as the intellectual equivalent of a photo album or home movies. Reading through my journal, as I have been doing while writing this essay, I feel like a man watching a slide show that features himself. Why, there I am being turned down, at the age of twenty-six, for a job I then much wanted at a New York magazine. Here I am, in his office at the City University of New York, chatting intimately with

Irving Howe, who was so kind to me when I was a young writer. Here I am again, pleased to receive a pleasant letter from Anthony Powell, a novelist I much admire, saying kind things about an essay of mine in the *TLS* and noting, in my journal, that such pleasure as my essay may have given him is "small quid for large quo." There I am marking the onset of boorishness in myself, at age thirty-nine, after a lunch with a young academic, about which I note that I have done most of the talking and said nothing that I have not said many times before. Here, there, everywhere, I am making firm resolutions I shall not come close to keeping—learning ancient Greek among them. And yet is this slide show any less boring than one given by a middle-aged suburban couple of their recent trip to Europe? I don't know, but I do know that, in my case, the host is having a swell time.

How is it that so many otherwise highly productive writers, in the midst of turning out novels, poems, essays, and criticism, have also found time to keep extensive journals or diaries? Ralph Waldo Emerson, Samuel Butler, Arnold Bennett, Theodore Dreiser, André Gide, Virginia Woolf, Evelyn Waugh, H. L. Mencken, and Edmund Wilson are but a handful of prominent names among such writers. One might have thought their already copious literary production would have been sufficient, but, no, they all needed to spill still more ink in notebooks, journals, and diaries. Having already used gallons of ink on their public thoughts, they poured out quarts more on their private ones. Enough, one would have thought, was enough—and yet for these writers it wasn't.

Are we talking here about the writer's disease known as graphomania? This is a disease that can take many forms. For some, graphomania takes the form of simply being unable to put the pen down—the authorly equivalent of logorrhea. For others—those, I should say, who have the disease in its advanced stage—it takes the form of needing to write everything down because anything that hasn't been written down isn't quite real. My guess is that Edmund Wilson had an advanced case. I know of no other explanation for the fact that Wilson felt the need, and acted upon it in his journals, to record his sexual congress with his own wife, which I find at once astonishing and repulsive (quotations on request—send self-addressed plain brown wrapper).

Were he alive today, Anthony Comstock, organizer and special agent for the New York Society for the Suppression of Vice, could read my journal without missing a pulse beat. No future biographer, in the unlikely event that there is to be one, figures to find evidence in my journal for establishing the thesis that I am, say, a suppressed lesbian. And yet unsympathetic as I am to Edmund Wilson's chronicling of his conjugal sex life, as a journalist and something of a graphomaniac myself, I half understand his impulse to do so. It is the impulse to make one's days a matter of record—"no ink, no life," is the graphomaniac's slogan. Reading through my own journals I am sometimes amazed at how little in the way of stimulus I require to journalize:

5-2-78 a.m.
    Yesterday: wrote a few pages of my [Maxwell] Perkins essay. Translated my Yourcenar passage. Graded some student papers. Had a call from Caedmon records to write 750 words of album jacket copy for a record of Saul Bellow reading from *Herzog;* fee: $100 and some records. I chose not to do so.

Not exactly a day in the life of Ivan Denisovich, I grant you, but still I felt the need to record it.

On the other, larger hand, many are the private thoughts that a journalist can confide only to his journal. In *Samuel Butler's Notebooks,* which are mostly given over to general

thoughts about art and life, there is an odd entry entitled
"Myself at the William Rossettis." In it Butler records his ill
feelings about Mrs. Rossetti's family, the Madox Browns,
whom he used to visit but "who wanted me to climb my pole
too much and too often before they would let me have [a bun],
and it was not a good bun when it came. . . ." Nevertheless,
when he is invited to visit, Butler pays his call and it is all rather
a botch, even though he is on his good behavior. Before he
leaves, though, Butler notes: "I had a few words with William
Rossetti. I said how beautiful his pictures were; in reality I
hated them, but I did all as I should, and it was accepted as
about what I ought to have said." Here we have a fine example
of the use of a journal as a personal corrective to what is
deemed to be the world's necessary hypocrisy. Butler has gone
through his paces, paid his false obeisances, but reports his true
feelings in his notebook. Let the record show, then, that Samuel Butler found the Rossetti and Brown families a great pain
in a soft place.

What record? you might ask. In Samuel Butler's case, of
course, the record is the printed record, since his notebooks
have been judged worthy of publication, in both complete and
abridged form. Yet I believe that not only do few people keep
a diary or journal for themselves alone, but most people who
do keep a journal, even if they are not professional writers, at
least half hope that theirs, too, will one day be published.
Stranger things have happened. The great diarist Samuel
Pepys, who earned his living as a naval administrator, wrote a
diary that lay unpublished for some hundred and fifty-six years
after he ceased keeping it; first published in abbreviated form
in 1825, it has since been republished in various incomplete,
bowdlerized, and complete forms time and again. A very rich
and rather unpleasant man named Arthur Inman made the
maintenance of his diary his life's work and left enough money

to Harvard University to make certain that it was published, as it was in 1986. William Saroyan, a relentless diarist, left a good portion of his estate to the William Saroyan Foundation, which maintains his diaries and other papers. "In effect, he left his estate to himself," his son Aram Saroyan wrote. "He took it with him." The rest of us journalists and diarists have to trust to luck for posthumous publication of our journals and diaries; but my guess is that most of us are ready to do so.

While patiently awaiting the condition of posthumy, to be followed at a decent interval by posthumous publication, those of us who keep journals and diaries keep scribbling away. I note that in my own journal I once copied out an apposite line from Chamfort: "Quand M. de R——a passé une journée sans écrire, il repéte le mot de Titus: 'J'ai perdu un jour.' " Although I know exactly what M. de R——and Titus meant, I must confess that I do not write in my journal every day. On many days the world is too much with me and my life is too crowded even for a brief entry. I generally write in my journal in the early morning, before setting out to earn my livelihood. Sometimes I write down a paragraph or two after lunch, but I scarcely ever write in it at night, by which time, as an early rising man, I am usually drained of such mental powers as I possess. But when I do write something in my journal, I feel rather more complete, in the way I suspect an observant Moslem might feel for having done his ablutions. Not that journal writing elevates me—it doesn't, usually—but I do feel upon having made an entry in my journal as if I have done my duty, completed, in effect, an act of intellectual hygiene.

"I can no more recover one of my days in memory," wrote Amiel, "than a glass of water poured into a lake; it is not so much lost as melted away." I do not often look into my journals, yet whenever I do I am impressed by how much experience has slipped through the net of my memory. I note the name of a student in one of my classes whom I describe as "easily the most intelligent" I have come across during the then current academic year, whom I go on to describe physically, yet whom today, a mere seven years later, I cannot call to mind. I had quite forgotten having read a life of Voltaire by Jean Orieux, "a life that," as I recorded it in my journal, "in Orieux's telling, seems to have been made up of carefree fornication and witticisms, with a moment out here and there for writing." I completely forgot once describing a review I had to write of the book of a touchy acquaintance, an exercise I described as resembling "eating spaghetti while on a tightrope —and with chopsticks." At table on a Greek-owned ship on the Mediterranean, my journal reminds me, a companion at dinner, a tall, blonde, rather raffish woman, a producer for the BBC, announced "I then began to understand that the real interest in Yoga was the hope that one would develop body control enough to reverse one's ejaculations and levitate oneself"—an unforgettable bit of table talk, one might have thought, except that I seem to have forgotten it. I seem to have forgotten, too, that when a young intellectual, rather baldly on the make, stopped to visit me on a trip to the Middle West, I wrote in my journal: "I am for him an item (rather a minor one) on what I gather has been an extended tour of intellectual sight-seeing—on this tour I am the intellectual equivalent, perhaps, of Siena." That was in 1978; I was smarter then.

I suspect that anyone who keeps a journal must believe that the world revolves around himself. All autobiographers are liars, Orwell once said; quite possibly all those who keep journals or diaries are convinced of their own importance. When a figure from the world of letters dies, for example, I feel it essential that I record it in my journal and offer my opinion of his worth. On August 8, 1980, I wrote:

Kenneth Tynan died last week, at 53, of emphysema, in Los Angeles. He was not a writer I admired, but I generally read him with interest. He was the bright young man come down from Oxford, all marked out for success; but like so many such young men—beginning at least with Cyril Connolly—he did not quite come up to expectations. He was apparently a leftist of the decadent kind—for the people and for pornography, too. He had a pretty good roll of the dice, I suppose, as theatre critic for *The Observer* and *The New Yorker* and Literary Manager of the National Theatre. . . . [Here I cite a piece of exotic gossip about him.] His, Tynan's, seems an agitated life; he is still now.

"Excuse me, buddy," I hear a voice with a strong Yiddish inflection inquire, "but who asked you should put in your two cents?" An interesting question, except that the person asking it clearly understands nothing about the impulse felt by the keeper of a journal, who is a man with a bottomless pocket of pennies and who, in his heart, feels that his, and not *The Times* of either New York or London, is the true journal of record. The phrase "a modest journalist," referring to anyone who keeps a journal, is an oxymoron. It may well be that no man is a hero to his valet, but neither is any man a pip-squeak to himself, and especially not the man—or woman—who keeps a journal.

As the journal of record—the record, specifically, of my own opinions and impressions—my own journal is not without a certain edge. Reading some of the things about contemporaries that I have written in it, I seem rather stronger in the line of cutting comment than I had thought. I am not so strong as the Brothers Goncourt are in their journal, but then I hadn't their opportunities. Paging through my journals I cannot miss a certain enthusiasm on my part for a well-turned insult. I see that I have described an English writer as "almost always wrong and frequently original"; a certain American intellec-

tual as someone about whom I can never be certain if he is a
man of principle or an opportunist, since his principles seem
generally to run along the same track as his opportunities;
another English writer, a man now in his seventies but still
very much on the sexual attack, I have described as "a bent
rake"; after attending a lecture by a famous but disappointingly
dull scholar, I wrote that "I did not have to shield my eyes from
the dazzle." And these comments, you understand, are all
about people who have never done me the least harm; they are
the result of sheer verbal exuberance, the rising thoughts of a
journalist after a good night's sleep. Imagine, then, my journal
entries about people whom I feel are my enemies. Vengeance,
the Italians say, is a dish best served cold. My plan is to serve
mine posthumously, which is to say, when I, the cook, am cold.

But who is to eat from this dish? The longer I live, the more
I write in my journals and the lengthier they become, the less
I can expect them ever to be published. My only hope is that
standards continue to fall at the same splendidly alarming rate
as they have been for some years now, so that I become a fit
subject for a doctoral dissertation or a candidate for a book in
an author series that has already exhausted such authors for the
ages as Kurt Vonnegut and Philip Roth. Vengeance, then, I
fear, will first be served not to my enemies but to some hapless
graduate student or junior professor who will have to repair to
bed bleary-eyed after reading the hundreds and hundreds of
pages that I rose, dewey-eyed in the morning, to write in my
journal. Perhaps an advance apology is in order. Sorry, fella,
I had quantities of ink and a sturdy fountain pen and not all
that much else to do but fill up all these notebooks. Nothing
personal, which, if you will permit me to say so, is the way I
hope (against hope, I realize) that you will write about my life.

After reading through my journals, what sort of man is this
graduate student or professor likely to discover? Forgive me

for saying so, but the man he finds there will not quite be me. He will find my literary opinions, many views on writing and writers, portraits, antipathies, criticism, invective, even sadness. He will, I believe, find a writer but not a man. I quote an entry from my journal on March 18, 1978, that reads: "Insofar as a journal is supposed to be the true record of a person's days, this one fails, for the main event of my life over the past five months or so has been the disintegration. . . ." and I then go on to mention, briefly, the breakdown of an important relationship in my life. Again, my journal touches scarcely at all on my family life. Although she is often mentioned as being with me at this dinner or on that trip, my wife, who is the central figure in my life, is never talked about at any length in my journals, nor is my love for her discussed or analyzed, but then neither do I write about my appetite for oxygen. Lengthy though these journals of mine are, the most important truths of my life do not have much place in them.

At the same time, I would maintain that everything I have written in these journals is true—or at least as true as I could make it at the time I wrote it. Lying as such is not, I believe, a question in my journal: I do not claim to have met famous people I have not met; I do not deliberately falsify emotion to show what a bighearted fellow I am. Yet the truth of a journal of the kind I keep is truth of a proximate kind. Sometimes I discover, upon rereading, that I have simply not been smart enough, and thus have made judgments about other people that are inaccurate, or inept, or oddly askew. Sometimes I am too hard on people; sometimes I am not hard enough. Then there is the problem of self-deception. I do not think I brag in my journal, but neither do I specialize in modesty. I hope that the habit of self-mockery has helped me to elude the trap of self-inflation. I try, when writing in my journal, to keep in mind the twin truths that I am someone of the greatest importance to myself and that I am also ultimately insignificant. This is not always easily accomplished.

One of the reasons I think my journal is not too greatly marred by falsity is that in writing it I have had very little at stake. Unlike other journals, especially those of politicians, mine has almost nothing in it of the tone of self-exculpation. No reason it should have, since I have not been accused of anything more serious than having strong opinions with which some people have disagreed. As a writer, I do not feel in the least unappreciated; I feel very nicely appreciated—and quite lucky in this as in many other regards. I haven't, in sum, a case to make, but am instead a rather happy graphomaniac, a mere journalist with inky fingers and many blank notebooks and a taste for endlessly making distinctions and discriminations.

Harold Nicolson once remarked that a man should keep a diary or journal for the amusement of his great-grandson. I find that fellow rather difficult to imagine, let alone to write for. Although like every other man or woman who has kept a journal or diary I wish some portion of my journal will one day be published, just now it is being written for a good-natured and highly appreciative audience of one—me. Highly appreciative is quite accurate, for I tend to be partial to the younger man who wrote in my journal. (Will I like as much the middle-aged one who is writing in it now?) He could be gloomy, this young man, but he also understood that there was no point in letting his gloom get him down. He was forever imploring himself to work harder, and at one point he quotes a culture hero of his, Henry James, who, on the subjects of depression and work, wrote: "If only I can concentrate myself: this is the great lesson of life. . . . When I am really at work, I am happy, I feel strong, I see many opportunities ahead. It is the only thing that makes life endurable." After entering this quotation, my young journalist wrote: "Ah, those James boys!"

Sometimes I am astonished at the items that find their way into this journal of mine. On Tuesday morning, June 12, 1979, after noting that I had finished the first volume of a biography of Bernard Berenson, I also note the death of John Wayne. After remarking that, though I had no special reverence for him as an actor, as one of the larger-than-life movie stars of my youth, he had become, I wrote, "part of the furniture of one's life. The first half of one's life, it strikes me, one fills up one's rooms with such furniture; the second half one watches this furniture, piece by piece, being removed." My journal, in this connection, has served as a running inventory of my days, and I am pleased to have kept it. It has made life seem rather less the dream that I sometimes fear it may be.

"Life can only be understood backward," wrote Søren Kierkegaard, himself a journal-keeping man, "but we must live it forward." Too true—and a little sad. Yet a journal does provide backward understanding. Like the rewind button on a videocassette recorder, it is a great aid in replaying segments of past experience, in running over important and even trivial events, in recollecting moods and moments otherwise lost to memory. A journal is a simple device for blowing off steam, privately settling scores, clarifying thoughts, giving way to vanities, rectifying (if only to oneself) hypocrisies, and generally leaving an impression and record of your days. And when you are through with it, when the time has come to leave this mud pie, as my own journal recently reminded me that Mencken used to call the earth, you can even pass the damn thing along to your as yet unborn great-grandchildren. It is an extraordinary invention, better even than an American Express card, and I don't go anywhere without mine.

They Said You Was High-Class

KARL, FRIEDRICH, FORGIVE ME, fellas, for never having taken much interest in your class struggle, but the truth is that for the better part of my life I have been a bit unclear about what class I myself belong to. If the phrase didn't imply that I was of a higher social class than I am—and make me sound like an Englishman into the bargain—I should call the whole thing a frightful muddle. More than a mite confusing it is, though. How nice to be able to say with confidence, as George Orwell once did, that one is "lower-upper-middle class." Yet, unless I am quite wrong, such terms have now lost much of their descriptive power. The social pace has quickened; nowadays people move in and out of social classes with greater rapidity than ever before. Sometimes I wonder if today social class, at least as we used to think of it in this country, has about as much relevance as an electric salad fork and as bright a future as a cha-cha instructor in Montana.

Social mobility—the jumping or more commonly sliding from one class to another—is scarcely a new phenomenon. Chekhov, to cite an interesting instance, had a grandfather who bought himself out of serfdom and a nephew who became a Hollywood producer. I myself have a cousin, ten years older than I, named Moe and a niece, thirty years younger than I, named Nicole; and to go from Moe to Nicole in only forty years is in some respects to travel further than the Chekhovs did from Voronezh Province to Beverly Hills. Other evidence of our whirring social flux can readily be adduced. The janitor of the apartment building I live in has published a book; it is not, granted, a slender little volume on the poetry of the Comte Robert de Montesquiou but instead a book about the martial arts; yet the same man is a janitor and a published author. The other day, in Manhattan, I had the bite put on me by a panhandler wearing a rumpled but still a real Ralph Lauren shirt; and it occurred to me shortly afterward that, should I ever hit the skids, I may not have the wardrobe to go on the bum. Just when you begin to think you understand a thing or two about the drama of life, they change the scenery and send in a whole new cast of characters.

Cracks, major fault lines, in the class system may be a worldwide phenomenon. Peregrine Worsthorne, the British political writer, recently noted in *The Spectator* that "the class system has changed out of all recognition in my lifetime." Certainly, social distinctions in America have become vastly less clear in my own. When does a child first notice such distinctions? My own first realization that the world was a place filled with social differences might have been the gross recognition that some people lived rather better than we and others rather worse. It might have been owing to the woman, whose name was Emma, who came in to clean for us on Tuesdays, for I seem to recall thinking it peculiar that someone would clean a place not her own. It might have had to do with automobiles, for we lived on a street that was a thoroughfare, and the first organized knowledge I acquired as a child had to do with telling the difference between cars; and it could not have been long before I also learned that some cars (Cadillacs, Packards, Lincolns) were held in higher regard than others (Fords, Studebakers, Plymouths). These were the years of World War II, during which my father drove a green 1942 Dodge sedan.

If our family had a crest, that green 1942 Dodge sedan ought to be at its center. That car placed us—socially, financially, and stylistically—and where it placed us was slam-bang in the middle. Our family was not so much socially uninteresting as socially uninterested. If life is in some sense a status race, my parents never noticed the flag drop. While we owned possessions roughly comparable to those owned by our neighbors, we showed no passion for the subtleties of social life. Even when the money was there to do so, it would never have occurred to my parents to join a city club or country club or to move to a fashionable address—a residence with social resonance. Their notion of the good life was to live comfortably, always well within their means, and insofar as possible never to pay for pretension. Then as now that seems to me quite sensible—though I must add, I myself have not had the character to live up to it.

I have omitted a social fact of no small significance and even greater complication. The fact is that I am Jewish. I was born thus, and thus I shall remain; and it is exceedingly difficult to be Jewish and not have a somewhat heightened sense of social and class distinctions. Not for nothing was the keenest modern observer of such distinctions, Marcel Proust, half-Jewish and fully homosexual; after all, a man who is in danger of being despised from two different directions learns to devise sensitive antennae. Another sharp observer of social graduations, Anton Chekhov, was neither Jewish nor homosexual; but he was low-born, the son of a bankrupt grocer, the grandson of a serf, and that put the antennae permanently on his roof. In a famous letter to his friend and publisher, Alexey Suvorin, Chekhov explained his own social unease when he wrote that "what aristocratic writers take from nature gratis, the less privileged must pay for with their youth," adding that he had had to squeeze "the slave out of himself drop by drop" before "he finds that the blood coursing through his veins is no longer the blood of a slave, but that of a real human being."

Let me hasten to insert that I never for a moment felt the least like a slave. Doubtless this was in large part owing to having a father who was successful yet in no way tyrannical or crushing, on the model, say, of Papa Kafka. My father, along with giving me the reassuring sense that I was working with a net under me, encouraged me to believe that I came of a family capable of serious achievement. But my father also alerted me early to the alarming fact that people might detest me for reasons having nothing to do with my character or conduct and everything to do with my religion. I must have been four or five years old when the potential social consequences of being Jewish were thus impinged upon me. In the 1940s and early 1950s the word—the euphemism, really—for de facto anti-Semitic arrangements was "restricted"; and in those years many neighborhoods and suburbs, clubs and resorts, fraternities and sororities were restricted.

I would be a liar if I said that knowledge of such things

didn't bother me. But I would be an even greater liar if I said
that it bothered me very much. When I was growing up, we
lived in neighborhoods that tended to be at least 50 percent
Jewish, and the same was true of the public schools I attended.
If anything, this encouraged me in the belief that Jews were
rather superior—a belief based, unknowingly, on social class.
What I didn't know was that the non-Jews who remained in
the neighborhoods we lived in were mainly people who for one
reason or another were probably unable to depart them. In
other words, most of the non-Jews I went to grade school and
high school with were the sons and daughters of the working
class or the lower white-collar classes, while the Jews tended
to be among the newly surging middle classes, still very much
on the make.

Although so far as I know I have never been the victim of
any serious anti-Semitic acts, the first time I recall feeling
rather out of the social mainstream because I was Jewish was
during a year I spent as a freshman student at the University
of Illinois in the middle 1950s. Illinois was very much a school
of fraternities and sororities—a "Greek campus," as it was
called—and I, who had not yet developed socially to the point
of knowing there was something in the world called non-
conformity, accepted an invitation to join what was thought to
be the best of the Jewish fraternities. (All non-Jewish fraternities and sororities at Illinois were then "restricted.") The reigning spirit at the University in those days, far from being the
Jewish and metropolitan one I was used to, was Protestant and
small-town—a middle western, somewhat more yokelish version of the muscular Christianity that George Santayana found
several decades earlier prevailing at Yale. The student who
seemed to me best to represent this spirit was a young man
from Peoria named Hiles Stout. Stout was a Sigma Chi and
played three major sports for the University and resembled

e. e. cummings's conscientious objector Olaf only in being "more brave than me: more blond than you"—though perhaps it would be more accurate to say that he was "more Hiles than me: more Stout than you."

I did not so much feel out-classed or declassed at the University of Illinois as I felt myself on the outside of a house I had no particular desire to enter. For while attending the University of Illinois, I had informally enrolled at good old Mencken-Lewis-Dreiser University, where I learned a haughty if not especially original disdain for the middle class, that inartistic and uninspired group also known as the booboisie—that is to say, a disdain for the social class and culture from which, apart from being Jewish, I myself had derived. From M.L.D.U., beloved alma mater, I learned not to join the class struggle but instead to disassociate myself, insofar as possible, from my own class.

As a step in that direction, I transferred to the University of Chicago, which was perhaps as close as I have ever come to living in a classless society—I refer to the student segment of university society—and rather closer than I ever again care to come. A few fraternities remained at the University of Chicago at that time, but far from being thought in any way admirable, the chief attitude toward them was a mixture of mild contempt and apathy. Wealth and genteel birth counted for naught at the University of Chicago; apart from books and classical records, material possessions were thought the sign of a cramped spirit. Physical beauty and social graces were held to be beside the point, and the standard joke of the day had it that a panty raid on one of the women's dormitories netted a fatigue jacket and a single combat boot. A passionate bohemianism was what the University of Chicago student body aspired to; a grim scruffiness was what it often achieved.

Intellectually, the University of Chicago strove much

higher, holding four tasks in life to be worthwhile: to be an artist, to be a scientist, to be a statesman, or to be a teacher of artists, scientists, or statesmen. In this regard the University of Chicago was not anti-middle class in the abrasive manner of Sinclair Lewis and H. L. Mencken; it was para-middle class by its tacit implication that there were higher things in life than getting a good job, earning a living, raising a family, and getting on. Chamfort once said that society was divided between those who had more dinners than appetite and those who had more appetite than dinners, but at the University of Chicago the world was divided between those who loved art and learning and those who did not, and those who loved it were thought better.

If the University of Chicago was relatively free of conventional social-class considerations, the United States Army, the institution in which I was to spend the next two years of my life, was, at least formally, as class-bound as any society I have ever lived in. The first—and chief—class distinction was the patent one between officers and enlisted men. Officers ate, slept, dressed, and were paid better. Obeisance needed to be paid them in the form of salutes and in addressing them as "sir." Theirs was a strikingly better deal; one didn't have to be Alexis de Tocqueville to notice that. As an enlisted man who as a boy was never required to learn the habits of obeisance, I could not help marveling at the vast social discrepancies between officers and enlisted men. I did not so much resent them as wonder how career non-commissioned officers managed to tolerate them, especially in a peacetime army, when an officer's responsibilities were less and the call on his bravery non-existent. Confronted for the first time with a codified class system, I found myself more of a democrat than I had imagined.

At the same time that the U.S. Army was rigidly hierarchical and held together by the idea of rank, no American institution was, at its core, more democratic. Well in advance of the larger society of which it was a part, the U.S. Army had integrated its facilities and was color-blind in its promotions and other procedures. As an enlisted man, one was really thrown into the stew of American life. In my own basic-training platoon I lived with Missouri farmers, Appalachian miners, an American Indian auto mechanic, a black car salesman from Detroit, a Jewish lawyer from Chicago, a fundamentalist high-school teacher from Kansas, and others no less varied but now lost to memory. It felt, at moments, like living in a badly directed screen version of *Leaves of Grass.* Although I groaned and cursed, questioning the heavens for putting me through the torture in tedium that I then took my time in the Army to be, I have since come to view that time as one of the most interesting interludes in my life—among other reasons because it jerked me free, if only for a few years, from the social classes in which I have otherwise spent nearly all my days. It jerked everyone free from his social class, however high or low that class may have been, and yet somehow, despite the jolt, it seemed to work.

Or at least it seemed to work most of the time. A case where it didn't was that of Samuel Schuyler III, whom I worked with as a fellow enlisted man in the Public Information Office at Fort Hood, Texas. The Third, as I always thought of him, had gone to the Wharton School of Business, hungered for the country-club ease he was missing while in the Army, and drove a black Cadillac convertible, the current year's model. Despite the numeral affixed to his name, the Third was without social pretensions; he was a simple hedonist and a straight money man. How he had come to own that Cadillac convertible at the age of twenty-three I never discovered—my own

social-class manners, I now suppose, prevented me from asking
—but he played the stock market fairly often, calling his broker
in Pittsburgh to place his orders.

What was not difficult to discover was the Third's contempt for everyone around him, officers and enlisted men both.
(Only a few acquaintances, of whom for some reason I was
one, were spared.) Forms through which to express this contempt were not wanting to him. The Third had developed a
salute that, while formally correct, made every officer to whom
he tendered it think at least twice about it; there was about this
salute the faint yet almost unmistakable suggestion that its
recipient go forth to exercise an anatomical impossibility upon
himself. Driving on the post in his black Cadillac, the Third
was everywhere taken for the post commander—who himself
drove a more modest car, a Buick—and everyone, even up to
the rank of bird colonel, dropped everything to salute him,
only to receive in turn the Third's own extraordinary salute.
The Third even dressed with contempt. If there is a word that
is the antonym of *panache,* I should avail myself of it to describe
the deliberately slovenly way that he wore his uniform. In
mufti, meanwhile, no muted Ivy League dresser, the Third
preferred draped trousers, alligator shoes, and in shirts showed
an unfortunate penchant for the color known as dubonnet.
Toward the close of his enlistment, the Third was promoted
from Pfc to Sp4c. but refused the promotion on the grounds
that the additional money wasn't worth the trouble of sewing
new patches on his uniforms. No gesture better summed up his
refusal to partake of military class arrangements; he scoffed at
them every chance he got, making clear that, short of doing
anything that could land him in the stockade, he chose not to
play the game. His lofty contempt earned him a great deal of
not-so-lofty hatred. The Third knew he was hated and felt

about this much as he did about his promotion—he could not, that is, have cared less.

I cared rather more, in the Army and elsewhere, because social class has always seemed to me intrinsically fascinating. I have inevitably been interested in attempting to take the measure of any class system in which I found myself, though when young I must often have been, as Henry James might have put it, destitute of the materials requisite for measurement. A fantasy about social class said to be common among children, especially children fed ample rations of fairy tales, is that one's parents are not one's real parents but instead that one is much higher born—and is probably, as will surely one day be revealed, a prince or princess. My fantasy, taken up in early adolescence and not quite dropped to this day, is that I can roam freely from social class to social class, comfortable everywhere and everywhere welcome. Sometimes I think it would be more realistic to believe that one is the last of the Romanovs.

Not that I am a proletarian-fancier, the American equivalent of a Narodnik or a Slavophile. There is something inherently condescending in assigning special qualities to the lower class. Dorothy Parker, after being told that Clare Boothe Luce was always kind to her inferiors, is supposed to have asked, "And where does she find them?" But I like to view myself as being able to slip from class to class because I detest the notion of one's destiny being absolutely determined by birth and social upbringing; I readily grant the importance of both but not their decisiveness. I myself dislike being labeled too easily, being understood too quickly. Neither a strict Marxist nor a straight Freudian be—such is the advice of this old Polonius; accept the possibility of all influences, reject the fiats of all absolute determinism.

The old, received wisdom about social class is that one is

supposed to dislike the class just below one's own and gaze
yearningly upon those above one's own. But I find that the
only class whose members can sometimes get me worked up
are the upper classes, or what is left of them after taxes and the
Zeitgeist have done their work. A plummy upper-class English
accent with nothing behind it but enormous self-satisfaction
can, in the proper mood, still bring out the residual Red in me.
My Anglophilia, which may have had behind it a certain social-
class longing, seems to have slipped badly in recent years;
today, apart from being somewhat regretful about not having
gone to an Oxbridge college when a boy, I have only one
regret about not being English, which is that, because I am not,
I cannot be permitted to use the word "whilst" without seeming affected. The upper class of my own country now seems
to me, when it is not sad, mostly comic. The traditional
WASP-ocracy seems to have left the field without firing a shot;
they resemble nothing so much as white Russians, with the
serious proviso that they appear to have been forced into exile
without actually leaving their own country. One reads about
them nowadays at play in Newport or in Charleston, or in
repose at the Somerset Club in Boston, or sees them decked out
for a photographer from *Town & Country*, but they seem
rather desiccated and plain tuckered out.

It is a bit difficult to have a serious class system when, as
in this country at present, you don't have a convincing upper
class. So long as there is a convincing upper class, other classes
in the society at least know what to imitate, however absurd
the imitation. I can attest to this when I recall that, in 1950, as
a boy of thirteen growing up in a middle-class, mostly Jewish
neighborhood, I and several of my pals attended a class in
ballroom dancing called "Fortnightly." It was held at the field
house of a public park, was taught by a couple of very correct
posture and general deportment whom I now think would be

best described as "shabby genteel," and, despite the name Fortnightly, met every Saturday afternoon. What we did in this class was, in effect, prepare for a cotillion none of us would ever attend. Young ladies sat on one side of the room, young gentlemen on the other; young gentlemen crossed the room to ask young ladies to dance, and to dance waltzes, foxtrots, and other, rather intricate dances and steps that this young gentleman, aging fast, has still never had to press into service.

The decisive moment in the defeat of upper-class, capital-S Society may have come when, in newspapers all over the nation, what used to be called the Society page was replaced by the Style section. The old Society page, with its accounts of engagements and weddings, charity balls and coming out parties, tended to be boring and silly; while the new Style section, with its accounts of designer clothing, gourmandizing, and the trend of the moment, tends to be lively and silly. The Society page, like Society itself, began to go under sometime in the middle 1960s, which was not exactly a felicitous time for establishments of many kinds. Not that the sixties did away with class consciousness; it attempted instead to reorient such consciousness in favor of other classes. The animus of the sixties generation, expressed in its popular culture, was against both upper- and middle-class life. In their place it wished to substitute ethnic pride and, as expressed by such groups as the Beatles and the Rolling Stones, something of a working-class ethos, with sexual freedom and drug use added. Even in England, that most traditional of class-bound countries, according to the English journalist Jilly Cooper, "working-class became beautiful and everyone from Princess Anne downwards spat the plums out of their mouths, embraced the flat 'a' and talked with a working-class accent."

Not many people outside of it are likely to have been sorry to see the old upper class in this country pushed rudely to the sidelines. The upper class had a lot to apologize for, and in many ways it is still apologizing. In wealthy Fairfield County, Connecticut, in the town of Darien (the setting for Laura Hobson's novel about genteel anti-Semitism, *Gentleman's Agreement*), a local newspaper, according to the *New York Times*, ran an article by a high-school girl attacking the town for its lack of social diversity. "I am," this girl wrote, "a white Protestant living in a basically white Protestant community. I lack the richness and cultural background gained from a diversified environment. What are you, the townspeople, going to do about it?" Few things so lower the morale, and raise the gorge, as being lectured to by one's own children. One of these things may be being lectured to on the same grounds by the clergymen of one's church, and no church in America has gone at this task more relentlessly than the Episcopalian Church, once *the* church of the old upper classes if there is truth in the one-sentence sociology of religion that holds: A Methodist is a Baptist with shoes, a Presbyterian is a Methodist who has gone to college, and an Episcopalian is a Presbyterian living off his investments.

Although much that was once thought to represent upper-class life appears to have been routed, much more lives on, often in attenuated and snobbish form. Contemned the old upper class may be, yet the line of people hopefully awaiting their children's enrollment in such formerly exclusively upper-class prep schools as Choate, Groton, Exeter, and St. Paul's has not, my guess is, in any serious way diminished. Most middle-class students who have a wide choice will tend to choose universities favored by the old upper classes; and most university professors, given a similar choice in institutions, will do the same—a tenured professor who has left Princeton for Purdue, or Harvard for Hofstra, or Yale for Ypsilanti Community College is a fit candidate for the now defunct television show called "That's Incredible."

Freud said that it was better to be an ancestor, which he turns out to have been, than to have ancestors, which he lacked. But surely better still is both to be an ancestor and to have ancestors. In literary life I can think of at least three living writers whose careers owe more than a little to upper-class cachet: Gore Vidal, who at every opportunity brings his family connections into his writing; William F. Buckley, who attempts to live like an aristocrat, though without much in the way of aristocratic leisure; and George Plimpton, whose many autobiographical books on the subject of sports have about them something of the aura of slumming. (I do not count Louis Auchincloss, a novelist whose subject is often the eclipse of the upper class in which he grew up.) All three men are, in accent, neither chummy nor unplummy.

If he were still alive, I should most certainly count in Robert Lowell, whose ancestors were reputed to speak only to the Cabots, who themselves spoke only to God and who, before his death, was generally conceded to be this country's first poet. Without for a moment claiming that Lowell set out to exploit his upper-class genealogy, neither can one for another moment disclaim the importance of that genealogy to Lowell's poetry. Elizabeth Bishop once told Lowell: "All you have to do is put down the names! And the fact that it seems significant, illustrative, American, etc., gives you, I think, the confidence you display about tackling any idea or theme, *seriously*, in both writing and conversation. In some ways you are the luckiest poet I know." Was Elizabeth Bishop correct? Let us change some of those names she claimed Lowell had only to mention. What if Lowell's poem "My Last Afternoon with Uncle Devereux Winslow" were instead entitled "My Last

Afternoon with Uncle Morris Shapiro," or his "Terminal Days at Beverly Farms" were instead entitled "Terminal Days at Grossinger's"? (Actually, given that resort's famously rich provender, any day at Grossinger's could be terminal.) Not quite the same, perhaps you will agree.

But then neither is anti-Semitism in the United States quite the same as it once was, or else I could not make the kind of easy joke that I just did about the titles of Robert Lowell's poems, at least not in print. Whether anti-Semitism is today less, whether racism has greatly diminished, cannot be known with certainty; my sense is that they both are much reduced. But what can be known is that neither is any longer officially recognized in restricted or segregated arrangements, and this, along with marking impressive progress, has made for significant changes in the American class system. Whereas the retreat of the old upper class has blown the roof off the system, the demise of official and quasi-official discrimination has uprooted the basement. The metaphor I seem to be building toward here is a class system that resembles an open-air ranch house.

Strange edifice, this, but then socially many strange things appear to have taken place in recent years. In many industries union wages have placed many union workers, financially at least, into the upper reaches of the middle class, while attending college, once the ultimate rite of passage into solid middle-class respectability, no longer inevitably accomplishes this task —owing doubtless to the spread and watering down of higher education. There is a great deal of senseless and haphazard luxury in the land. Athletes and rock stars, many of them made millionaires before they are thirty, are removed from the financial wars for all their days. Meanwhile a servant class has all but disappeared. A daughter of the working class uses part of her wages from working at the supermarket to buy designer jeans, while a son of Scarsdale comes into Manhattan to acquire his duds at a Salvation Army thrift shop. The other day, in a parking lot near where I live, I noted a rather dingy Saab automobile, with an antenna for a telephone on its roof, an Oberlin College decal on its back window, and bumper stickers reading "National Computer Camp" and "I Support Greenpeace." Now there is a vehicle with a lot of class—and, symbolic of our time, a lot of class confusions.

If that car isn't owned by someone from what today passes for the upper-middle class, I'll buy you a salmon mousse and a manual on how your children can raise their SAT scores fully thirty points. "The upper-middle classes," writes Jilly Cooper, "are the most intelligent and highly educated of all the classes, and therefore the silliest and most sensitive to every new trend: radical chic, health food, ethnic clothes, bra-lessness, gifted children, French cooking." The members of the upper-middle class that Miss Cooper has in mind are mostly newly risen and, not always sure where they are, insecure about where they are headed. This upper-middle class is not to be confused with the nouveau riche. The former tends to be rather better educated, immensely concerned with what it understands to be good taste, and serious if also a little worried about culture—very little that one could think of, in fact, would be more wounding to members of this upper-middle class than to be taken for nouveau riche. I think I know what I am talking about here; this upper-middle class is my milieu—or, as the writer Josephine Herbst used to call it, my "maloo."

When I say that the upper-middle class is my maloo, I do not mean that I am quite of that class. Strictly speaking, I am fairly sure that I do not qualify financially. I do not drive a BMW, a Mercedes, or a Jaguar; I do not dream of driving such cars, and if I leave the earth without owning one or the other of them, I shall not, for that reason, die with a frown on my face (I cannot otherwise promise to depart smiling). I own no works of art, nor do I aspire to own anything above the level of an unnumbered print. No espresso machine sits on the counter of my kitchen, no mousse molds sit upon the shelves of my cabinets. From the tax standpoint, I do not earn enough money now, nor do I soon expect to earn enough, to cry out, in the words of the rock 'n roll song, "Gimme shelter." Do not get me wrong. I should not in the least mind driving off in a Mercedes 380 SL, a Turner watercolor locked in its trunk, on my way to have a cappuccino with my tax lawyer. But my mind, that great wanderer, does not linger long on such things. Expensive good taste, that sine qua non of the new upper-middle class, is not my sine qua non. I do not despise it; I am not in the least uncomfortable around it; but I do not live for it.

What, then, do I live for? Apart from love for my family and friends, I live for words. I live for the delights of talking and reading and writing. I am content when talking with people I adore or admire or at least feel I can learn a little something from; I am happy when I am reading something fine or subtle or powerful; and I am delirious when I am writing something of which I am not altogether ashamed. If one's social class is defined, at least in part, by one's wishes, then I ought perhaps to be defined as a member of what I think of as the verbal class—someone, that is, who both earns his livelihood and derives his greatest pleasure from words. Membership in the verbal class has its advantages and its disadvantages: the hours are a bit crazy, but, like the village idiot posted at the town gates to await the arrival of the messiah, at least you are never out of work.

The term "verbal class" is meant to be almost purely descriptive; nothing, certainly, honorific is intended by it. Orwell, who did not use the term "verbal class," did once refer to "the new aristocracy" of professors, publicists, and journalists who in large part comprise the verbal class; he did so in the portion of *1984* that purports to be from Emmanuel Goldstein's manuscript, where this new aristocracy is described as "less tempted by luxury, hungrier for pure power" than their opposite numbers in past ages. In Chekhov's time, the verbal class of our day and the new aristocracy of *1984* would have been described as the intelligentsia. This is the same intelligentsia of whom Chekhov, in a letter to a friend, writes: "I have no faith in our intelligentsia; it is hypocritical, dishonest, hysterical, ill-bred, and lazy." Which made them, in Chekhov's view, quite as wretched as any other social class, though perhaps a bit worse because the pretensions of the intelligentsia were more extravagant and its complaints better formulated and more insistently expressed. Read Chekhov and, in questions of social class, one soon becomes a Chekhovian. "I have faith in individuals," he wrote. "I see salvation in individuals scattered here and there . . . be they intellectuals or peasants, for they're the ones who really matter, though they are few."

Yet my sense is that the verbal class has risen slightly in recent years. It has not done so, near as I can make out, because of any improvement in its members' general mental acuity or civic valor. The verbal class appears instead to be rising by default. Members of the verbal class, odd fish that they are, seem able to swim easily through a fluid social scene—and the American social scene at present seems extremely fluid. John Adams spoke of his studying "politics and war that my sons may have the liberty to study mathematics and philosophy," but what would he have thought of men who studied real estate and the stock market that their daughters may have the liberty to study Marxist historiography and their sons become, through downward mobility, carpenters in Vancouver? He would probably think his wife Abigail very clever for describing the American people as "the mobility."

"Classless Soviet Is Far Off, Siberian Scholar Says." So not long ago read a headline in the *New York Times*. It is difficult to doubt such authority, for surely one of the quickest ways of telling that a classless society is far off is merely to live in Siberia. My guess is that a classless society is roughly as near completion in the Soviet Union as it is in the United States—which isn't very near at all. Not that this even remotely suggests the need for intensifying the class struggle. Take it from a member of the verbal class, in a real class struggle one is lucky to end up with a draw, except that it inevitably turns out to have been a very bloody draw.

I see the serious class struggle as that of men and women singly fighting off being entirely shaped by the social class into which they were born. Insularity, unimaginativeness, self-satisfaction—each social class has its own special drawbacks, blindnesses, vices. "Vices" reminds me of a story a friend of mine, a man born into the English working class, used to tell about a shop class he was required to take at a grammar school in London. It was taught by a flinty little Scotsman who, when he wanted the class's attention in order to make an announcement, used to cry out, "Stand by your vices, boys!" When we think too exclusively as members of our social class, we all, essentially, stand by our vices. I should have thought the trick of becoming a human being is to stand away from them.

Tea and Antipathy

I MAGINE MY CHAGRIN at learning, as I not long ago did, that a writer whom I rather blithely despised for what I take to be his fraudulent self-righteousness and utterly self-assured hypocrisy, had cancer. Until then I had so enjoyed loathing him, my distaste for everything about him had seemed so complete, so pure, so uncomplicatedly pleasant, and now it was incomplete, alloyed by his misfortune, complicated by my own sympathy for his illness. This was a real setback. I had counted on being able to continue disliking him for another decade or two. It was as if someone had removed a wall against which I had happily grown accustomed to banging my head.

"You know," I explained to a very dear friend, "while I dislike quite a few people, I do not really wish them to undergo physical pain and certainly not death." "I understand," she said, "you merely wish those you despise to feel more stress." That was it precisely. More stress is exactly what I wished for those whom I consider my enemies. By stress I mean I wish that their children will grow up to dislike them; I wish them trouble with the IRS, sharp reductions in the status that is so vital to their well-being, perhaps a bit of public humiliation—all the little things that cause, as my friend so delicately put it, "more stress."

I suppose this makes me a pretty good but not a great hater. I should rather not be a hater at all, of course. I respect people who struggle against permitting themselves the indulgence of hating. It is much grander, I realize, to be above such mean feelings. Lofty amusement leading on to generalizations about the flaws in human nature seems to me a finer response to people whom one finds repugnant. How much better to accept people as we find them! Yet I find that to love one's neighbor often involves an effort of will, whereas to hate one's enemy seems to come so naturally. What does not come naturally to me is ready forgiveness for injuries suffered. On those occasions when I have made an earnest attempt to turn the other cheek, in that other cheek I have inevitably discovered my tongue inserted. Hating exacts such a strong feeling that it can be a serious distraction; indulged in a concentrated way, it can even diminish one's own high opinion of oneself. Hating can skew the judgment, furrow the brow, take the bloom off one's complexion. Getting one's knickers in a twist, as the English used to call being in an agitated state, tends to remove the crease from one's trousers. It ain't, kiddo, good.

I have never been fond of the prospect of myself hating someone, and early in life I tried my best to avoid doing so. Like everyone else, I encountered people I did not like. Usually I was able to register my distaste for their selfishness or their cruelty or their crudity and then avoid them whenever possible; as with sand traps and water holes on a golf course, I shot around them and played on through. But all this changed when, in my late twenties, I became enmeshed in intellectual life. Something there is about the nature of intellectual life that seems to encourage rivalrous and rancorous feelings. Edward Shils, a thinker who does not fall back regularly on psychological labels, has said that paranoia is the reigning psychological condition of the intellectual, and I believe he is absolutely correct. Anyone who has worked among scholars knows that, in the humanities and social sciences, there is no academic subject, from numismatics on up, that does not have its politics, and these politics can sometimes be internecine. Such politics do not discourage paranoia. "Even paranoids have real enemies," famously said Delmore Schwartz, who was himself certifiably paranoid. Not every intellectual is a paranoid, but I have yet to meet one who did not claim to have real enemies. And this is especially so among literary intellectuals. "I don't know how it is in other professions," says a character in George Gissing's *New Grub Street*, "but I hope there is less envy, hatred and malice than in this of ours."

In intellectual life sticks and stones are not thrown, but well-aimed words can pierce the skin. By now the intellectual insult has acquired nearly the status of a genre. It has been going on long enough for Penguin Books to bring out not one but two collections of famous literary insults. Pride of place in this line perhaps ought to go to Alexander Pope, who in *The Dunciad* set down 1,670 ten-syllable lines, not a false rhyme among them, blasting away at his contemporaries for "dullness," a comprehensive term Pope meant to include shoddy reasoning, bad taste, and general stupidity. Much of the time Pope felt he was returning insult for injury; and no target was too minor for him to knock off, for, as he put it, "It would vex one more to be knocked on the head with a piss-pot than by a thunderbolt."

William Hazlitt—"pimpl'd Hazlitt" to his enemies—is another English writer who gave rather better than he got. Perhaps it is more accurate to say, when he got, he gored, for he had a lovely knack of combining fury with precise formulation, with which he could rip an opponent wide open. When Hazlitt's book on Shakespeare was attacked by William Gifford, the editor of the *Quarterly Review*, Hazlitt replied in a forty-

page "Letter to William Gifford, Esquire," in which he described the *Quarterly Review* as the "receptacle for the scum
and sediment of all the prejudice, bigotry, ill-will, ignorance,
and rancour afloat in the kingdom." The Goncourt brothers
made a specialty of dining out in Paris and returning home to
put down—in both senses of the phrase—the behavior of their
dinner companions in their famous journal. Chekhov claimed
to be "physically repelled by abuse no matter at whom it is
aimed," and wondered why journalistic critics "write in a tone
fit for judging criminals rather than artists and writers." Yet
even Chekhov, for all his vaunted "gentle humanity," could be
savage when confronting a point of view or an intellectual
position he thought spurious.

In our day some of the most vicious insults seem to have
been made by the intellectuals gathered around the magazine
Partisan Review. Their best shots were all fired behind one
another's backs in the form of comments that somehow always
found their way to their targets. The paranoia of Delmore
Schwartz, who was an associate editor of *Partisan Review*, was
in this sense planted in fertile soil. Schwartz himself is supposed to have said of Lionel Trilling that of course he was very
intelligent, but he wished Trilling didn't say even the most
obvious things in a tone of voice more appropriate for announcing a cure for cancer. Philip Rahv, one of the principal
editors of *Partisan Review*, was especially brutal at the behind-
the-back intellectual insult, and, when asked why he went in
for it with such vehemence, chalked it up to what he called
"analytical exuberance." In *The Truants*, William Barrett's
splendid memoir of the *Partisan Review* crowd, Barrett recalls
Delmore Schwartz remarking, " 'Analytic exuberance'—
Philip Rahv's euphemism for putting a knife in your back."
William Phillips, the magazine's other principal editor, used to
refer to Rahv's various wives and women friends as his "alter-

Iagos." Nobody escaped this kind of maiming remark. When some years ago I asked another member of the *Partisan Review* crowd how Harold Rosenberg (who was then still alive) was doing, he said, "You know Harold, still acquiring every expensive painting he can lay his hands on while waiting for Marxism to get its third wind." And they say words can't kill.

Do people say such horrendous things about me behind my back? In his essay "On The Pleasures of Hating," Hazlitt remarks, "I care little what any one says of me, particularly behind my back, and in the way of critical and analytical discussion: it is looks of dislike and scorn that I answer with the worst venom of my pen." I care rather more, but I suppose I must count myself lucky in having very few rough things that were said about me behind my back reported to me. When I was much younger I had a friend who used to say terrible things to my face, and then go and praise me behind my back —a strange reversal of normal procedure. Such insults made about me behind my back that have been reported to me have tended not to be well formulated but merely sincere expressions of heartfelt hatred. No one thus far has thought to say of me, "He writes very nicely. Do you suppose English is his first language?" Or: "He appears to have such confidence in his views. Looking at him, and given those views, I cannot for the life of me imagine whence this confidence derives."

I have been called some charming things in print, among them a "cultural terrorist" and a "Stalinist." I was once called a "racist" for writing that my own children, before they had developed table manners, ate like Apaches. A vastly overheated third-line literary critic once led off an essay about me and two other writers who share some of my views with an epigraph from Hemingway that made reference to "yellow bastards." On more than one occasion people have asked, publicly, that I be fired from my job. In every one of these instances I believe

I understood the motives behind such behavior, but for me, I am sorry to report, to understand all is not to pardon all. I shall doubtless forget many of these insults, yet I have not truly forgiven any that I can remember. *Dieu les pardonnera,* to paraphrase Heine. *C'est son métier.*

I prefer not to meet the people I dislike. Perhaps this is because, being an intellectual, I tend to dislike them for their ideas, and to discover, upon meeting them, the ideas made flesh can be disconcerting. One is likely to discover some quality in them, even some defect, that curbs one's distaste. I not long ago attended a conference at which I met an editor whose magazine encourages just about everything I find lamentable in public life. If the ideas promoted in his magazine were to win through, this country would become an exceedingly unpleasant place for me. At a session of the conference at which I spoke I had no trepidation about attacking these ideas. But at the break for lunch I found myself walking ten or fifteen yards behind this editor, from which perspective I noticed that he had bad feet. He walked funnily; he wore special shoes; he lived with real discomfort, possibly persistent pain; he became more human for me. I could no longer dislike him with the same cheerful gusto. Making enemies is easy, William Dean Howells once noted, but keeping them is not.

I am reminded of a letter George Orwell wrote to Stephen Spender in which he explains how he had once been able to attack Spender but had changed his mind after meeting him. Orwell tells Spender that he regarded him as a poet whose verse meant very little to him as well as a Communist sympathizer—the letter was written in 1938—to whose views Orwell himself was hostile. He was able to think of Spender, as he puts it, "as a type & also an abstraction. Even if when I met you I had not happened to like you, I should still have been bound to change my attitude, because when you meet anyone in the flesh you realise immediately that he is a human being & not a sort of caricature embodying certain ideas." Orwell concludes: "It is partly for this reason that I don't mix much in literary circles, because I know from experience that once I have met & spoken to anyone I shall never again be able to show any intellectual brutality towards him, even when I feel I ought to."

Since reading that letter many years ago, I have had a few opportunities to meet Stephen Spender, but have gone a bit out of my way to avoid doing so. I have never treated him to the intellectual brutality that Orwell speaks about, yet the fact is that I prefer to hang on to my strong dislike of his writing, and do not wish to jeopardize it through personal encounter. I prefer to keep the possibility of intellectual brutality in reserve, for I find I cannot meet someone, pretend to like him, and then attack him in print—I cannot do so, that is, without a strong sense of acting hypocritically. On the other hand, I note a number of people who have not allowed personal meetings with me to keep them from treating me with intellectual brutality afterwards. (Can it be that my personal charm is not quite foolproof?) On the third hand—we complicated thinkers sometimes require four or five hands to make our point—I greatly admire those few writers I know who can go on the attack, or take an attack, no holds barred, and have drinks afterwards with the very people with whom they have just engaged in intellectual combat. Such writers seem to be able to hate certain intellectual positions without hating the people who hold them—to hate, that is, the sin but not the sinner.

Nature, remarks Hazlitt, seems "made up of antipathies: without something to hate, we should lose the very spring of thought and action." Hating, it is discouraging to report, may be more interesting than loving. Certainly the range of emotions associated with hatred is much greater than that associated with love, and its language is correspondingly richer. Indignation, rage, scorn, disgust, loathing, fury, vengeance, grudge, contempt, jealousy, contumely, malice, wrath, embitterment, and let us not forget our old friend *schadenfreude*—now here is a vocabulary a fellow can work with. Think of the writers who, were it not for hating, would be out of business. Swift comes immediately to mind, for all strong satire begins in hatred. Dostoyevski hated in the name of Christianity. Strindberg and Ibsen blew a cold wind of hatred down from the north. None of these, I must confess, is among my favorite authors. But other authors whom I adore hated, so to speak, selectively. The English critic D. W. Harding wrote an essay on Jane Austen entitled "Regulated Hatred," in which he argues that Jane Austen had very mixed feelings about the society in which she lived. Dickens believed in evil and despised it wherever he described it. Max Beerbohm, who once said that anger was "a rare feeling for me," nonetheless deeply disliked, if he did not actively despise, George Bernard Shaw. And Karl Kraus, whose satirical lashings appeared in his own Viennese journal *Die Fackel*, to which he eventually became the sole contributor, said, "I no longer have any collaborators. I used to be envious of them. They repel those readers whom I want to lose myself."

Things worth hating in the world are never in short supply: hypocrisy, cowardice, cruelty, disloyalty. Then there are world-class villains, among whom Stalin and Hitler remain permanently hateful. Hatred between nations is far from scarce: the Greeks hate the Turks, the Koreans hate the Japanese, the Irish hate the English, and there is no love lost between the Pakistanis and the Indians. Nirad C. Chaudhuri, the gifted Indian writer, has written about what he calls "the real East-West conflict," the hatred of the Third World for the West, which, "arising from historical experience, has bitten into the subconscious to become a self-propagating emotion capable of discovering ever new grievances to feed itself." Chaudhuri wrote that in 1957, and I should like to show anyone who believes that things have improved since that time some choice real estate in downtown Managua.

Politics provides the clearest channel for hatred. Tell me your politics and I shall tell you whom you despise: Qaddafi or Botha, Arafat (Yasir, that's my baby) or Pinochet. Yet impersonal hatred is sometimes difficult to sustain. The larger the object of hatred, the less concentrated the emotion one can bring to it. There are of course men and women who can hate entire peoples. Anti-Semites are an ugly example. ("He who hates the Jews," Eugen Weber has written, "hates mankind.") But I know a woman, a Polish Jew from Lodz who was in Auschwitz, who not only hates the Germans but also hates the Poles; and, when the Russians were bearing down on the Poles during the rise of Solidarity, I recall her remarking that, remembering how cruel the Poles were to the Jews during the Nazi era, she could feel no sympathy for them now as victims of the Russians. Yet her hatred was not impersonal—far from it. There are hatreds one doesn't approve but has to respect.

Easily the most hated American political figures of my lifetime have been Franklin Delano Roosevelt and Richard Nixon. I was seven years old when Roosevelt died, and never felt any special animosity toward him, then or since. To this day, though, I run into old-line Republicans whose fuse goes off at the mere mention of his initials. Nixon, for me, was a different story. As a youthful reader of *The New Republic*— weekly strolling, as S. J. Perelman once put it, down "the *couloirs* of the House and Senate, aghast at legislative folly"— I early decided that Richard Nixon was the villain of villains. (I am now a middle-aged reader of *The New Republic*, but one who, as my next paragraph will make plain, appears to have run out of aghast.) Nixon's political victories left me sullen, his setbacks brought me a refreshed belief in the progress of humankind. I detested him deeply and comprehensively.

When Richard Nixon lost the gubernatorial race in California in 1962, I greeted the news in the manner in which the Hasidim greet the Jewish holiday known as Simchas Torah—with dancing in the streets. After he announced his retirement form politics, however, telling journalists assembled for a news conference that they would no longer have Dick Nixon to kick around, I became nervous. Without Richard Nixon to despise, what would I now do with my spare time? As history shows, I need not have worried. Another decade of reverse ecstasy awaited me. Yet at Richard Nixon's greatest defeat, Watergate, I discovered that, somehow, my scorn had flown, my fury had grown flaccid. The events surrounding Watergate brought other Nixon haters paroxysms of pleasure; one sensed that, during the Watergate hearings, they could scarcely wait to pop out of bed in the mornings to watch these hearings on television and, baby, let the good times roll. I found I could not join them. I should have felt the delight associated with consummation, but instead felt only sadness. Unrequited love may be a bore, but hatred, I suspect, may never allow for a satisfying conclusion.

Richard Nixon is a man who did not wish to be hated, but more interesting to me are those people who do not seem to care whether they are hated or not. Some among them seem not merely unconcerned about having enemies but appear actively to seek them out, and usually have no difficulty in finding them. F. R. Leavis was evidently such a man. Always kind to his students, he could be crushing to colleagues or to anyone else who didn't agree with his views. Simon Gray, the playwright, who was a student of Leavis's at Cambridge, has recalled another of his teachers asking him what he thought of

Leavis. Gray reports: " 'Yes,' he said fretfully, when I'd nearly got into my stride, 'I do wish he'd hurry up and die.' " Yvor Winters, the American poet and critic, lived out his days in roughly the same combative condition as F. R. Leavis. In an essay about his friend the poet J. V. Cunningham, Winters wrote about "the doctrine of hatred, or anger," arguing that "it is no accident that so many great writers have sooner or later retreated from society," from which they feel excluded. Hating and being the object of hatred is not the gentlest way to live, a fact that Winters knew well enough to write a lovely poem on the subject entitled "Hymn to Dispel Hatred at Midnight," whose final lines run:

> Hence unto God, unsought,
> My anguish sets. Oh, vain
> The heart that hates! Oh, naught
>   So drenched in pain!
> Grief will not turn again.

Although Leavis and Winters clearly had what used to be called "a natural cussedness," it is more important to note that both men lived against the intellectual spirit of their times. So, too, did William Hazlitt and Karl Kraus live against the spirits of their respective times. To say no, to go against the flow, is a most efficient way to accumulate enemies. I fancy myself a man who in some respects sails against the Zeitgeist, yet I do not fancy myself someone who hungers for intellectual combat or derives real delight from having enemies (though I do have a few enemies that I am rather proud of). When I used to get a piece of hate mail, or find myself saying something that I knew would bring me the enmity of other people in the room, it would cause my stomach to churn. Nothing much for it, however. An intellectual is finally the sum of his opinions, especially if these opinions add up to a point of view; and he cannot change them to suit the company he happens to be with at the moment. But I had better stop before I begin to sound like Lillian Hellman in trousers.

Bandying about a variety of strongly held opinions may in some ways influence people, but it is not the surest way to make friends. Where possible I try to keep my own opinions in check. Difficulties arise when others come forth with confidently put opinions opposed to my own. Along with reflexes, muscle tone, and a few other items, tact departs with age; and in such situations I find it increasingly difficult to hold back from saying precisely what I think. I was not long ago in the company of an editor of a journal of opinion who was in the habit of using such introductory phrases to his sentences as "On balance" or "To be fair," after which usually followed statements that were neither particularly balanced nor fair. I found I could not resist pointing out to him his little tic of using falsely impartial phrases, and thereby made, I feel confident, another lifelong friend.

Certain subjects make for natural enmity and can turn polite society into impolite society—fast. If one is looking to save on fuel bills, politics is likely to heat up a room quicker than just about anything else. In certain circles, the subject of educational reform will turn the trick. In recent years, discussion of the women's movement can be depended upon to send the thermostat up thirty or so degrees. (In Barbara Pym's novel *Some Tame Gazelle*, I find this lovely line: " 'I shall never understand women,' said Dr. Parnell complacently.") Similarly, certain names have acquired a built-in explosive quality. In this connection, the name of Henry Kissinger is an almost foolproof land mine. In intellectual quarters mention of the name of Norman Podhoretz, Susan Sontag, or George Steiner is guaranteed to get the conversation off small talk. When he was alive the conductor Georg Szell, famous for his autocratic behavior, could inflame anyone he worked with. Once, when Szell stormed out of the Metropolitan Opera, someone said that he was his own worst enemy. To which Rudolf Bing responded, "Not while I'm alive." But one doesn't have to be alive for one's name to continue carrying the power to raise blood pressure. I was seated some years ago at a dinner with nine people, most of us strangers to one another, when someone brought up the name Robert Hutchins. A mild-looking, bespectacled man queried gently, "May I ask, is there anyone at this table who is Robert Hutchins's son-in-law or niece or anything of that sort?" When no one allowed having any such relation to Hutchins, the man leaned in and hissed, "I hate everything about that s.o.b."

A distinguished university president, upon retiring from his job, is said to have remarked about the people with whom he worked, "I don't hate anyone, but I must admit that I despise a great many people." That very precise formulation reminds me that I have been using the word *hate* in rather a baggy-pants fashion—that is, so loosely that almost any unpleasant feelings can be fit into it. Yet the range of distaste of a healthy hater is vast, subtle, and topographically intricate. It is, for instance, perfectly possible to like someone without in the least respecting him, and just as possible to respect enormously someone one doesn't in the least like. Then there is that rather ample body of people whom one neither likes nor respects but who do not come near qualifying for one's hatred. The university president is correct; one can despise a person for acts of cowardice or duplicity or shameless self-promotion —I restrict myself to standard despicable academic behavior— without hating him. Despising is much to be preferred; hating takes up too much psychic energy.

Many other things in life are not worth despising but instead simply tick one off. Some among them are obvious: ineffi-

ciency, incompetence in high places, empty language, vandal-
ism, waste, and so forth. Where things that tick one off become
interesting, though, is where the rational gives way to the
quirky and the quirky to the slightly mad. In one of the essays
in *The Crack-Up*, F. Scott Fitzgerald drew up a list of things
that, during a bad time in his life, he could not bear: "I couldn't
stand the sight of Celts, English, Politicians, Strangers, Vir-
ginians, Negroes (light or dark), Hunting People, and middlemen in general, all writers (I avoided writers very carefully
because they can perpetuate trouble as no one else can)—and
all the classes as classes and most of them as members of their
class." Even for someone in the throes of a nervous breakdown,
that is an impressively comprehensive list of antipathies. I have
never put together such a list of my own, but if I did, one of
the items on it would be people who make too great a fuss
about the stylishness of F. Scott Fitzgerald.

Unlike Fitzgerald's antipathies, which tend to fall into categories, my own are almost exclusively particular. Too fancily
cut beards, for example, will set me off, but so will unkempt
ones. I was not long ago pleased to see this antipathy shared
by the late George Balanchine, who noted that beards, which
were authentic in his father's generation, today are the essence
of stylelessness: "All right, somebody wants to look like Christ,
you know—the hair and all. But it's silly, it looks silly on
people. It's all a fake." Vanity license plates on cars can get me
worked up. And people who have installed telephones in their
cars "tick me to the max," as the kids say nowadays. When, in
my own car, I see someone driving alongside me talking into
a car telephone, it is all I can do to refrain from asking him if
he would mind terribly calling my wife to tell her that I shall
be late for dinner.

Parents who express their own pitiful yearnings for elegance and give their children a poor start in life by awarding

them pretentious names—Ashley or Brandon, Fairfax or Tiffany—seem to me blinkin' awful. Although it is probably the sheerest economic jealousy on my part, it lifts my spirits to discover that someone driving a Rolls Royce looks sad. In traffic I never give such people a break; nor do I give a break to people who drive Cadillacs, Mercedeses, Jaguars, or BMWs; I figure that they have already had their breaks in life. I secretly hope that people who militantly pursue culture never find it. All the world loves a winner, it is said, but I find myself regularly pulling against too-consistent winners: the Boston Celtics in basketball, the Los Angeles Dodgers in baseball, the Dallas Cowboys in football. Such is the complexity of these matters that I sometimes find my antipathies deeply divided: when, for example, Gore Vidal and Norman Mailer argue, or Barbara Walters interviews Lauren Bacall, or General Westmoreland sues Mike Wallace and CBS. As you can see, a man with strong antipathies is seldom bored.

Shared antipathies can sometimes be the basis for friendship, especially when the antipathies give one the feeling of belonging to a select minority. This has happened to me on more than one occasion. Living in the South in the late 1950s and early 1960s, I found myself falling in with a social set whose single defining characteristic was its strong anti-segregationist sentiment. More recently, as a contemner of much of the new literary criticism and social theory now rampantly fashionable in universities, I have found myself warming immediately to those who share my strong views. "Of course, I loathe all that garbage," said a young teacher, a new acquaintance, over a Chinese lunch. Here was a sentence that added great flavor to my Mongolian beef and tea. Tea and sympathy is nice, but tea and shared antipathy is even better. But behind shared antipathies even greater sympathies must lie.

When antipathy replaces what was once sympathy, sadness

results. The hatred for each other of parties to a divorce is perhaps the most obvious example. "Of all the objects of hatred," wrote Max Beerbohm in *Zuleika Dobson*, "a woman once loved is the most hateful." One has first truly to have loved another person to be able to hate him or her in the way that divorcing couples are often able to hate each other. In a divorce all the weapons for effective hatred are nicely in place: knowledge of each other's desires, fears, and unpleasant little secrets, all of which can be brought into play for vengeance or betrayal. At a lower level of intensity are friendships that have been sharply broken off or have been allowed to go sour. When this occurs the chain of emotion runs, or at least it has in my experience, from anger, to sadness, to regret, to antipathy, to apathy, to cold indifference, to no longer giving a damn. I recently learned that a former friend was to undergo a divorce in a marriage that was crucial to him; and what I felt at learning this sad fact was—almost nothing at all. Even *schadenfreude*, the malicious enjoyment of another's misfortune, would have been preferable. In some situations hatred seems much more human than simple indifference.

In half a century of middle-class living, I believe I have felt a fairly full range of the feelings, grand and petty, that are usually subsumed under the category of hatred. I have felt jealousy, envy, and rage; I have felt petulance, distaste, and irrational prejudice. But I do not believe that I have ever felt that emotional condition known as self-hatred. ("Why should he feel self-hatred," I can hear someone about whom I have written wounding things say as he reads that last sentence, "when my hatred for him is surely enough for both of us.") I have been angry with myself for committing foolish errors, ashamed of myself for insensitive behavior, disgusted at myself on those occasions when I have failed to meet other people's quite reasonable expectations for me—but sustained and pervasive hatred of myself, this I have come nowhere close to feeling. The conventional wisdom about self-hatred is that it is the hatred internalized by those people—minority groups, deviants, etc.—who feel themselves despised as outsiders in their own societies. Yet I wonder how true this is. I have known people with a talent for self-destruction; I have known people who were ashamed of their backgrounds; I have known people who have attempted suicide, but I am far from certain that any of them qualifies as a true self-hater. Then there are those people who seem to spew up so much hatred that one assumes that it must derive from a volcano of hatred for themselves. It would be gratifying if this were so, but I am not convinced that it is.

When I think of the strong haters I have known, the ugly, the really lethal haters, they have almost always been sorely disappointed people. Life, they somehow feel, has let them down. They are not where they want to be, not doing what they want to do. Things have gone awry, things are askew, all's wrong with the world—and everyone else is to blame. Their argument is with Fate, but they quarrel with you and me. Disappointment embitters, and embitterment sups comfortably with hatred.

Although I have said more than a few kind words for hating in this essay, I hope I do not qualify as a serious hater. I know I have not been disappointed by life—quite the contrary. As Philip Rahv assigned his propensity for poisonous remarks about his colleagues to analytic exuberance, so do I assign my manifold antipathies to what I prefer to think of as "nice discrimination." ("You are, sir," says Sydney Greenstreet to Humphrey Bogart in *The Maltese Falcon*, "a man of nice discrimination.") Sometimes I fear my discrimination has become too nice. Recently, for example, a friend offered to put forward my name for a club whose membership is made up of men who work in the arts, publishing, journalism, and government. Reading down the club's membership roll, I discovered that, among those whose names I knew, there were more members I disliked than liked—and thus I declined the generous offer to join this club. I believe this qualifies me as distinctly unclubbable, something I had never intended to become.

As I grow older, my guess is that my antipathies, dislikes, peeves, and prejudices (rational and irrational) will not grow fewer. Shall I gradually become a curmudgeon—am I one already?—and end my days as a full-blown crank? It is not, I confess, quite what I had in mind for my old age. Yet I must also confess that I have never worked so well until I learned what it was I detested in life. "Hate must make a person productive," Karl Kraus wrote, "otherwise one might as well love." And Chekhov has a character, in his story "Gooseberries," who exclaims, "I am old and not fit for the struggle; I am not even capable of hatred." For myself, it was only when I came to know what I hated that I came to love intensely those things that matter most to me in life. Hatred is finally only productive in the name of love. That, I recognize, comes near to being a paradox, which is unfortunate, because, as it happens, I hate paradoxes.

An Older Dude

FIVE-O. ROMAN NUMERAL L. Half a century. Five big ones, baby. I refer to my age. This year I turn fifty, with no hope of turning back. It is a bit of an amazement to me. Him Tarzan, me boy, or so I used to think, except that now I am decades older than the inarticulate ape-man himself and a good deal less agile even than Jane. I, a stripling, a mere lad, only yesterday a fine broth of a boy, shall soon have fifty winters under my belt. The evidence for my age is there. I look in the mirror and, like an actor in a long-running play, I know my lines; also my wrinkles, pouches, and circles. Recently, filling out a bureaucratic form, I was able to supply my birth date, height, weight, and eye color readily enough, but when asked the color of my hair I instinctively lifted my cap to let the clerk decide for herself on brown or gray. On a good day, when the light is right, I do not look a week over forty-eight, though where I live there are not that many good days. But enough of these little self-deceptions. I am fifty, and, realist that I am, I must now conclude that my life is at least a third over.

St. Augustine says that "we should not underestimate the significance of number, since in many passages of sacred scripture numbers have meaning for the conscientious interpreter." In my own life, I have paid little attention to the number of

my years. The supposedly great decade markers—twenty,
thirty, forty—whirred past, and I paid them no more heed than
as a boy I did to the Burma-Shave signs along the highway: I
noted them, smiled, and drove on. Owing perhaps to my having become a father fairly young—I had charge of four sons
by the age of twenty-six—I was unable to linger overlong on
the glories of youth, except in fantasy. I tended to be precocious in other, less important ways. Perhaps it was the era into
which I was born, but I never looked upon youth as an occupa-
tion or religion or social class. It was instead something one
enjoyed—if one was lucky—while passing through it.

"Act your age," mothers would say to their children when
I was a boy. "Be a man," fathers would exhort their sons. "Aw,
grow up," older sisters and teenage girl friends would exclaim.
In fact, growing up didn't seem like a bad idea. A goodly
number of grown-ups walked the streets in those days. Think
only of the movies. Edward G. Robinson, Humphrey Bogart,
Cary Grant, James Cagney—these were men who appeared on
screen in suits and ties, hats, black shoes. Grown-ups. Robert
Redford, Dustin Hoffman, Robert De Niro, Harrison Ford—
these are men who, at the same age as Robinson, Bogart, & Co.,
one thinks of as characteristically in jeans, sneakers or boots,
loose collars. Graduate students. One could make a similar
comparison of actresses. Compare Bette Davis and Jane Fonda,
Ingrid Bergman and Meryl Streep. All are fine actresses, but
the former are women, the latter girls who continue to grow
older. Nowadays there aren't so many grown-ups—just a lot
of older dudes. It is, apparently, what the culture calls for just
now. I happen to be writing this in a short-sleeve rugby shirt,
chino pants, and tasseled loafers. I'm an older dude myself.

Just as I have never been able to think of Hugh Hefner as
a playboy—he has always looked to me like an insurance salesman—so neither can I quite think of myself as an older dude,

all physical evidence to the contrary notwithstanding. Not that I wish to remain forever young. Unlike Philip Larkin, who once declared that not having to get mixed up with children more than compensated for having to start earning a living, I rather enjoyed my childhood and adolescence. But enough was enough. Becoming grown-up, with its promise of freedom, was always more alluring to me than anything youth could promise. The allure was there when I was very young. At the age of seven, at most eight, I used to watch a man named Sid Carter play softball in my neighborhood, and he represented, at least for me, some of the promise of growing up. Sid Carter must have been only in his early twenties, but from the perspective of age seven or eight that was plenty old. A marvelous athlete, he could hit a softball from Farwell Beach in Chicago roughly to Bessarabia. Tall, slender, tanned, his sandy-colored hair brushed straight back, he was dapper even in softball duds. In street clothes he was never less than perfectly turned out; elegance and flair came naturally to him. He drove a cream-colored Plymouth convertible. I recall thinking that, when I grew up, I, too, would own a convertible.

I never have. I suppose I never shall. My eldest son does, though. Not long ago he traded in his car for a high-powered British sports car. He called to report this to me, with what I sensed was a slight trepidation in his voice lest his square old man think him frivolous. "Dear boy," I said, "I'm glad that you have a sports car. I want you to have all the things I never had: sports cars, a beautiful Chinese girl friend, lots of foreign languages." If you sense some yearning here, you are probably correct. If you sense serious regret, you are mistaken. I shall muddle through all right if I never drive down the Pacific Highway, the top down on my Porsche, gently teasing the lovely Dai-yu in Persian. Yet growing older does remind one of all the things one is now unlikely to do, or have, or be. I believe I have come to grips with the distinct possibility that I will never be a United States senator, or own a horse in the Kentucky Derby, or write a novel as long and as good as Proust's. I can live with these deprivations. I don't want your pity.

What I would prefer is that you find a way to stop the clock from running. When one is young, one lives as if one had a thousand years to go. Once one hits fifty, as E. B. White, a considerable hypochondriac, once said, one feels one has about twenty minutes to live. One is humming the damn "September Song" all the time. In this morning's paper I read that Robert A. Comfort, one of the five men who robbed the Hotel Pierre in 1972, died at age fifty-three. Alexis de Tocqueville—Mr. T. himself—was taken out of the game at the same age. Philip Larkin, a man who seemed to have had the gift of perpetual middle age, while in his fifties (he died at sixty-three) once remarked: "If you assume you're going to live to be seventy, seven decades, and think of each decade as a day of the week, starting with Sunday, then I'm on Friday afternoon now. Rather a shock, isn't it?" It is. It also forces one to place a whole new interpretation on the notion of T.G.I.F.

As I turn fifty, it occurs to me that, unlike Tocqueville or Robert A. Comfort, I shall never write a great book or take part in an adventure such as a three-million-dollar heist. Neither shall I slam dunk a basketball nor publish a translation of Horace. Some of these things are technically possible—the robbery and the Latin translation—but more and more un- likely. I recently met a man who all his life wished to fly a plane; at sixty-four, upon his retirement, he learned to do so; and now, nearing seventy, he is about to fly solo to Europe. Impressive. I should love to learn to play the harpsichord, and with the injection of large sums of money in lessons and even larger sums of time given over to practice, my guess is that I could learn to play "Clair de lune" with a proficiency that, should a person with good manners be listening to me, would doubtless bring on in him a hemorrhage owing to violently suppressed laughter. But I am certain not to attempt to learn to play the harpsichord. There are too many other items on my agenda that are more pressing. Reaching the age of fifty may not confer wisdom—that honorary degree is given to few and never at commencement time—but it does allow one to understand rather better the poet Joseph Brodsky's remark that "every choice is essentially a flight from freedom."

The fact is that I am a man on a schedule. Some people are and some people aren't on a schedule, and the people who aren't are probably luckier. Those people who are on a schedule—who plan to be millionaires by the age of thirty, publish ten books by the age of forty, or hold serious economic or political power by the age of fifty—always hear the clock ticking, feel the light breeze caused by the turning of calendar pages, sense footsteps (whose?) following them. My own schedule is far from clear, though in some loose way I have always kept one. Its chief purpose appears to be to convince me that I am, inevitably, a bit behind. In college, not long after I somewhat inchoately decided I should like to become a writer, I met a classmate who, at the age of sixteen, had already published a short story in *New World Writing*, a magazine with a paperback book format that included among its contributors Federico García Lorca, William Carlos Williams, and Ignazio Silone. Not yet out of the starting gate, I already felt myself several furlongs off the pace. Henceforth I carefully noted the birth dates of published writers younger than I, and, while I did not wish them ill, I did hope they would slow down.

My classmate who published a story in *New World Writing* at sixteen has not, so far as I know, published anything since. What happened to him? Having opened so grandly, did he then draw bad cards: a fatal illness, an automobile accident, alcoholism? Or did he instead forego life lived on a schedule? Did he come across the advice of Lambert Strether? In Henry James's *The Ambassadors*, Lambert Strether tells the character little Bilham, "Live all you can; it's a mistake not to. It doesn't matter so much what you do in particular, so long as you have your life." When issuing that sound advice, Strether was fifty-five, or five years older than I—and Henry James, when putting the advice in Strether's mouth, was himself fifty-eight. Good advice though it is, is it available to one who is on a schedule? The question is, of course, one that occurred to Henry James—what serious question didn't?—for James himself was on a schedule, piling up book after book, so that in later years he wondered if he had allowed himself to live as fully as he might have done. As Strether goes on to tell little Bilham, "Still, one has the illusion of freedom; therefore don't be, like me, without the memory of that illusion. I was either, at the right time, too stupid or too intelligent to have it; I don't quite know which. Of course, at present, I'm a case of reaction against the mistake; and the voice of reaction should, no doubt, as always be taken with an allowance."

The only other American writer as good on the subject of middle age as Henry James is that great klutzy genius Theodore Dreiser. After Dreiser lost a decade of his writing life to a mental collapse and to regaining his confidence following the failure of *Sister Carrie,* he wrote like a man on a very strict if often confused schedule. Dreiser created the most powerful portraits of middle-aged men in American literature: Lester Kane in *Jennie Gerhardt,* Frank Cowperwood in the so-called *Trilogy of Desire,* and, most memorably, George Hurstwood in *Sister Carrie.* What is astonishing is that Dreiser created Hurstwood, the quintessence of the middle-aged man in crisis, while he, Dreiser, was still in his twenties. It was Dreiser who, in

Hurstwood, depicted the mid-life crisis fully seventy years before it became a cliché in the thick-fingered hands of the popular psychologists, thus confirming Freud's famous statement that psychology has most to learn from the poets.

I am pleased to report that I myself have not yet had anything resembling a mid-life crisis, at least as such episodes are advertised in popular culture, and I plan to go to my grave without one. Merely because the label is there doesn't mean everyone has to paste it upon his forehead. Besides, with the span of life increasing, it is no longer quite so clear where mid-life is. *Life Begins at Forty* was the title of Walter B. Pitkin's bestseller of 1932, a book written in cheerful reaction to the then-prevailing notion that senescence first began to set in at forty. Nowadays it more often seems that not life but adulthood begins at forty—sometimes between obtaining an MBA and acquiring a condominium. A great deal in contemporary culture permits one to indulge the delusion that one is still youthful well into one's thirties and even one's forties.

The moment of truth will arrive. However young one may feel, one is no longer young when in the eyes of the young one is not young. Somerset Maugham tells, in *A Writer's Notebook*, that the moment of truth came for him when, one day in his early forties, he got into a cab with a woman and her niece, and the niece took the strapontin, or tip seat, leaving the more comfortable seats for her aunt and him. (If you can recall tip seats in cabs, you are no longer so young yourself, darling.) A bachelor friend of mine noted that the moment of truth came for him when a younger woman he was out with suggested that they repair to a bar that had "a really knock-out sound system." Another friend marked the moment when, after a day spent outdoors, he returned home to discover that, owing to thinning hair, the top of his head was sunburned. My own moment came when, delivering a lecture on Theodore Dreiser to a class of college freshmen, I began by saying that "Dreiser was the first major American writer from the other side of the tracks." No sooner was the sentence out of my mouth than it occurred to me that my class could have no notion about what tracks I was talking about. I was thirty-seven, and obviously old well before my time.

My time was part of the problem. I was born in 1937, which means that in 1965 I was twenty-eight years old. I mention 1965 because that was the year that the era known—with chronological inexactitude—as the "sixties" got under way in earnest, with the prominence of the Free Speech Movement at the University of California in Berkeley. Virginia Woolf famously (and rather dubiously) declared that human nature changed in 1910; I am quite certain that human nature did not change in 1965 either, but one of the things that did begin to change in that year was the way people thought about age. Suddenly to be young was everything, and even not very young people became aggressively, even militantly, youthful. The ground for the apotheosis of youth was prepared by the election of John F. Kennedy and the orgy of publicity given our young president and his youthful staff. By the middle 1960s this apotheosis of youth had taken a rivalrous, slightly nasty turn. Old geezers among us will recall one of many slogans of the day: "Don't trust anyone over thirty."

I was not yet thirty, and hence technically trustworthy, but exceedingly ill-prepared to join the kiddie corps. I had a family and a well-paying job; I had, for crying out loud, a mortgage. Wearing my hair in the style of George Eliot or pulled back in a ponytail like Debbie Reynolds did not seem to be, as people said at the time, "my thing." I prefer to think that I had too much irony—and, I hope, iron—in my makeup to smoke pot with either a straight or a laughing face. I rather liked to wear a necktie; had I wished to wear bell-bottoms, I should have joined the Navy. Allen Ginsberg was not my idea of a serious writer, nor Timothy Leary of a clear thinker, nor Herbert Marcuse of a profound philosopher. The sixties, when you got right down to it, was not my idea of a nice time.

With the arrival of the sixties it was as if a curtain—I believe a man named Churchill has already used up the metaphor of an "iron curtain"—had descended that divided the young from those who chose not to be young. Age had less to do with it than temperament and condition: John Lennon, the head Beatle, for example, was only three years younger than I and a year or two older than George Will, the conservative columnist and a grown-up. Natural predilections of temperament put me on the side of the not-young—E. T. A. Hoffmann, not Abbie Hoffman, was my idea of a hero—but, temperament aside, having a family clinched it. Experiments with high-powered drugs of the kind that went on in the sixties may have been interesting, but psychological interest was not the first thing to come to mind when I learned that a friend of my adolescent step-son had killed himself with an overdose of LSD. The sexual freedom of the sixties was also enticing, but, such are the limitations of human nature, it, too, did not come without cost. If I found myself on the not-young side of the curtain, others my age and older chose the young side, and many of them have remained there, living out their days as post-hippie Dorian Grays.

At fifty you can no longer claim that you are young, the way you might, say, at forty-five, and get away with it. At fifty, however young, even immature, you may feel, you have to begin regarding yourself as middle-aged, early middle-aged, if that adjective makes you feel any better, but middle-aged nonetheless. At fifty you can look much younger than you are, if that is important to you (and if it was not important to lots of people, health clubs and plastic surgeons would be out of business). At fifty you can, with training, run a marathon, play serious tennis, swim the English Channel. At fifty, again with training, you can have a lover of twenty-four. (I once knew a man in his early fifties who was married to a woman of twenty-three, but this same man also kept a mistress of forty-five. When I remarked on this unusual reversal of procedure, and asked him why, with so young a wife, he needed an older mistress, he put out his hands, palms to the heavens, and replied that he had to have someone to talk to.) At fifty you can still be in pretty good shape—*for fifty.*

Middle-aged—the English language contains jollier words, surely. Middle-aged has something of the ring of the end of the party about it. It suggests loss of hair and gains in flesh, stiffening of joints and loosening of teeth; it suggests a dimming of vision and memory, of physical and mental powers generally. It is a Bosporus, a Golden Horn, of the life span, where not east and west but age and youth meet; and like Istanbul, the city on the banks of the Bosporus, middle age can be filled with not always charming surprises: you make it through fewer and fewer nights without arising to inspect the plumbing; in winter the hair departs your shins; the clerk at the hardware store, with irony you could live without, refers to you as "young feller"; you cannot remember what you had for dinner on Tuesday, but you can remember the lyrics to Vaughan Monroe's hit songs. You don't recall having booked passage, but you appear to be, very slowly, sailing to Byzantium, which, as Yeats seems to imply, is the country of timelessness.

On the positive side, at fifty, if life has been kind, leaving you with no serious illnesses or permanent disappointments, you begin to get the feeling that you are playing, as the sports announcers say, "in control." You see more going on around you. Setbacks are easier to take; victories are no less pleasant, but you know that the sweet taste they bring does not last long.

Baggier and saggier though your skin may grow, you feel more comfortable in it. Things that used to outrage you can now sometimes amuse you. You do not expect so much from other people, or from yourself. You care less about what other people think of you. This last point is similar to one made by Somerset Maugham, who was always a rigorous registrar of his own age. In *A Writer's Notebook* Maugham wrote: "That is what makes youth unhappy, the vehement anxiety to be like other people, and that is what makes middle age tolerable, the reconciliation with oneself." I hesitate to use the word, lest I be thought to be claiming it for myself, but middle age does sometimes give one the faintest suggestion that one may be acquiring "perspective."

Yet is it perspective that explains what I can only describe as my loss of awe for the living? When I was younger, it seemed that giants walked the earth: Churchill, Gandhi, de Gaulle in politics; Matisse, Stravinsky, Thomas Mann in art; Einstein, Fermi, Planck in science. The last figure for whom I felt a similar reverence was George Balanchine. The only living figure for whom I feel anything approaching such regard is Solzhenitsyn. Still, I wonder: Have I grown larger, smarter, surer in my perspective, or have men and women grown smaller in some indefinable way? I continue to respect what I take to be solid achievement in art and scholarship, but age has brought with it a loss of the capacity for adulation.

It was Evelyn Waugh who, having submitted himself to a painful and less than altogether necessary operation for hemorrhoids, claimed that his motive for doing so was perfectionism. I cannot claim to have had any serious standing as a perfectionist, but, now at middle age, any tendency in that direction has departed (gone perhaps to the same place to which the hair on my shins departs in winter). I am also through with self-improvement programs. But I do note around my apartment the presence of a plastic jump rope, two ten-pound barbells, and racquetball equipment—all there to testify to my hopes for one day getting into shape. What shape? At fifty, I suppose an oval is most likely. Intellectual self-improvement programs, too, are over for me. All I wish now is to become a little less stupid in the years left and to become more than a little better at my craft. As people close to me will tell you, I was never much good at self-improvement anyway.

From the perspective of fifty, I can now see that I have been extremely lucky. Lucky not to have been seriously ill, lucky to have been born in an interesting and free country, lucky even in my generation. Mine has been a generation that has missed having to go to war, which, in the present century, is like having lived out of doors in the rain and somehow avoided getting wet. My generation was much too young for World War II, still too young for Korea, and then too old for Vietnam. Having come of age in the United States in the 1950s, we missed the excitement of generations that came of age before ours—excitement, however, that carried certain penalties with it. The twenties, for example, when Prohibition was in force, produced an inordinately large number of alcoholics, largely because, as a man of that generation once explained it to me, drinking was inseparable from the idea of the illicit, and hence inseparable, too, from excitement. The thirties, with its crunching Depression, left a great many people hostage to anxiety over money all their lives, while a great many other people lapsed into the swamp of sectarian politics, from which they, too, never quite re-emerged. To have come of age in the forties was to have one's maturity marked indelibly by World War II. But to have come of age in the fifties was to miss being swamped by public events, to be a little out of it, and, when you came right down to it, to be a little out of it was not a bad place to be. To be absolutely in it, to be altogether with-it, brought its own disadvantages, not least among them the loss of perspective. (Must remember to supply the antecedents for all those *its* at a later date.)

Tolstoy had no problem with the antecedent for *it*. In "The Death of Ivan Ilych," *it* is death, impure and unsimple. "It alone was true," Tolstoy has Ivan Ilych reflect. "Face to face with *It*," Tolstoy later writes. "And nothing to be done with *It*. Only look and shudder." I recently reread Tolstoy's terrifying story, and not the least terrifying thing about it, to someone who is about to turn fifty, is that poor Ivan Ilych, in the story, is only forty-five. And "the thought had suddenly come into his head: "What if in reality my whole life has been wrong?" Ivan Ilych's whole life, as Tolstoy leaves no doubt, has indeed been wrong, wasted on the inessential and the irrelevant, which is what makes his death so bitter. The power of Tolstoy's story is of course in making every reader above a certain age—forty, let us say—ask that same question of his own life: "What if in reality my whole life has been wrong?"

There really is no way around asking that question, though there are endless ways of providing elusive answers to it. I do not so much ask the question of myself directly as consider it indirectly through the yearning to change my life, or at least my work, which comes upon me periodically. A few years ago, for example, I felt a powerful urge to drop all intellectual work —to continue reading, to continue writing (though much less than I now do), but to take a job that would put me more in the stream of daily life. One day I confided this to a graduate student, who, I rather insensitively failed to consider, longed to do exactly the kind of work I was contemplating leaving. "My God," she said, "if you are not happy, I may just commit suicide." I tried to explain, but am fairly certain that I did not succeed. You live, an old saying has it, and you learn. You live, I myself find, and you yearn.

If you are anything like me, you yearn above all to go on living. Unlike Ponce de León, I have never searched for the fountain of youth, but I should be heartily pleased if I could find a way to freeze time. Unlike, too, Mr. John McSorley, the founder of McSorley's Old Ale House (written about so splendidly by Joseph Mitchell), who, upon ceasing to drink at age fifty-five, was supposed to have announced, "I've had my share," I feel nothing of the kind about life. "If you're fifty-five and retired," runs the beginning of a commercial for an insurance company, and every time I hear it I think, "Wait a minute, I am fifty and have only begun." It's a fine age, fifty, an age when one begins to feel a certain ease in the world and mastery over one's environment, and I should like to remain at fifty for another twenty or thirty years. Somehow I have the sense that this will not be permitted.

At fifty one begins to be comfortable with oneself, but the more comfortable one feels, the more uncomfortably one feels time running out. The minutes, the hours, the days go as slowly as ever; it is those damn weeks, months, and years that now speed past. While I remain as youthful and beautiful as always, why, I cannot help ask, have so many of my contemporaries grown to look so old? It feels as if I have just arrived at the table, and they are already bringing out dessert; I have just stepped out onto the dance floor, and the band is getting ready to play "The Party's Over." Hold the waiters! Stop the music! I like it here. I don't want to leave.

And yet am I ready to do everything possible to stay? It is not always easy to distinguish between the love of life and the fear of death. ("It" again.) Nor are love of life and greed for it quite the same thing. I have acquaintances who—out of a love of life? a fear of death?—are slowly but rather systematically eliminating life's little physical pleasures: cutting out tobacco, alcohol, caffeine, red meat, cholesterol-laden food, all sugar. Soon their meals will be reduced to three dandelions and a nice cup of boiled water. These same people also generally torture themselves with exercise. (I like very much the saying that jogging extends one's life—but only by exactly the amount of time that one spends jogging.) Why do I find all this mildly upsetting, if not slightly obscene? It strikes me as greed for life, as opposed to love of life; it is a demonstration of people whose greed makes them willing to do anything for duration; and greed, even for good things, is not very pretty.

When I think of the distinction between the love of life and the greed for duration, I think of the writer A. J. Liebling. With the aid of his fork, Liebling had early joined the ranks of the obese, an army he was never to leave. Like many of the Frenchmen he knew of the generation before World War I— "the heroic age" of dining, he called it—Liebling never developed "the ulcers that come from worrying about a balanced diet." He did what he wanted to do; went where he wanted to go; wrote extremely well on those subjects he wished to write about; and lived with the throttle full-out—though a more appropriate metaphor would be "the plate always heaped up." Doubtless he would have lived longer had he lived more carefully. But had he lived more carefully—eaten less, drunk less—he would not have been A. J. Liebling. He had his fill and enjoyed the show, paying the check and leaving the table in his fifty-eighth year. Between the dandelion-and-boiled-water set and A. J. Liebling, a compromise position is possible. My own preference would be to live like Liebling and last until age ninety-seven. There is a contradiction here, I realize, but then, fortunately, the law of contradiction is not enforced, lest the jails overflow.

I can't supply a drumroll to go with this cliché, but the fact is that we human beings are the only species born with the painful foreknowledge of our death. Should this foreknowledge slip our minds, age is there as a perpetual crib, or pony, to remind us that life itself is a terminal illness. That at any rate is one way of looking at it. Another is to disregard age, as did Johnny Nikanov, a.k.a. King Cockeye Johnny, the gypsy who also appears in Joseph Mitchell's *McSorley's Wonderful Saloon* and who, when asked about his age, answered, "Between forty-five and seventy-five, somewhere in there. My hair's been white for years and years, and I got seventeen grandchildren, and I bet I'm an old, old man." There is something immensely appealing about that—about, more specifically, living outside age.

Most of us, I suspect, live our lives between these two possibilities, recalling that life is a terminal illness while at the same time forgetting our age. Our age seems incidental, something that has happened to us that we hadn't a great deal to do with, or that happened while we weren't looking. Sometimes our age frankly astonishes us; it is as if it were a strange country we suddenly find ourselves in. Fifty, one says. How the devil did I get here? If one thinks of age as a phonograph record, for many people the needle of their spirit seems to have stuck well before their actual age. I know a woman in her eighties who carries herself as if she were, tops, thirty-four. Despite the depredations of time and the ravages of illness, she is still, somehow, in spirit, sexy. I knew a man in his seventies in whom the mischievous eyes of a boy of eleven shone. My problem, if problem it be, is that I am and feel and look—fifty.

As ages go, and as long as one has to have some age, I am rather fond of fifty. It has a nice middling sound to it. It qualifies for the French phrase *d'un certain âge*, which I render, idiomatically, as "not so young." Yet neither is it all that old. It is roughly two-thirds up the mountain, not a bad place to view those thirty years below as well as those thirty or more

years above. Fifty is an age old enough for one to have suffered
serious disappointments, yet young enough not to be completely out of hope. Proust, who died at age fifty-one, wished
to recapture time, and came as close in his great novel as
anyone is likely to get; I, at fifty, will settle for allowing time
to continue to run. "Miles to go before I sleep," the poet wrote,
and I hope his words apply to me. Even now I am planning
on being a colorful elderly dude, filled with rich and dubious
stories. Should I achieve eighty years, I just may claim to have
played ball with Jackie Robinson, to have danced for Diaghilev, to have been Anton Chekhov's gin-rummy partner. At
that time, feel free to call me a liar, an outrageous old codger,
even gaga. But call me a senior citizen and you had better carry
dental insurance.

My Friend Martin

Y OU CAN NEVER KNOW for certain what the next person thinks of you, but my guess is that Martin thought I was smart enough to get my work done and make a small name for myself in a large world, yet not as smart as he, who understood how hopelessly complicated the world was, an understanding which only rendered him impotent to make any sort of dent in it at all. Why some people are able to chug along without second thoughts and seem to get the best out of themselves, while others are stopped by interior obstacles, blocked by irony, or entangled in the skein of their own deep dubiety, this undoubtedly was a question that Martin spent long hours contemplating. No longer, however. The other day, in the last paragraph of what was otherwise a business letter from a man who was also a friend of Martin's, I read: "Martin died a few weeks ago. It was as bad as it could have been at the end: he developed brain tumors and aphasia. I kept talking to him but was never sure how much was getting through. He never had a chance to make up his accounts with the world."

About sixteen months before, Martin had phoned. I assumed he was in from London on a business trip, hawking one or another of his publishing projects in New York. When he was in the United States, sometimes he called, sometimes not. Inconstancy, if not exactly a part of his charm, was very much part of his standard operating procedure. As long as you weren't Martin's wife or business partner or boss or lover, this inconstancy was tolerable. Not that you had any choice in the matter; nagging Martin somehow did not seem the correct approach. When he was ready to see me, I was ready to see him.

Our friendship, it occurs to me now that he is dead, was completely disinterested. What I mean by this is that we neither took nor expected anything from each other. We did no business together, asked no favors of each other, shared no common past and hence no nostalgia, confided rarely if at all. In fact, I can hardly recall what we talked about, though our hours together always passed very pleasantly, even delightfully. What is more, unlike in so many friendships, in ours no obligation was built up on either side. No, the only reason, the only motive I can make out for our friendship was that we liked each other without complication.

When Martin told me, sixteen months ago over the phone, that he had cancer and of a kind that could not be operated on, my first response was to ask him if he needed any money. A friend who was with him in the last year of his life reported to me that Martin was much touched by my offer. But in truth the offer came less as a gesture of generosity than as one of dumbfoundedness—my usual response—in the face of impending death. He told me in that same phone conversation that he intended to stay in New York, where his older sister was a physician and where oncological treatment was said to be more advanced, leaving his wife and young child in London for the present. We would, he said, stay in touch. He was, I believe, forty-five years old.

That would have made him thirty-two or thirty-three

when I first saw him. The setting was a large boardroom with dark wood and black leather appointments at the offices of Encyclopaedia Britannica, Inc., in Chicago. He was part of a crew whose project it was to develop, out of the amplitude of the *Encyclopaedia Britannica,* a core of material that could be supplemented with local, national, or regional material to provide encyclopaedias to be sold in Asia, the Middle East, Latin America. Quite a crew it was, too. Its chief was a Greek of great suavity, a man who claimed to have been brought before and survived a Nazi firing squad; a dazzling beautiful young woman, another Mediterranean type; a tidy English lady who spoke, most tidily, in an Oxford accent: and Martin. Martin, who spoke in a basso voice, was less readily pinned down. He gave off an international aroma. He might have been an Israeli educated in Europe, except that he dressed too well for an Israeli. He could have been a Dutchman, or a dark Dane, or from Andorra, or the more cosmospolitan circles of Buenos Aires. In fact, Martin was a Jew from New York.

Martin was a man who had made himself, or rather remade himself. I never knew, and had had only the faintest hints of, the original version, the boy and young man friends who knew him from the old days in his neighborhood or at Bard College called Marty. The secret of life, it has more than once been said, consists of being absolutely oneself. What, though, if it is a self one is not very comfortable with, or even much likes? I do not know about Martin's original self, but his remade self seemed to me highly interesting. He was, for example, a handsome man, though he really had no right to be. He was quite short —5′4″ at most—and had early lost most of his auburnish hair. But he had strong bones, supremely intelligent eyes set deep behind high cheekbones. He combed his remaining hair forward. He grew a mustache, and this well before your local accountant or every NFL field-goal kicker wore one. Short he

was but strong, not wiry but muscular. His weren't the muscles of the natural athlete; they were those of the man who
works out alone, a bit grimly perhaps, the muscles that come
not by courtesy of nature but as a result of discipline.

His clothes were elegant, and not quite like anyone else's.
They looked as if they might have been French or Italian. His
suits and jackets were mostly of browns, his ties were like
Venetian tapestries, though dusky, muted. His shirts were
gray, or blue, or taupe. When he came to work for Britannica
in Chicago he brought along a brown leather coat, fur-lined
and with a fur collar, that he had bought in some second-hand
shop in New York. Looking like the kind of coat some German general might have had made to order in anticipation of
spending the winter on the Russian front, it must have
weighed at least fifteen pounds. "Now there," I said when I
first saw him in it, "is a serious coat." I think he was a little
pleased at my recognition that this was a special piece of goods.
In later years, after he moved to London, and when a year or
two would pass without our being in touch, when he would
call or we would meet, I would always ask, "So, how's the
coat?" "Holding up nicely," he would say. "It's kind of you
to inquire."

The Martin I knew was a character in some mythical movie
set in the Balkans, with actors like Peter Lorre, Oscar Ho-
molka, and Akim Tamiroff in the cast. Another friend of mine,
a Berliner, said he thought Martin a character out of E. T. A.
Hoffmann. Certainly he had some extraordinary, as we should
say nowadays, moves. When he smoked a cigarette—lung-
ripping Gauloises were his brand—you could scarcely take
your eyes off him. Like a gourmand eating a pigeon stuffed
with truffles, so Martin taking down smoke—he seemed to
enjoy the hell out of it. He wasn't a heavy smoker, either, but

a controlled one; it seemed he got so much out of every cigarette that he didn't need a lot of them. He handled money with
an interesting sensuality, rubbing the bills when he removed
them from his wallet between his thumb and index finger as
if they were of cashmere or vicuna. His fingers, short, broad,
powerful, were not elegant but what he could do with them
was.

Martin's manner and general demeanor made him seem
like nothing so much as a spy, but if I were a casting director
I shouldn't have wanted him in my movie for his being, in the
role of double-agent, perhaps a shade too obvious. But cast as
an associate editor at Encyclopedia Britannica in the late 1960's
he was scarcely noticeable. Britannica was then undergoing an
enormous reworking, under the direction of Mortimer J.
Adler, who had conceived the absolutely novel and quite Won-
derlandish notion of rewriting *Encyclopaedia Britannica* by
creating its index first. A crew of oddballs and misfits—out-of-
work theologians, disgruntled academics. St. John's of An-
napolis graduates, free-lance writers, down-on-their luck
scientists—myself among them, were hired to attend Dr.
Adler's daily tea parties, where the subject was how best to
organize, or rather reorganize, knowledge. It was unintention-
ally comic but the pay was excellent. Martin was our legal
editor.

How does one get to be a legal editor? One way is to go
to law school, fail the bar exam, even though one is exceedingly
intelligent, then refuse to take it a second time. This at any rate
was Martin's way, and friends of his, meeting soon after his
death, seemed to feel that first flunking and then not retaking
the New York bar exam was the great turning point in Martin's life. I am not so sure. I cannot imagine Martin ever mar-
shaling the patience for the intricacies required in tax law or
estate planning; nor can I envision him sitting, in a Queens

County courthouse, conferring with and calming down a female client in a divorce case. Martin's mistake might not have
been in failing to take the bar examination but in having gone
to law school in the first place.

Does life really have turning points, or is it instead for most
of us one long, fairly straight road riddled with more or fewer
bumps and potholes, nails and broken glass? I don't know for
certain but my guess is that Martin probably was a straight-
road man. Ten or so years after I met him he made a casual
passing reference to "my shrink," and as a man in psychoanalysis Martin no doubt believed less in turning points than in
straight roads of destiny; for what else is so much of psychoanalysis but a trip back down the road in the attempt to discover
when and where the scrapes and misalignments and blowouts
occurred? Yet I thought at the time Martin mentioned "my
shrink" that the psychoanalyst who had Martin for a patient
certainly had a couchful.

He was so very intelligent and so very devious and so very
intent on bungling his life. Intelligence first. An example is
wanted. In those days, late in the 1960s, a time when Britannica
was filled with people in their twenties and early thirties who
were at work on the great revision, political rallies of one kind
or another were fairly frequent. One day in particular a rally
was to be held on the plaza outside the building in which
Britannica had its offices. People going to the rally—it was an
anti-Vietnam war rally—were excused from work, and those
who planned to go wore black arm bands. I heard a very
earnest young Jewish girl, a secretary, who was wearing an
arm band, say to Martin: "Aren't you going to the rally?"
Martin replied: "No, Naomi, afternoons such as this I generally spend at the graveside of Santayana."

Now I submit that this reply, so characteristically Martin,
was perfect. That the young woman would not have known

who Santayana was, that, too, was artful, for the true artist
doesn't require an immediate response or even an appreciative
audience. Sometimes I have thought that Martin was an artist,
and that the sadness of his life was that he had no art to convey
—except perhaps the creation that had become himself.

Consider for a moment his reference to Santayana. Had
Martin read much Santayana? He must have read enough of
him to know that citing a figure noted for his serenity at a time
of tumult was exactly right. But whether Martin had read and
admired Santayana or any other writer I have no way of knowing, for we never discussed books or bookish things. Before law
school, he had gone to Bard, one of those small schools—
Antioch in Ohio and Reed in Oregon were two others—in
which the liberal arts were taught as though they were a religion. Usually the people who have gone to these schools never
quite get over them, but Martin did and he scarcely ever mentioned Bard, except once to tell me that the teacher he most
admired there was Heinrich Blücher, the husband, as he has
since become known to history, of Hannah Arendt. Once
Martin told me that, finding himself in a great bog of depression while an undergraduate, he had come to Blücher to announce that he intended to take his life because he could not
find any reason for wanting to live. "Don't take your life,"
Blücher told him, "we'll find you a reason."

I assume that Martin read widely while at Bard, but, I
suspect, he had pretty much stopped reading by the time I met
him. Not only did we never talk about books, but I never saw
him carrying a book. In his London apartment there were a
few books, though these could have belonged to his wife. He
may have thought that he had gone as far as he could with
bookish knowledge, and that if he were to discover any of the
world's secrets he would have to extract them directly from
life. Besides, although there was nothing jittery about him,

although all his gestures seemed deliberate, he had not the temperament for repose; he was a social being, a city creature, a man of and in the world.

About the world he could be very penetrating. When he spoke with you, at least upon the first few meetings, you felt rather as if you were under investigation—and you were, for Martin was taking your intellectual measure, estimating your philosophical weight. Were you a serious person? An interesting person? What were your flaws? What was your con? What might your personal fantasies be? How did you view life? These, you sensed, were among the things he was trying to get at as he spoke with you.

Martin specialized in the oblique insight. He would say that a certain woman would never love a man above a certain size. He was very efficient—that is to say, unfailingly correct —at spotting closeted homosexuals. He could scent malice, insecurity, cowardice in another man. He was almost a pure observer. He seemed to have absolutely no nervousness about status. At Britannica, I was a senior editor, he an associate editor, but he never had any difficulty talking down to me when the mood was upon him.

Martin may or may not have been an original, but this much at least must be said of him—like Hazlitt, he never listened to the echo. He came by his views on his own. He was, for one thing, well spoken, his speech utterly free of both cant phrases and jargon—and hence his mind was free of trendiness and clichés. His politics, for another thing, were like no one else's I have ever met. Not that he ever laid them out for me in any detail, but my sense was that while disliking what he felt was tinny or vulgar about American life—he never, so far as I know, owned a television set—he felt no need to knock these things; and, what was more, he had a true respect for entrepreneurs and tradesmen, who he felt were the backbone of this or any other healthy nation. This is all the more interesting when you consider that, in the late sixties, to be an intellectual, or even to be interested in intellectual things, was to be, except for odd pockets, on the Left. Heinrich Blücher, an old German radical, may have been Martin's mentor, but Martin's mind was his own.

If Martin had read this last line, he might have replied, "Surely no one else would want it." I fear I may have made him seem a little humorless. But only to the humorless was he humorless. Part of his charm was in the playfulness of his mind. I went through a divorce during the time Martin was living in Chicago, and, though mine was an uncontested divorce, under the legal requirements of the day I needed two witnesses to attest to my fine character. I chose Martin for one. He came through splendidly, though I remember thinking, while he was on the witness stand, that I rather wished he looked less like an agent provocateur and hadn't a hotel for an address. After the courtroom business was over, we walked across the street —it was only a quarter to eleven in the morning—for drinks. I bought two rounds of Bloody Marys, and toward the end of the second round Martin slipped into a sweet little bit about being a professional witness, and having three more cases to go through that afternoon. "I'll be glad when the divorce season is over," Martin said, "and we can get back to witnessing criminal cases." A moment later, looking at me, he said: "Shit, boy, I could regale you with stories about Kahn here and I doing three-hour stints on the witness stand without time out even for so much as a leak." He would slide off into these vignettes at any time.

But if Martin had a playful mind, it could also play against itself—and wickedly. Although he was a New Yorker by birth, and a world city man by inclination, Martin did not despise Chicago. Not knowing many people in the city gave him freedom of a sort he valued. He lived in a hotel, which certified him as, in the phrase he once used to describe himself, "a permanent transient." He went to parties with various among Britannica's youngish editorial workers. He must have put in a certain amount of time in Rush Street bars. He had a lady friend. Yet he was performing badly at work, missing deadlines, showing up late in the day (usually near lunch), causing by his general behavior a good deal of ill-will against himself in the man for whom he worked. Meanwhile, he strolled the corridors and cubicles of Encyclopaedia Britannica, Inc., clearly doing little work or having much in the way of business on his mind, a flaneur but one on the payroll. As he let deadline after deadline go past, it began to be rather apparent that he had a taste for trouble, perhaps even for self-destruction.

One Friday afternoon he strolled into my office to announce that he planned to spend the weekend in New York and while there thought he might get married. Since he had never before mentioned any romantic connection in New York, this came as news to me. What, he wanted to know, did I think of this notion. I said I thought that, theoretically, marriage was a very sound idea, though, as a recently divorced man, I could not help noticing that, practically, in marriage one sometimes encountered certain little difficulties. But did I think he ought to marry? I don't know what you have in mind, I said, and I have never met the woman you plan to marry. Still, I was a pro-marriage man. "Where shall I send it?" he asked. "Send what?" I replied. "The check for this consultation, of course," he said, departing my office.

A few weeks later I met Martin's wife, whom he had brought back to Chicago and who was beautiful. She was Dutch, an Amsterdamer, with lovely skin and good humor and fine intelligent eyes. She was a jewelry designer who worked in gold. She spoke English with complete fluency, and only a slight accent. In some ways she seemed rather more American than her husband, to whom, it became evident on the instant of seeing them together, she was devoted. He was quite gallant around her and most solicitous. She, though, seemed to me perhaps more made for the world than he. Seeing them together it occurred to me that of course Martin would never have married anyone other than a European woman. They are a special breed, American men who marry (outside of wartime) European women, they entertain certain special ideas about themselves, like white American women who marry black men.

Martin and his wife and I and the woman I am now married to began to spend time together as a foursome. We got on well together, I thought, everyone liking everyone else. Usually we would drive out into the country on a Sunday. Once he took us to a very good restaurant he knew in Wisconsin, just over the Illinois border. More often we picnicked. Martin was a city man, but he seemed to me to ease up, to relax, in the country. Sometimes we dined at my apartment—Martin and his wife still lived, in fairly close quarters, in his hotel—and once I recall asking him if he had any difficulty finding a parking place. "Never," he said. "Always remember that there are two open parking places on every block in America: one where the fire hydrant is, the other at the bus stop."

I don't know for a fact that Martin did rack up scores of parking tickets, but it would not surprise me if he had. Every so often in the Chicago press—as I am sure in the press of other cities as well—a story will appear about a man being brought to court to pay $12,682 in accumulated parking tickets and fines. Martin might have been such a man, except that I suspect he knew he never would live long enough in Chicago to have been caught. When he spoke of himself as a permanent transient, he meant it; as with so many of his seemingly tossed-off phrases, this one too had precision. He and his wife continued to live in their furnished room off Rush Street. There was no talk of their settling in. The feeling of their time in Chicago had about it an atmosphere of camping out.

And then Martin did something that put finis to the Chicago chapter of his life—a thing that is extraordinary and that requires explanation. What he did was get himself fired from his job at Encyclopaedia Britannica, Inc.; and fired not for producing work at too slow a rate, nor for disrupting others while on his *flâneur*ish rounds, but for being caught going through the desk and files of Britannica's editor-in-chief. Coming in late in the mornings as he did, Martin frequently stayed an hour or so after everyone had already gone home. Evidently he must have thought everyone had already left for the night when he entered the editor-in-chief's office for a casual inspection of his most recent correspondence and memoranda. Unfortunately the editor-in-chief's secretary had not yet left for the evening but had been in the ladies' room. When she returned to her desk she discovered Martin going through her boss's desk. Next morning she reported this to the editor-in-chief, who asked no explanation but announced: "Call down to personnel. I want him out of here before the day is over." And so, most efficiently, Martin was.

What could he have had in mind in going through another man's private papers? Had he gone through other people's files, including my own? I should not have been shocked if he had. But what was his motive? Let me say right off that self-interest probably had very little to do with it. Scarcely anything in the editor-in-chief's papers could have made reference to Martin. As I suppose every large corporation is, Britannica was shot through and always hot with rumor and gossip. My guess is that, in digging into the editor-in-chief's papers, Martin was searching for a bit of inside information. He wanted to know what was really going on. He was interested to discover how this large company operated, its interweavings and its inner dealings at its higher levels. He was, in a word, curious, but in a detached sort of way—as a child might be curious, or an artist.

Was this behavior self-destructive? The more I stare at the phrase self-destructive the less certain I become of its meaning. I don't for a minute think that Martin wished to be caught in what was a fairly humiliating circumstance. At the same time he had to have known that there was a chance of his being caught. But then Martin often seemed to be playing a game of Russian roulette with himself. He was, for example, a mad driver, and I can think of a number of roller coasters from my youth that compared favorably for feelings of comfort and security with being driven in a car by Martin. After his death, I learned that he had been gambling steadily. He wasn't, I gather, a bust-out gambler but apparently, frequenting the gaming clubs in London, lost at a steady and serious enough clip. He had a taste for playing at the brink: taking the curve at seventy miles an hour, missing the fourth deadline, highrolling on a modest salary, grabbing his trousers only when he heard the husband's hand turn the doorknob, always when possible taking the wild chance. Is such behavior self-destructive? Or is it instead the behavior of a man who may have felt himself deadened in his soul and knew no other way than risk-taking to assure himself he was still alive?

Meanwhile, Martin had effectively slammed the door on himself in Chicago. He was, it seems, building up an impressively disastrous little resumé. There were events that couldn't be accounted for easily to a prospective employer—"What happened again in law school?"—years that yawned vaguely— "You say you worked at Encyclopaedia Britannica, Inc., then,

but you'd rather we didn't get in touch with anyone there?"
—questions for which straight answers were simply not available. Martin hung around Chicago for a while, trying to pick
up free-lance editorial work, but perhaps no one was less suited
for such work. Finally, he had made a connection with the
Dutch publishing firm of Elsevier, for whom he was to work,
on a new encyclopaedia project, in London. To have gained
the job he must have done some very artful interviewing.

I felt pleased for him. London, a great world city, an increasingly international city with the vast decline in English
power, seemed right for Martin—for his clothes, for his man-
nerisms, for his cosmopolitan notion of himself. Perhaps his
wife, though she had never complained in my presence, would
be happier there, too. No mention was made of London's being
a temporary arrangement; no talk about returning in three or
five years. In an odd way, when Martin left to live abroad I felt
as if he were, at last, returning home.

Would Martin be more at home abroad than, so to speak,
at home at home? I pictured him aloft on planes for Amster-
dam, Frankfurt, Rome, a Gauloises and a Campari on the tray
before him, at ease, if not yet in Zion then at least on his way.
Why mightn't Martin make a tidy success in publishing? So
many doltish men I knew made large sloppy ones. There was
a man at Britannica who, I once said to Martin's pleasure,
seemed quite crass all right but not very commercial. He was
able to retire in his fifties. Wasn't there room out on the margins somewhere for Martin to score a few victories? Clearly,
intelligence was not wanting. Why not Martin?

We fell out of touch. Martin, as might be imagined, was not
much for correspondence. Sometimes, though, I would hear of
him at second- or third-hand from someone who had been to
and seen him in London. Shreds of information had come

across. One was that he had left Elsevier. Another, much more
significant in every way, was that Martin and his wife had had
a child, a boy named Gabriel. This struck me as an extraordinary item. Martin as a father did not quite fit within the frame
of the permanent transient within which I had always pictured
him.

Not long after this my wife and I were in England for a
visit. Before departing I had written to Martin to say that we
would like to see him while we were in London. He wrote
back to say come ahead and that we would be welcome with
or without a salami. We took a long cab ride from our hotel
on George Street to their apartment out near Hampstead
Heath. The boy-child Gabriel was then perhaps eighteen
months old. He was blond and ran about naked and was very
beautiful. Martin's brother happened also to be there. Apart
from his winning sense of humor and obvious high intelligence, he neither looked nor spoke as Martin did—further
evidence, in my view, that Martin had made himself. The
self-made man was, on this occasion as on nearly all others,
very dependably late. His wife greeted us at the door, in fact,
by saying that Martin had just called and would be a little late.

The apartment was hardly grand but it was pleasant. It was
an apartment in which a small child reigned. The boy's toys
were everywhere and so was he. All hope of order had been
surrendered to this child. Yet no one seemed to be suffering
very much. Everyone seemed to live, as it were, around him.
I am not very sentimental about small children—or animals or
good causes—but this child seemed to me rather special. He
had much mother love but also, it became clear when Martin
arrived home, father love. This man who seemed, from the
angle at which he had allowed me to view him, so ill-suited to
fatherhood was quite good at it. Martin was not a fawning
father, but a father who seemed to know very much what he

was about—to know what parts of this golden child were sheer animal spirits and had best be given way to, and what parts needed to be carefully molded and developed. For all his other difficulties, one sensed that Martin felt that, in this child at any rate, he had been blessed.

We ate in the garden behind their apartment. I had long since departed Encyclopaedia Britannica, Inc., but my wife still worked there, and she brought Martin up to date about those people there who interested him. After dinner, I told him some jokes I had recently heard, and he remarked that the English don't tell jokes. He wasn't very high on the English generally. He had few English friends, it turned out, but saw mostly Americans in London. He thought the English as a nation were doing all they could to make themselves negligible, and were succeeding handsomely. Martin had an apocalyptic streak, and when it would show up, as it did from time to time, I tended to tune him out. Now, with a grim look on his face, he told me he was searching for a place to live with his family when Europe fell apart.

London was clearly not going to be the answer for Martin. Seeing him unhappy there gave me a sharper sense of the malady of permanent transience. Martin had only to be in one place for his heart to yearn after another. His was the condition of the interior exile: take him to Paris, he cries out Rome; in Rome, he wants Athens; in Athens, Jerusalem is the name of his desire. He doesn't like it here. It looks better there. Anywhere you go, an old saying has it, there *you* are! The permanent transient doesn't quite believe it. Or, if in his heart he does, he isn't ready to act on it.

Yet Martin stayed on in London. He was locked into his business—manufacturing reference books of various kinds for larger firms—and seemed able neither to leave it nor to succeed in it. When we met on our next trip to London, he took us to a French restaurant in the neighborhood of his apartment, and between drinks and starters his wife told us that she had recently been operated on for cancer. Later Martin drove us back, at an insanely fast clip, to our hotel. At stop lights we heard Arabs standing on street corners chatting in their sing-song native tongues. At the hotel Martin and I walked and talked for a bit. He told me what a lout his partner was. His situation was far from enviable. His wife was ill, his business seemed to be going nowhere, he lived in a vast city that seemed to belong to no one. When he drove off that night I thought I knew of no one lonelier.

The last time we were together he was late again, of course. He was driving up from London to meet us in Cambridge, where we had been lent the house of a friend. His wife couldn't join him but he was bringing his son. When they arrived Martin looked a little seedy but then so did England. The boy Gabriel, though, was dazzling. He must at this time have been five years old. His head was very round and very blond, his face full of lively intelligence. He spoke in a lilting English accent, with occasional Cockney touches. Later, when I had pretended to steal a cigar from his father's pocket, he said, imploring me to do it again, "Joe, do it. Nick Martin's cigar." The boy called his father by his first name. Although I don't usually feel quite comfortable about this practice, in this instance it didn't feel wrong. Perhaps the reason was that, as the afternoon unrolled, it became apparent that Martin, along with being the boy's father, was also something like his older brother.

We took a rowboat out on the Cam, behind the Cambridge colleges, the four of us, my wife and Gabriel, Martin and I. It quickly became apparent that Martin and his son shared a fantasy world. As we rowed among the inlets and streams down well past Peterhouse, they referred back and forth to a

special world—of knights? of pirates? of gremlins and trolls?
—which, clearly, only they inhabited. Martin was relaxed and
at his best: filled with wit and penetrating observations and
courtliness. The four of us lingered on into dusk, when Martin
announced he had best get the boy back to London. He had
promised his wife he would be back much earlier. Late again.
As they drove off, the boy leaning out of the window, Martin
waving, the battered red Mercedes clunking down the narrow
Cambridge street, my wife turned to me. "What a pair they
are!" she said. "What a pair!"

When I didn't hear from Martin for four or five weeks after
his call telling me that he had inoperable cancer, I telephoned
his brother in New York to ask how things were going. Martin
seemed in good mental shape, at least as good as could be
expected, his brother said, though it was of course much too
soon to know what effect the therapy was having. A few days
later Martin called. He seemed, for the only time in our acquaintance, shaken. "I have got to find the faith to believe I can
defeat this thing," he said. "I have to make that leap, and I don't
know if I can." I muttered a few platitudes about having no
choice but to make the fight. He said he might come to Chicago
in a month or so. He would, I said, of course stay with us. It
was the last time we spoke. For his own good reasons, he never
came to Chicago and he never phoned.

Martin spent the last year of his life in New York. His older
sister, a physician, lived there and aided in his therapy. His
young brother, who had recently married and whom he loved,
lived there as well. He spent long sessions with a boyhood
friend, with whom he had gone to Bard and who himself had
had a severe heart attack and thus a close glimpse of death, in
Bardishly philosophical discussions on the meaning of life.
Still, it could not have been comfortable for a man so intelligent
as Martin, so alive to life's manifold ironies, to walk the streets

of Manhattan with death so closely at his heels.

Not long after learning that Martin had cancer, in an autobiographical volume of Peter Quennell's I ran across a reference to cancer as "the disease of the disappointed." I wonder what Martin would have thought of that notion. I suspect he might slyly have remarked that the reference was certainly apt insofar as having cancer was clearly disappointing. But in fact this was the kind of theoretical point Martin loved to play with. Was he, before he had been brought down by cancer, a disappointed man? Did he have a plan: to become rich, to be utterly free, to live according to the highest conception of himself? If he had, then no doubt he was a disappointed man, but in this he only joins the great majority.

Disappointed Martin may have been, yet—and here he was of a very select minority—he himself rarely disappointed. To be with him was almost always to be reminded of life's larger possibilities, which is the service performed by people who are original for the rest of us. And Martin, even though he was self-created, was finally an original. I think this is why I find myself so affected by his death. When a man or woman of originality dies the subtraction seems somehow even greater than the loss of a friend, which is subtraction enough. Martin died much too soon. As the friend who wrote to me about his death said, "He never had a chance to make up his accounts with the world." Yet, in the gift of his originality, Martin may have left behind a great deal more than even he could have known.